# That Was When People Started to Worry

## YOUNG WOMEN AND MENTAL ILLNESS

# NANCY TUCKER

ICON

First published in the UK in 2018
by Icon Books Ltd, Omnibus Business Centre,
39–41 North Road, London N7 9DP
email: info@iconbooks.com
www.iconbooks.com

This edition published in the UK in 2019 by Icon Books Ltd

Sold in the UK, Europe and Asia
by Faber & Faber Ltd, Bloomsbury House,
74–77 Great Russell Street,
London WC1B 3DA or their agents

Distributed in the UK, Europe and Asia
by Grantham Book Services,
Trent Road, Grantham NG31 7XQ

Distributed in the USA
by Publishers Group West,
1700 Fourth Street, Berkeley, CA 94710

Distributed in Australia and New Zealand
by Allen & Unwin Pty Ltd,
PO Box 8500, 83 Alexander Street,
Crows Nest, NSW 2065

Distributed in South Africa
by Jonathan Ball, Office B4, The District,
41 Sir Lowry Road, Woodstock 7925

Distributed in India by Penguin Books India,
7th Floor, Infinity Tower – C, DLF Cyber City,
Gurgaon 122002, Haryana

Distributed in Canada by Publishers Group Canada,
76 Stafford Street, Unit 300
Toronto, Ontario M6J 2S1

ISBN: 978-178578-448-4

Typeset in Perpetua by Marie Doherty

Printed and bound in Great Britain
by Clays Ltd, Elcograf S.p.A.

# CONTENTS

Voice to the Voiceless
*page 1*

**Abby** – Depression
*page 13*

**Yasmine** – Bipolar Disorder
*page 45*

**Georgia** – Self-Harm
*page 85*

**Freya** – Anxiety
*page 127*

**Beth** – Disordered Eating
*page 165*

**Holly** – Post-Traumatic Stress Disorder
*page 201*

**Maya** – Borderline Personality Disorder (also known as
Emotionally Unstable Personality Disorder)
*page 243*

Presences and Absences
*page 279*

References
*page 291*

Acknowledgements
*page 295*

# Voice to the Voiceless

'People say mental health isn't discussed, and that's why no one understands it properly. That's bullshit though. I can't go on Facebook without seeing ten or twenty posts about mental health. Maybe this is just me being blind and privileged, and I'm sorry if that's the case, but I feel like mental health *is* discussed more and more these days. And yet still no one really understands. You cancel arrangements because you're physically ill, and you're unlucky. You cancel arrangements because you're mentally ill, and you're flaky. You're "always bailing". You take time off work for physical illness, and it's unavoidable; you take time off work for mental illness, and you're slacking. The posts about mental health that get shared on Facebook and retweeted on Twitter – a lot of them are great, but more of them are awful. They say nothing – nothing at all – and then at the end they say "STIGMA" or "RAISING AWARENESS" or "IF THIS JUST HELPS ONE PERSON", as if those words were anything more than empty buzz-phrases. What's wrong with contemporary representations of mental health? Well, for starters, they shouldn't be called "representations of mental *health*", because mental *health* is just the state of the inside of your head, the same way "diet" doesn't actually mean "weight-loss plan", it just means "what you eat". If we're talking about mental *ill*-health, we're talking about mental *illness*. So what's wrong with contemporary representations of mental *illness*? They're sanitised. They're superficial. They're tokenistic. A lot of the time, they're

1

just inaccurate. I know I sound horrible saying this, and don't get me wrong, it *is* really great that we're working towards a better understanding of psychiatric as well as physical disorders, but … I don't know. I just feel like … we're not there yet. Yeah. To put it mildly, we're not there yet.'

Laura, 23

On the 31st of March 2015, I was flitting around a crowded bookshop like a scrawny, nervy star. There were stars on my dress and stars on my earrings and stars behind the lids of my eyes when I moved too quickly because I hadn't eaten in three weeks. I was all sharp edges. There were stars on the cover of the book I had written about eating and not-eating and self-discovery and self-destruction. Tiny, hopeful, yellow stars. *I'm flying*, a tiny, hopeful, yellow voice tinkled in my ear. *I'm flying, I'm flying, I'm flying.*

On the 31st of July 2015, I was tethered to earth by a hollow tube, harnessing me to a tall, metal stand. Salty fluid chilled my arm and swilled the poison from my blood. My edges were gone, swallowed up by flesh I had thought I would never see again. Loose, hateful flesh, weighing me down like sand in a doorstop. All around were puzzled faces, furrowed brows: 'You wrote a book? You have a job? You're going to university? What's wrong with you? Why do this?' When I met their gaze, I felt the sharp points of a thousand shattered stars prickle behind the lids of my eyes, and I crossed and re-crossed my arms over the body I had tried so hard, and so repeatedly, to exterminate. *I'm falling,* a repetitive, unexterminated voice scratched in my ear. *I'm falling, I'm falling, I'm falling.*

On the 31st of December 2015, I felt as if I were buried deep underground, earth and rock and paving stones pressing down on my tired body. You can only fall so many times before you start to fracture. I was disintegrating into splinters of a soul, the raging voices thrumming in my ears a cacophony of blame and bile. *Useless! Disgusting! Failure!* When the nurses stitched up the patterns carved into my arms, they forgot to knit together the great, gaping wound in my chest. I walked out of the hospital, all fixed up, spilling dirt and desolation from the gash between my ribs. *I'm broken,* a dirty, desperate voice droned in my ear. *I'm broken.*

This is mental illness. It is vicious waves slamming you onto a rocky shore, and your tired body dragging itself up, and vicious waves slamming you back onto the rocks, and your tired body dragging itself up, over and over, until you think you might as well lie down on the sharp edges and let the water subsume you. It is smiling faces in the distance, bobbing above a picnic blanket, rolling their eyes and raising their hands: *Why don't you just stand up? Stand up – come and join us! It's gorgeous over here!* It is unexpected strength and unusual luck and an uninterrupted string of steps. Knee-deep, then ankle-deep, then the sun on your face and salt on your tongue. When the next wave comes – an unannounced, unkind fist – it knocks you forwards. You wipe grit from your eyes and swipe blood from your knees and cough mud from your lungs. In the distance there are smiling faces and raised hands: *Why do you **keep** falling over?! Just **stand up**! It's **gorgeous** over here!*

At the beginning of 2016, I was marooned on the rocks. The previous year had seen me soaring, giddy on the high of self-confession and self-discovery and an ever-present undertone of self-destruction, until – running out of momentum mid-flight – I had come tumbling from the sky. Swathed in shame and bruised from the fall, I had walked into my university room three months after walking into a room on the psychiatric ward which had tried to stick me back together again, and I felt no more at home in the former than the latter.

3

'What went wrong?' people asked, six weeks into term, when I crumbled spectacularly and was bundled back home. 'What was it you couldn't cope with?'

I wanted to say: *I couldn't cope with being me. I couldn't cope with finding myself in a brand new setting and being unable to turn myself into a brand new person. I couldn't cope with the myriad hours I spent frantically, privately filling and emptying myself, or the blades I carried in my pencil case, or the search history crowded with questions about how many paracetamol tablets I would have to take to definitely die. I couldn't cope with the drone in my head telling me: 'You don't deserve to be alive. You don't deserve to be happy. You are a horrible, terrible person.'*

I didn't say that. I said there was a lot of pressure, and I struggled to keep up, and I felt homesick. And some people smiled and said: 'Yes. You poor thing.' And other people smiled and said: 'But everyone feels like that when they leave home.' And other people said: 'Running away never helped anyone.' And other people rolled their eyes and wrinkled their noses and thought: *God. What a fuss.*

I was terrified by what was happening in my mind – but I had already given my brain a book of its own. My insides had been scraped out and plastered onto the page, and my eyes needed to be swivelled outwards. So I rolled up my sleeves and prepared to sink my hands into the dark, gruesome innards of mental illness in the wider world. I wanted to climb into the grimiest corners of the unwell mind, and open the curtains keeping those corners trapped in gloom. I wanted to invite outsiders to peek through the grubby windows and see 'what it's really like'. I wanted to give voice to those whose internal demons rendered them dumb.

Over the following months, I contacted and met 70 young women – of all classes, colours and creeds – and heard stories of pain so visceral it knotted itself around my own nerves.

We met in pubs and coffee shops, bedrooms and university houses, kitchens and living rooms. We talked about transformations from happy child to tortured teenager to hardened twenty-something. We talked about difficulties that had been waiting in the wings from birth, ready for a grand entrance. We talked about settled, 'normal' younger years, disintegrating to disarray in adulthood. These women allowed me to slip through tiny gaps in their armour, and stand shoulder to shoulder with the most bruised and battered parts of themselves, usually concealed from the melee of the outside world. The experience was harrowing, heartening and humbling.

Although the 100+ hours of interview I collected comprised the unique stories of unique women, their experiences clustered around certain core themes. A subset dwelled on difficulties with food; another on difficulties with mood. A handful relayed stories of alarming impulsivity; others of frightening compulsivity. While some described the agonies of post-traumatic stress, others painted pictures of psychotic duress. Although psychiatric diagnoses were not applicable in all cases – and, in any case, such diagnoses tend to mingle with one another like ambitious millennials at a networking event – most women's experiences fell within the bounds of one 'label' or another. And so, I created characters embodying each of the major difficulties my interviewees described: depression (Abby); generalised anxiety disorder (Freya); borderline personality disorder (Maya); self-harm (Georgia); disordered eating (Beth); post-traumatic stress disorder (Holly) and bipolar disorder (Yasmine). *These characters are not real people: they are composites of real people.* To have transposed individual interviews directly onto the page would have been unethical (and the resultant product would not have been a book). However, every significant experience my characters undergo, every significant belief they hold, every significant conversation they have is a real event, recounted by a real person. Each character's 'story' is a potted memoir of *lives*; it is not a potted memoir of *a life*.

Why women? Put simply, women are more vulnerable than men to many common mental health conditions. The Adult Psychiatric Morbidity Survey (APMS), which has been conducted every seven years since 1993, offers some of the most reliable data for the trends and prevalence of mental illnesses. The most recent APMS (2014) found that all types of common mental health problems, including depression and generalised anxiety disorder, were more prevalent in women than in men. The discrepancy was most marked among young people: 26 per cent of women aged 16–24 reported symptoms of a common mental health problem, compared to just 9.1 per cent of men of the same age.[1] This survey sampled people from England only, but similar gender patterns have been found in Wales,[2] Northern Ireland[3] and Scotland.[4] Young women also report higher levels of self-harm and suicidal thoughts than any other group.[5]

This is not to say that male mental health is not important and worthy of exploration. In 2014, the Office for National Statistics reported 6,122 suicides in the UK, of which 75.6 per cent were male.[6] Given that suicide and suicide attempts are associated with a psychiatric disorder in 90 per cent of cases,[7] men are clearly suffering. Further, young adult males experience greater personal stigma surrounding mental health problems than their female counterparts,[8] resulting in a possible reporting bias: men may resist admitting to a mental health problem, hence statistics concerning this population may be inaccurate. This is before considering the mental health of transgender people, or those with a complex gender identity, who may face elevated levels of both psychological distress and stigma.[9] A book exploring mental illness within these populations would be highly relevant – but I would not be the person to write it.

Why young people? A 2005 prevalence study carried out in

the USA predicted that 75 per cent of mental health problems are established by the age of 24.[10] Therefore, it must be of paramount importance to learn more about the wellness or illness that develops during this early chapter of life.

To me, these seemed objectively sound reasons for choosing to focus on this specific population, but it would be naïve not to acknowledge that personal interest played a part. In my experience, being a young woman is, at best, challenging and, at worst, agonising – and I was interested to learn whether or not this sentiment would be echoed by others of my age and gender who suffer from mental health problems.

Before I began interviewing, my primary concern was whether the conversations would constitute a basis for engaging writing. I knew I would find these young women's stories interesting, but I did not know whether they would translate into readable material. As readers, we tend to look for stories that are wide and full and exciting – but mental illness is often small and empty and dull. By the time I had finished interviewing, my primary concern had morphed: my interviewees' experiences were *too* vivid; *too* shocking; *too* dramatic. I was convinced no one would believe that these things had really happened. There is little I can do to challenge this state of disbelief, except to reiterate: it is all true. It is all real. These things happened. These things happen.

I am aware that there may – still – be those who look upon these stories as a collective indulgence of 'first-world problems'. Although the women involved in this project by no means represent a single social class, none came from abject poverty or deprivation. They had roofs over their heads and enough food to eat. Most were educated, employed and in good physical health: they had at least some degree of 'privilege'.

However, I see no value in comparing the pain entailed by mental illness with the pain entailed by, say, those involved in warfare, national disaster or persecution. To do so suggests that there is some universal ranking of suffering, which puts one type of distress above another. It is ludicrous to compare forms of pain, expecting to discern a 'worse' and a 'better'. It is also absurd to suggest that privilege should preclude or invalidate unhappiness: one's crushing depression, all-consuming suicidality or paralysing anxiety cannot be discounted because one is white, heterosexual or middle class.

Where is the value in comparing their struggles? We move through the world within the bounds of our own experience, which has peaks – the most intense happiness we know – and troughs – the most intense misery we know. The scope of this experience varies widely: one person's lows may be another's middle ground, and the distance separating the depths from the apex can be vast or small. The location of the low is less important than its position within the 'experience space': being at the depths of said space, *for anyone*, feels wretched. For this reason, comparing two people's nadirs – *Things aren't really that bad for you; just think what others go through!* – is unhelpful. I have treated all stories as equally valid, because they *are* equally valid.

Recently, I was berated for referring to those experiencing mental illness as 'sufferers'. 'You can't say that,' the person said. 'It's judgmental. It's politically incorrect.' They were mentally well, but had assumed offence on behalf of the affected party. Who has decided that the suffering entailed by mental illness must be hidden? In my experience, it's not the mentally ill themselves. My interviewees were united on this front: their illness caused them to suffer. They were sufferers. To say, 'a person living with a mental illness' implies harmonious co-existence between the disorder and its host – and this is inaccurate and ignorant. Societal rejection of the word 'sufferer' is indicative of a much larger problem: unwillingness to accept the true scale of the duress involved in a mental health condition. *Yes, by all means, have a mental health problem, but, for goodness' sake, don't* **suffer** *from it. What's the point in having it unless it's going to enhance you? I only want to hear that your depression has made you grateful for sunny days, that your anxiety has made you sensitive to others' feelings, and that your eating disorder has made you glad to be alive. I don't want to hear about the* **unpleasant** *bits. I don't want to hear about* **suffering.** In this book, I refer to sufferers *as* sufferers, not out of disrespect, but in recognition of torment they face.

My aim has always been to present stories honestly. For this reason, the book contains passages some might find upsetting – particularly those with personal experience of mental illness. I have provided a broad overview of the conditions described in each chapter in the table of contents, but it is inaccurate to suggest that symptoms restrict themselves to a single disorder so neatly. Discussion of self-harm, for example, occurs in *Georgia*, but also *Yasmine* and *Maya*. Disordered eating is the core pathology in *Beth*, but there are references to weight and body image in *Abby*, *Holly* and *Maya*. In *Holly*, there are descriptions of sexual assault, but sex and relationships also feature in *Yasmine* and *Abby*'s stories. These descriptions are – I hope – never gratuitous, but nor are they deliberately moderated. I have simply recounted thoughts, feeling and incidents as they were recounted to me. If you are concerned about the impact of such material on your own mental health, I urge you to think carefully before continuing. There is no pressure or urgency. Books will always be there; your vulnerability may not. A further content notice: the stories and reflections that make up the bulk of the narrative are book-ended by 'guides'. As I hope is evident, these are not intended as literal instructions on how to develop or recover from mental illness, far less a representation of my own opinions. Rather, they serve to highlight the common misconceptions my interviewees felt surrounded their conditions. At times, they are humorous; at times, they are harsh, callous and inappropriate. This is because those experiencing mental illness are all too often treated harshly, callously and inappropriately.

The women who make up the characters captured between the following pages did a brave and remarkable thing in contributing to this book. They set aside their impressive outer shells, and in so doing uncovered something more affecting than any competent, capable façade. The selves these women revealed were flawed, messy, achingly vulnerable and deeply real. It is this mess of flawed, vulnerable reality that I am honoured to share.

# *Abby*

7.33.

I have been awake for three minutes, and have had enough of today.

7.36.

I have been awake for six minutes, and have had more than enough of today.

7.39.

I will get up in one minute.

7.41.

I have missed the opportunity to get up in the 40-minute slot. I will get up at 7.50.

7.53.

It really makes no sense to get up before 8.00 now.

8.03.

I have left it too late. If I get up now, I will be rushed. When I swing my legs over the side of the bed, the tension will spread upwards, through the soles of my feet, into my calf muscles, around my pelvis, up to my chest. It will be tight and squeezing and sore. It will be like stepping into a bodysuit of tension, and I won't have time to shower, and not showering will make me more tense, and I will scuttle around the room like a crab, ferreting clothes from the piles crouching in the corners. They will smell stale and sour and will be too creased to wear without ironing.

8.09.
There is no way I have enough time to get out the iron, let alone the ironing board.

8.11.
I can't iron this morning, so I have nothing to wear, so I can't get up.

8.16.
If I get up now, I will be *really* rushed. Maybe I still have a fresh shirt hanging in the wardrobe, and if I wore trousers the creases might not show as much as they would in a skirt ...? But then I would have to brush my hair, and it's been four days since I washed it now. The spines of the brush would leave oily indentations between the strands. What if I pulled it into a ponytail without brushing? Could that work? No, of course it couldn't, don't be ridiculous, don't be *absolutely fucking ridiculous*, Abby.

8.22.
I have to leave the house in eight minutes. I have to leave the house in eight minutes in order to arrive on time. I have to leave the house in thirteen minutes in order to arrive late-but-not-so-late-it's-an-issue-late, and eighteen minutes in order arrive pretty-fucking-late-but-maybe-possibly-hopefully-only-late-enough-to-warrant-a-raised-eyebrow-and-not-a-'Can-I-have-a-word?'-late. But calculating that has taken two minutes. So now I have to leave the house in six minutes or eleven minutes or sixteen minutes, and—

8.25.
I can't breathe. I can't fucking breathe. There is a corset laced up around me, but it is laced up too tight, crunching my ribs together like a rattle of xylophone keys and grasping upwards,

14

upwards, upwards, clenching around my chest, clasping around my throat, squeezing so fiercely that all the air inside me is forced out …

8.27.
I can't get there on time. I can't be late. But I can't get there on time. But I can't be late. And I can't … I can't … I can't I can't I can't I CAN'T I CAN'T I CAN'T I—

8.29.
There are billions of burning, blistering beetles crawling up the back of my neck, over the top of my scalp. My skin is melting, sizzling and splitting under their feet. My head is on fire, and my tongue has swollen, thick and slimy, and my heart is banging the blood away from my limbs, away from my lungs and into my eyes, my ears, my mouth, until all I can see and hear and taste is the hot, thick slime of my tongue …

8.30.
Silence. Stillness. Soft and sad as a soggy cornflake, softening sadly in chalk-white milk dregs.

8.31.
I can't get to work on time now. Even if I rocket up, stuff un-socked feet into uncomfortable shoes and leave the house trailing an armful of clothes, ready to button myself into 'competent professional' mode on the train, I won't make it. If I leave for work now, I will be late. I can't be late. My manager has already had to 'have words' about my lateness, and the words that she has had have left me fairly sure that they are not the sort of words she enjoys having, and that if she has to have many more of them she will make sure the need for those words to be had is eliminated. If I am late, I will be eliminated.

I can't be late, but I can't go to work without being late, so the solution is clear: I can't go to work at all. Simple. Why didn't I think of this in the first place?

I am still lying, mummy-like, but the knots of panic trussing my insides begin to unravel. Like rainwater dripping from leaves, the tension gradually drip-drip-drips from my body. There is a dull ache across my shoulders and a throbbing ache at the back of my head and a gnawing ache between my ribs. I ache all over, as if I have just emerged from a boxing match with an opponent who has run rings around me. But my challenger was not a brawny sportsman – it was a dense mass of myelin. A three-pound lump of fatty grey matter that trounces me every time.

When I sit up, the weight of the duvet falls away, goose-bumps erupting across my arms. Harry's side of the bed is a shell of early-morning clumsiness and boy-smell – crumpled pillows and rucked-up sheets infused with testosterone and stubble. Harry sets his alarm for 6.00 in the morning. Harry is up by 6.15. Harry drinks a sludgy concoction of bananas and soy milk and whey protein on the way to the gym at 6.30. Harry does legs on Mondays and arms on Tuesdays and something else and something else and something else on Wednesday–Thursday–Fridays and showers in the nice clean gym showers at 7.30 and is at work by 8.00, and I don't because I'm not Harry and I won't ever be Harry, and sooner or later I won't even *have* Harry any more because I get tethered to my bed in the mornings by crumpled clothes and greasy hair. And, anyway, I never consume any whey. Harry smells of safety and relief. I will never smell like Harry.

I creep across the hallway, desperate to lock myself in the bathroom and scrub my skin raw. Porridgy breakfast-time chatter skitters up the stairs. When you squeeze six people into a five-person house, what happens? *It'll be fine!* we said, waving away raised eyebrows. *It'll be cosy!* we said, mouths distorting in exaggerated grins. *It'll be such a laugh!* we said, doubling over, grotesque caricatures of mirth. What actually happens is that there's noise, noise, noise everywhere, and the air is thickened by the smell of six different deodorants and six different dinners cooking, and the low, ominous hum of the washing machine is a constant, and there is never, ever an hour or minute or corner of a room that is yours and yours alone. It is definitely cosy, but rarely fine. And I very rarely laugh.

The trickle from the shower nozzle spills lazily over my too-big body in the too-small stall. It is not quite hot enough to stop me shivering. I am working Tropical Paradise-scented shower gel into the hair under my arms when there are two sharp taps on the bathroom door. They sound clipped and accusatory. I feel sticky and hairy and indecently fleshy, and I wish I didn't smell so strongly of Tropical Paradise.

'Abby? Is that you?' Ellie-from-across-the-corridor doesn't speak: she chirrups. It is unmistakeable and inescapable. Her voice sounds like her face: round and smooth and perpetually hopeful. When I open the door, cold air prods at the nakedness under my towel. Ellie has been standing right up against the wood, listening, and for a moment we are almost nose to nose. As she stumbles back, her brown eyes come into focus, the smooth skin between her plucked brows puckering.

'Oh, hey? Yeah, so I've got a seminar starting at 9.30? On campus?' Her persistent upwards inflection questionises every sentence. It is *infuriating*. 'I was just wondering if I could just …?' She gestures vaguely behind me to where her tooth-brush and toothpaste balance on the edge of the sink. Even her movements feel like questions. *Stop **asking** me things, Ellie*, I think as I lumber past her, like a great, apologetic hippo. *Can't you see I have no answers?*

Back in the bedroom I feel sticky as I pack myself into yesterday's clothes. I didn't rinse myself properly. The soap still coating my skin makes me stiff. I sit heavily on the bed, knees hunched up to my chest, and the day stretches ahead of me like a deserted racetrack. An ocean of unfilled time, to float in and swim in and wallow in. Surely there could be no greater luxury than a sea of blank time. What *freedom*. Only my unfilled day doesn't feel tantalising. It feels like a sentence. I can't look at my phone because I don't want to see the whingeing red dot above the voicemail icon and I don't want to listen to the whingeing grey voice of my manager. She will not be able to mask her exasperation at having to ask why, *yet again*, I have not *seen fit to grace the office* with my presence. I can't open the curtains, because I think it's sunny this morning. There is waxy yellow light bleeding through the un-curtained corners of the window, and it makes my ears ring and my throat feel thick and sore. When it is sunny you should be warm and colourful and *Shall we eat lunch outside today? Why the hell not?! We're young and free and beautiful! What's not to celebrate?!* You shouldn't be soapy and scratchy and indefinably sick.

I screw my wet towel into a ball and drop it by the bed. The laundry basket is three feet away, but those three feet look complicated today. The towel can sit in a grouchy ball until it starts to fur and reek. I fish a fat bottle of rattly tablets from the silt of my bedside table and twist off the childproof cap. One pink sleeping pill of dubious provenance purchased from eBay will have no effect on me. Three pink sleeping pills of dubious provenance purchased from eBay will make me drowsy. Five will knock me out. Six will leave me with a hangover. I count the pills in my hand – 1-2-3-4-5-6-7 – and swallow them with flat Coke that tastes of sugary dust. Then I pull the duvet up, over my head, and the world goes black until Harry shakes me awake in the evening.

When Harry shakes me awake in the evening, we don't talk about my greasy hair or my mouldy towel or my work shoes, lying exactly where they lay when he left this morning. He doesn't mention the seven texts he sent me over the course of the day and the seven replies he didn't receive. He doesn't ask why these days – the empty days – are starting to outnumber the not-empty days, and we don't acknowledge the fear that thickens the silence between us. Harry goes downstairs. I hear him laughing in the kitchen with the others, and I wish everyone in this house would stop *bloody laughing* all the time, as if they only laugh to highlight my not-laughing. He comes back upstairs later – quite a lot later – with two bowls of pasta and green pesto. The food feels pappy in my mouth. While we eat, Harry watches football highlights on his phone with his headphones in.

As the day ebbs away, replaced by a blue-black bruise of night, Harry showers and changes, and I put on last night's pyjamas and question why I took them off in the first place. We lie, limbs tangled with the covers, wishing for a breeze to buffet the curtains. We lie for a long time, not sleeping, not speaking. Eventually I shift towards him, and he loops an arm around me, and I rest my head on the ball of his shoulder. His breathing is very deep, and every breath sounds like a sigh, and there is a throbbing pain in my nose and throat as two tears slide down and wet his white T-shirt. There is nothing I can say that I have not said before, and the despair in the room is as close as the heat. We are too hot like this, wrapped in one another, but we do not move. Sweat gathers in the creases of my neck, and I want to lift my hair, but I do not move. Harry falls asleep, and his arm falls away from my back, but I do not move.

---

When I met Harry I was drunk and nauseated and normal. We caught spangled glimpses of one another in the strobe lighting of a horrible club, and mashed our bodies together to the beat of horrible music, and he stood and flapped his hands as I was horribly sick in the gutter outside. When I had finished spewing dark swirls of vodka and Coke onto the paving stones, I wiped my mouth with the back of my hand, straightened up, and cocked my head to the club's hungry music. 'We going back in then or what?' He looked at me, beer and confusion clouding his watery eyes, and said, 'What? Back in there? There's no way we'll get back in. You're so drunk.' And I tried to walk too fast on ridiculous heels and wobbled precariously and slurred, 'Try and stop me.' He hoisted me up and looked at me like I was the best thing in the world and said, 'You're fucking mental. You know that, right?'

The first university year was a whirlwind of books and bravado and Harry. We were charged particles, barrelling towards each other over and over again, never sure whether we would collide in an embrace or a blistering of bitter words. We fought and we pined and we didn't speak for weeks, and then we made up, faces fused by saliva and contrition, insatiable for whatever young, giddy derivative of love we had. We were electrons.

The weeks ran through my fingers like water. Second year swung up like a garden rake in a slapstick sketch, and I stumbled through the first term reeling from the thwack between my eyes. The safe, sensible schedule of day and night that had contained my life up to that point fell away, and I vacillated between weed-smoking, wine-glugging oblivion and keyboard-tapping, coffee-downing anxiety. I returned from raucous nights out in the early hours of the morning and collapsed, broken, into bed, then woke mid-afternoon and feverishly tried to catch up on weeks' worth of essays, watching the sun rise without leaving my desk to wash, change or even remove the smeared nightclub make-up.

I dealt with self-doubt and self-loathing through hair dye and piercings. 'Crisis piercings', I called them. When I kissed Harry goodbye one morning, my past-the-shoulder brown hair tickled his cheek, and he tucked a strand behind my single-pierced ears. Later, I lay with my head in his lap and he ran gentle fingers through bleached tufts, reassuring me over and over that he *did* like it, he really *did* think it looked good; it was just a bit of a *surprise*, that was all. He traced the loops of the five gold rings in each of my ears. His palms were sweaty and smelled of salt. When I cried he asked me why I'd done it, and I said I'd just needed a change. He smiled at me like I was the best thing in the world, but this time it was like he was realising that all the best things in the world are warped and strange at the edges. And he murmured, 'You're fucking mental. You know that, right?'

By the time I moved into the third-year house I was spiralling. Within weeks, the nauseating knot of dread once reserved for essay deadlines had set up permanent residence in the bottom of my gut, and I was dogged by a relentless sense of doom. Desperate, I made an appointment with the university counselling service, but as Therapy Day drew nearer I felt more and more incapacitated by fear. The fear was as intangible and illogical as it was intense. The clock ticked closer and closer to Therapy Time, and my body curled tighter and tighter into an embryonic ball, and I thought: *I cannot go. I cannot go.* I did not go. When Harry came home from his afternoon lecture, eager to hear how the session had gone, I collapsed on him in a slump of snot and anguish.

'You didn't *go?* What do you *mean* you didn't go?' he moaned, raking a clawed hand through his hair.

'I couldn't! I *couldn't!*' I howled, bunching myself into a knot. 'I was *too anxious!*'

The air filled with my sniffles and Harry's sighs and the ringing of obvious, unspoken words. Too anxious to get help with my anxiety? The tide in Harry's eyes ebbed weakly.

Spring term and six weeks of blank time leading up to a coursework deadline. For a month I deteriorated steadily, barely noticing the sheer drop on the horizon until I was tumbling down, down, down. I became almost entirely nocturnal during the final two pre-deadline weeks, snatching an hour of sleep at midday here, another two hours at 5am there, otherwise sitting so still at my desk I imagined myself putting down roots between the floorboards. When I did leave the house, it was to wander aimlessly through the streets – in the middle of the night just as easily as the day – my mind blank, senses dulled. I forgot how it felt to have a chest that didn't lurch and convulse with every breath, and a head that didn't buzz with low, insistent pain, and muscles that didn't tic and tense of their own accord. After thirteen days and 23 hours I had reached the end of the assignment and my tether. My tutor would be collecting hard copies of the coursework from his desk at 7am; the printer spat out my final page at 6.30.

'You're not going to get there if you walk,' said my housemate Chris, leaning against the kitchen doorframe, watching me struggle to tie shoelaces with uncooperative fingers.

'Oh. Well. I might,' I said, knowing that I wouldn't.

'No, you won't,' said Chris, knowing that I wouldn't.

'No. I suppose I won't,' I sighed, accepting that I wouldn't. I couldn't summon the strength to care.

'Take my bike,' said Chris, bundling me out of the door, and, in a daze, I did. The early morning air was crisp and refreshing, and I felt as though I'd been put through a laundry mangle in the night. My legs ached with the effort of propelling the bicycle wheels round, and my throat stung with the unfamiliar influx of oxygen, and suddenly one of my feet went cold, and then the other, and I heard something bump onto the ground; I looked down and saw that my shoes had fallen off and were lying in the road behind me, as if running a marathon independent of an athlete. My feet were bare on the bicycle pedals and the wind was whipping between my toes and I felt horribly, ridiculously naked, but it was 6.45 and I was ten minutes from where I needed to be and I had to keep forcing the bicycle wheels in jeering, spiteful revolutions.

When I got back to the house, Chris and Harry were sitting at the table, eating toast topped with sand-coloured peanut butter, drinking sand-coloured tea from mismatched mugs.

'Did you get it in?' Chris asked, teeth doughy.

'Four minutes to spare,' I panted. Chris whooped, then choked, and raised his mug in an elaborate gesture of triumph. Harry didn't. Harry looked at me.

'Where are your shoes?'

'Fell off. On the way. Couldn't stop. No time.'

Harry looked at me for a long, swollen moment. I was wearing a scrubby black coat over plaid pyjamas, feet mottled purple by the cold of the morning. Salt crusted from my nose to my mouth, and I tasted iron on cracked lips. I was shivering from head to toe, and my breath came in short, sharp gasps, and the blue-black bags under my eyes were so heavy I could feel them dragging down my lids.

Harry looked at me. He didn't look at me like I was the best thing in the world. He looked at me like I was a monster, or a deformed baby.

'You're fucking mental,' he whispered. The tears trapped in his throat made his voice as thick and gluey as the peanut butter collected at the corners of his mouth.

'You're fucking *mental*. You know that, right?'

---

If you had to draw a picture of a counsellor, you would draw Anna. If you had to cast a film featuring a counsellor, you would scour the country for an actress who looked exactly like Anna. If you were a woman who looked like Anna, it would be criminal to pursue a career in anything but counselling. Everything about Anna is soft and neutral and unthreatening. She is a remarkable feat of unremarkability. Middle-aged, middle-height, middle-build, dressed in thoroughly middle-of-the-road clothes and sitting in an office on the middle floor of a building in the middle of the street.

'Perhaps you'd like to tell me a little about what's brought you here today, Abigail?' Anna asks, in a middly sort of voice.

And I think: *Yep. I can do this one. I know the answer to this one. No revision, no panicked trips to the library – I've got this one **down**.*

'Yes. Well. I suppose I … The thing is, I …'

And then I think: *Fuck – I can't do this one. Fuck.* This is supposed to be the easy one. This is like the starter for ten, except *much* easier. Like the starter for five, or the starter for two, or … If I can't manage this one, how the *fuck* am I going to manage the rest of them? The really deep, probing ones? *Fuck.* Why am I here? I don't really have 'problems'. I mean, of course I have *problems*, because everyone does, but I only have *problems*, not *Problems*. I only have problems like, 'Oh no, I haven't done any washing in six weeks and have no clean underwear.' Like, 'Oh God, I really drank too much last night and now I feel like my tongue is made of carpet and my insides are made of mud.' Like, 'Oh fuck, I'm at work and I'm crying, and everyone can see me crying, and I don't know why I'm crying but I know I can't stop crying.' *Normal* problems.

In the waiting room, I saw a lot of people with real, serious *Problem* problems. The girl whose face was so red and puffy she looked like she was in anaphylactic shock. The boy whose heel tapped incessantly against his chair and whose fingers drummed out an anxious rhythm on his thigh. The girl whose legs were the width of my wrists, who bobbed from foot to foot in front of the notice boards like a lissom rubber duck, pretending to read the pinned-up leaflets about sexual health. They deserve to be here. I don't. I'm a fraud.

I am crying. Not civilised, blotting-a-tear-delicately-from-the-cheek crying. Sobbing. *Howling.* I am sitting opposite the queen of non-description in a chair and a room and a building designed to be nondescript, but I am not being nondescript. I can think of few times when I have been more demonstratively descript.

'What about that question makes you so upset, Abigail?'

*Oh, Anna. I don't know. I'm upset because there's too much to say, and I'm scared of saying it to you, because – bless you, Anna – I'm sure you're doing this job because you want to be kind and solve people's problems, and good on you for wanting to help, but the thing is, Anna, I feel like, with me, it's just not going to be that simple. Because with me, you see, Anna, I am the problem. I'm upset, Anna, because even though I don't know you, and I'm not supposed to care what you think, and you've clearly put a lot of effort into convincing me that you're a completely blank canvas, I really want you to like me, Anna. And I'm upset because, if I tell you what's brought me here, the fact is, Anna, you're not going to like me. If I tell you about the not-getting-out-of-bed-in-the-morning and the cancelling-plans-at-the-last-minute and the sleeping-through-the-day and the worrying-through-the-night and the being-horrible-to-poor-Harry, you're not going to like me, Anna. No one does, and no one should. Anna, I think I'm upset because I know it's all my fault. Everything. All of it. It's all my fault, Anna.*

I don't launch this torrent of words at Anna. I tell her about the overcrowded, over-noisy house and how *cosy* and how *fine* and how much of a *laugh* it was supposed to be, and how actually it's just a messy prison where I can't relax. I tell her about sweet, kind, patient Harry and how much better he deserves, and how I've started to wonder whether he might prefer to come home and find me dead than come home and find me asleep in bed. I talk and cry and shred tissues for 50 minutes, and when I go back to real life I feel as if I've been sitting in Anna's room for 50 years.

The doctor Anna sends me to see is hassled and has letters and prescription pads and half-drunk mugs of coffee all over his desk, and after alarmingly few words and an alarmingly brief questionnaire I find myself walking across the road to fill a prescription for antidepressants. The pills, shaped like tiny white bullets, are shame and comfort – proof that I am cracked and broken; hope that the cracks and breaks are fixable. For the first few days, gulping down a tablet every morning has little effect. After swallowing I sit, tense, on the bed.

*Is it working yet? Maybe now? Or maybe now? Do I feel as bad now as I did yesterday morning, when I hadn't taken a pill? If I do, is that definitely because of the pill, or could it just be that I slept better / it's a warm day / it's a Thursday? Do I feel better yet? Maybe now? Has it started working yet? How about now? Now?*

When it finally kicks in, the medication gives me the boost of a strong cup of coffee. I don't feel *happier* – not in a sunny, laughing-and-smiling way – but the murky sense of dread that has been underscoring my day-to-day life begins to peel away, until one day I realise it has been replaced with a liberating indifference. For the first time in years, I am not foggy: I am focused. Getting up with my alarm no longer feels like a mountain to scale – more a hummock to hop over. I can go to work and get things done and come home in the evenings and go to the pub and not care about the noisy house or the imperfect achievements or the gnawing pointlessness of it all. I can function, and functioning feels fantastic after aeons of fog.

At first, Harry is elated by the departure of the haunted spirit that has been using his girlfriend as host. Who *cares* if my sudden energy is bordering on mania? At least I'm not a lifeless slug any more! So *what* if I'm drinking a bottle of wine a night, clinging to the acidic habit like a limpet? At least I'm having a good time! Does it *matter* that my newfound functionality is becoming more dysfunctional with every passing day? At least it's *different!* Within weeks, the tide in his eyes has changed. His teeth gnaw at his lips. His eyes track the wine from bottle to glass to my lips. We are together – stoically, immovably together – but it is a taught, sour thing, crackling with negative energy. We are electrons.

One particularly messy morning after a particularly heavy night before – drinks and clubs and pumping music and little white pills under my tongue with no prescription – I open my eyes to a splintering headache and Harry's broad, T-shirted back, arched over as he runs his hands through his hair. I reach across the gulf between us, pressing the flat of my hand to his warm body, and for a moment I feel him flinch.

'How are you feeling?' he mutters, turning to face me.

'Like sick,' I yawn, forcing a smile that feels like a leer.

'Look. Don't you think … I mean, I don't know, Abs. I know I'm not inside your head. And I know it's not, like, easy, or whatever. But don't you think maybe these meds might be a bit … Are you sure they're a good idea?'

Indignation heats my cheeks. 'What? What are you saying? I don't know what you mean. I don't – I can't – Harry, what?'

'Come on, Abs. You *do* know. You *have to* know. You're out of control. It's not *working.*'

'What's not working? The meds? *My* meds aren't working for *you*? Sorry, Harry. I totally forgot that *you* were the one with depression. *You're* the one who didn't used to be able to get out of bed in the mornings and who couldn't leave the house for days, aren't you?'

'Abs, you know I'm not—'

'Actually, Harry, these are *my* meds. They're *my* meds because they're *my* feelings, and *I* think it's going *great*. I *love* these meds. They make *everything* better for me. Look at me: I can go to work now, and I can go see my friends now, and I can go out and have a good time now, and I—'

'*YOU'RE SO FUCKING SELFISH, ABBY!*'

I have been so caught up in my righteous tirade of reasons why Harry is wrong and I am right that I haven't noticed his muscles go tense and his jaw set hard and the tic at the corner of his eye start to dance. It takes me by surprise that there is suddenly a roaring volcano of a man standing over me, spitting resentful lava.

'You're the most *selfish person* I have *ever met!* Do you *realise* that? All you *ever* talk about is yourself! All you care about is *your* life and *your* problems and the things that make stuff easy for *you*! But you're not the only one in the world, Abby! There are *six* of us in this house, and there are *two* of us in this relation-ship, and only *one* of us has become a *fucking nightmare* over the past few weeks!'

'But I—'

'*No*! You don't get to say that any more. You don't get to say anything any more. You don't get to. You don't get to …'

His voice makes a sound as if it has been snagged by a fishing hook, and his face sags like a punctured bouncy castle, and he is jelly on the bed. He is sobbing, and I am sobbing, and we are holding onto one another like babies clutching fingers. We cry and cling for minutes, snot and sweat mingling on our skin, and I feel like the emperor, exposed by a child. My selfishness has shrouded me, protected my modesty, but now it lies wrinkled at my ankles.

'I want you to be happy, Abs.' Harry chokes, muffled by the swell of my chest. 'But I don't want you to be like *this*. I'm scared.'

28

I run my fingers through his thick, dishwater-blonde hair, and think maybe I am selfish, because maybe we're all selfish, deep down.

Harry feels young in my arms. He shudders with each breath. I feel heavy and tired and nothing more.

---

As it struggles to force its way through the leaves of the trees in next-door's garden, the sun casts patchwork shadows onto my legs. I am eating handfuls of dried cherries from a brown paper bag. They are sour. They stick my teeth together. On the narrow aisle of scrubby grass stretching out in front, Chris and Harry flick a dented football lazily back and forth. They are like lanky children, allowed out to play before bed.

I pour myself a second half-glass of red wine. It tastes soft and deep in my mouth. I won't drink any more after this. It's been a few months now, and the insatiable hunger for sensation that growled in the wake of the last medication hasn't returned. The new pills make me feel clear-headed and capable. There is no chaos around the corners.

Harry glances at me over Chris' shoulder, raising his eyebrows in a silent question. Harry still has anxious eyes. Beetle eyes. They skitter across my face. It is hard for him to accept my smile when he is the one to grip my hand and guide my breath at two in the morning, insisting over and over that I'm *not* going to die, that my heart *isn't* going to beat out of my chest, that I *can* breathe, that the world *won't* collapse in a heap of bones and rubble. But he is learning – we are learning – not to panic about the black days, or the dark thoughts, or the panic attacks. At my last session with Anna, I told her that Harry and I were going to stay together after all. That maybe it wouldn't be forever, but it would be for now. And she wasn't allowed to tell me what she thought, because that wouldn't be *middly* at all, and it was probably just refracted light ricocheting from window to iris, but I felt like her eyes twinkled approval.

I shift from the step to the ground, and let the sun fall onto my face. I'm not finding it so unbearable any more – the trope of a beautiful day. I don't feel young and free and celebratory, and I very rarely eat lunch outside, but I feel the gentle warmth of the sunlight, soaking into my skeleton, and I like it. The wine has left my lips tasting rich and slightly bitter and my brain feeling calm and slightly woolly, and I didn't sleep well last night so I feel tired but not frantically tired, and I made mistakes at work today so I feel guilty but not frantically guilty. There will be other nights and other days, and maybe they're not leading up to any grand denouement, and maybe there isn't much point to any of it, but it still feels good to have so much time ahead.

I last felt black – really, truly, bleakly black – about six months ago. Perhaps in another six months I will feel really, truly, bleakly black again. Perhaps it will happen every twelve months for the rest of my life, or perhaps it will happen more frequently than that, or perhaps it will happen whenever I try to come off my medication, or perhaps it will never happen again. I don't know. I can't know the future. I can only really know today.

Harry is still looking at me, and the water of his eyes is choppy. I smile, and the waves still. His nose crinkles, like it always does when he grins, and the waxy sunlight falls across half his face, and he looks safe and strong and real, and perhaps it won't be forever, but it will be for now.

I dip my chin towards my chest and squeeze my eyes in a cat's smile: a response to the silent question suspended between us in July evening air.

Yes. For now, I feel OK.

———

'But it's mainly just feeling sad, isn't it?
We all feel sad sometimes.'

## Depression: Your Three-Step Guide to the Way We All Feel Sometimes!

### Step One: Descending

One day, when you are sitting at your desk, or walking down the street, or chatting to a friend, you realise that the colour has started to bleed from the scene around you. It is as if, up to now, the world has been full of thick, brightly dyed liquid, but now someone has punctured the landscape at the bottom and the vivid fluid is dripping away. It happens slowly. At times, you doubt it is happening at all. At other times, you wonder whether someone has taken a pin to you too: pricked a hole in the sole of your foot and stood back to watch something bleed from you. What is it? This slowly dripping, day-by-day loss? What are you losing – your soul? Your spirit?

You tire more easily than usual. You get home from work and fall asleep on the sofa. You wake at bedtime, groggy and disoriented. Perhaps you go to bed and sleep some more. Perhaps you stay awake for most of the night, lost in the vortex of your phone. When you think of going to work the next day, your ears rush with inexplicable terror, and yet the world around you is so grey that even terror cannot put colour back where it belongs.

Wait – when did that happen? When did the slow drip-drip-dripping drain all the reds and blues and greens away, leaving only the grey? When did the oozing of energy from the soles of your feet turn into the flooding away of all feeling? When did everything get lost?

## Step Two: Defending

But you cannot feel this way. You have a wonderful life. You love your job. You love your family. There is *no reason whatsoever* for you to feel so darkly, debilitatingly bleak.

Perhaps you are ill. That's it. Anaemic, or infected, or coming down with something. Simple. Except that your blood is stubbornly replete with iron and white cells; your body obstinately free from infection. The promised 'something' never 'comes down'. You are not *ill*, but nor are you *well*. Your muscles ache. Your skin is dry. The beginnings of a sob crouch in your throat, but you do not cry: you leak. Tears sheet down your face. It is not *sadness* you feel – the sadness escaped through the soles of your feet. You feel grey.

But you cannot feel this way. There is nothing wrong with you. And so you carry on, one foot in front of the other, one day spooling into the next, and you contort your lips into a plastic smile when a colleague makes a joke, and you force your jaw to maul the leather-textured food in your mouth, and when you catch yourself researching 'suicide + reliable + failsafe' you shut down the browser before you can really register what you are doing. Because you cannot feel this way. Because there is nothing wrong with you.

## Step Three: Drowning

At some point, when you are crouched over your desk, or dragging your feet along the street, or propping open your eyelids as a friend talks at you, something breaks. The delicate thread tethering you to the world snaps, and you plummet downwards. Perhaps you feel panic. Perhaps you feel confusion. Perhaps you feel nothing.

When you get into bed that night, or that afternoon, or that morning, you are vaguely aware that you will not emerge for some time. How can you face the real world when you are not a real person? You are an empty outline, devoid of colour, devoid of an inside. You feel like a human sandbag. Where your body touches the sheets there is pain. When you open your eyes there is pain.

When breath fills your lungs there is pain. Wait – no – you were wrong. You *do* have an inside. Your inside is pain.

Perhaps there are people who try to talk to you. Perhaps there are people who try to extract you from the safe, excruciating cocoon of cotton covers and crisis. Perhaps there are people who say: 'But why do you feel this way? There is nothing wrong with you.' You realise your voice – your internal voice – has changed. It used to agree – *There is nothing wrong with me* – but it has changed. *Why wouldn't I feel this way? What isn't wrong with me?* You feel as if all the world's problems – all the cruelties and atrocities and brutalities of the seven continents – have been stuffed inside your empty outline. There is not 'something wrong': *I am wrong.*

You feel as if you have been dipped into a vat of boiling oil, then dropped into a bathtub full of liquid concrete. The grit worms into the sores covering your body and sets hard. You are trapped in a heavy mass, every inch of you burning, screaming, rotting.

> 'That's the thing. It's not just feeling
> sad. It's not like that at all.'

What *is* the relationship between sadness and depression?

Sadness is the swish of a paint-smeared brush in a cup of clean water: a dark silhouette dissipating into pale fluid. Sadness is transient and translucent. If sadness splatters your skin, it is cold and damp and unpleasant, but you blot it away with a paper towel and soon feel good as new. When the time is right, you can pour sadness away, and the ghostly ring it leaves in the cup disappears with a rinse of fresh water.

Depression is a thick slick of acrylic, slithering from paint tube to water cup, swirled and swilled until the fluid is tarry. Depression is opaque. It stains your skin. When the time is right, depression oozes lazily down the plughole, clogging the sink, sticking to the sides of the cup. Depression resists evisceration. Sadness is to depression as an unseasonably fresh April morning is to months of icy winter.

The false likening of depression to sadness is at the heart of one myth my interviewees were keen to dispel: that depression is a 'normal' state, experienced by everyone at some point. This is not true. Everyone feels *sad*, but few people have depression. Academically, mood disorders such as depression fall under the heading of 'abnormal psychology': they are, by definition, *not normal*. If everyone experienced depression, it would be considered 'normal psychology' (otherwise known as just 'psychology'). While the normalising of depression is usually borne of compassion – a desire to reduce sufferers' alienation – it is all too often interpreted as dismissive. *But **everyone** feels this way. You're experiencing nothing abnormal. Why are you making such a fuss?* Sadness is normal; sadness is universal. Depression is neither. The confusion between the former and the latter is understandable, and the distinction is difficult to pin down. The women I interviewed *did* describe feelings of sadness – of heavy-bellied, glass-eyed melancholy – but their sadness was encompassed by something bigger, darker, heavier. My own conclusion was this: it is not that depression sufferers are *not* sad; it is that they are *more than* sad. They are handicapped – rarely permanently, but often significantly – by a hounding presence that trails lethargy, terror and self-hatred. They feel the pain of being set on fire, and the confinement of being set in concrete.

There is no single, unifying 'recipe' for depression. Some of my interviewees traced its roots back to the distant past, describing child selves weighed down by world-weary, unchild-like preoccupations. Some pinpointed specific events – traumas, upheavals, bereavements – as the cause of their descent into murky fog. Many became visibly anxious when probed on the origin of the problem, nibbling their lips as deep furrows ploughed across their foreheads: the truth – that they *just didn't know* where it all came from – felt shameful. The desire to iden-tify a cause was widespread, and when there was ostensibly 'no cause' the guilt was palpable. *I shouldn't be like this, should I? Some people have been through horrendous things – they deserve to be depressed. But not me. I have no reason to be like this.* Again and again, a depression diagnosis was conceptualised as a badge to be earned, preferably through extreme hardship or suffering. One woman who could not identify a cause for her depression described feeling as if she, an able-bodied person, had been ran-domly assigned a disabled parking permit. *Why do I have this? I don't deserve this. At any moment, somebody is going to find me out …*

The notion that depression can only be acquired as a result of adverse circumstances is another pervasive myth. While certain illnesses *do* stem from traumatic experience – as you will see later, Holly couldn't be haunted by dark memories were it not for the dark experiences that spawned them – depression can take hold in response to something or nothing. In this respect, Abby represents the majority of my interviewees: although unaffected by poverty, bereavement or abuse, she finds herself mired in turmoil. Many of us now understand that depression can be caused by brain chemistry – namely, an imbalance of the neurotransmitters that influence mood[11] – and that genetic inheritance may also play a part.[12] In some cases, these biological factors are sufficient to trigger depressive episodes; in others, a gentle nudge from life sets the wheels of pathology in motion. A happy, balanced upbringing may reduce the risk of depression developing in adulthood, but it is not a vaccination – and becoming ill despite a happy, balanced upbringing (or in the absence of a family history of depression) is not a mark of weakness, ingratitude or poor character. It is simple bad luck.

I was staggered and saddened by the blame my interviewees heaped on themselves: for their own struggles, for the struggles of others, for the ills of the world. They assigned themselves the role of 'wrongdoer', and stooped under the weight of criticism hefted onto narrow shoulders. This is one of the many ways in which depression is a cruel catch-22: self-hatred is as much a part of the condition as hopelessness and pessimism, and relentless self-battering lowers sufferers further into the fog.

Exhaustion, too, is an inescapable symptom of the illness. I have never met a group of people for whom the word 'bed' is as loaded with connotations. *Staying in bed is lazy. Staying in bed is a luxury. Staying in bed is a choice.* Many of my interviewees became abashed when describing weeks lost to the island of mattress and duvet, sensitive to public perception of such behaviour. *Spending all day in bed?! Surely that's what we would all do if given the chance!* A day spent in bed with only depression for company is more akin to 24 hours on a torture slab than a period of blissful rest – not an ocean in which to wallow, but a sentence. Bed is a safe, predictable purgatory: under the covers, a ghoulish cabaret plays on repeat, interspersing '101 Reasons Why You Cannot Get Out of Bed' with '101 Reasons Why You Are a Terrible Person for Not Getting Out of Bed'. This captures the cruel, but common, intersection between depression and anxiety: the tension of the latter prevents relaxation, while the apathy of the former squashes any motivation to act. The brain is abuzz with knowledge of the million tasks one should be completing, but the body is inert: Abby is patently aware that she *should* be at work, keeping to the commitments piled in the corners of her conscience, but 'indefinable sickness' tethers her to the mattress. The depression/anxiety cocktail sends its victims crashing into closed windows like bumblebees, as desperate to escape as they are trapped.

While those whose depression confines them to bed face allegations of indolence, when sufferers persevere with 'normal life' they fly head first into a different accusation: fraudulence. *Are you sure you're not making this up? I mean, you don't seem depressed* ... On one level, this is a reasonable argument: if we accept depression as a debilitating condition, surely its sufferers should *seem* debilitated? Over the course of this project, I often found myself listening to accounts of agonising internal duress and struggling to reconcile them with the bright-eyed composure of their narrators. Understandably, we like packaging to match contents: it makes the world make sense. However, in the case of depression – and mental illness more widely – we have to accept that *seeming* is a very poor indicator of *being*. While some can mask the condition, others cannot; while some find themselves tethered to their beds by inertia, others do not. Attempting to place sufferers in a hierarchy according to their symptom manifestation is unhelpful – those who maintain a 'healthy' façade are no more or less unwell than those who do not; nor are they more or less 'admirable'. They are affected in a different way. What I can say with absolute confidence is that people do not 'pretend' to have depression, and that the phrase 'but you don't seem depressed' has no place in our handling of the condition.

Abby not only embodies the internal turmoil of depression, but also the havoc it wreaks on relationships. A depressed loved one can seem self-indulgent, stubborn and – yes – selfish. Realising just how many of my interviewees had had this accusation levelled at them forced me to consider whether it holds a grain of truth: is depression a selfish condition? Analyses of speech and writing show that depression sufferers use personal pronouns more than their non-depressed counterparts.[13] Is the illness, at its heart, a disorder of self-obsession? If selfishness is the state of being at the centre of one's own universe, then of course sufferers are guilty – *everyone* is guilty. *Everyone* is at the centre of their own universe. This self-centration may be exacerbated in depression sufferers, but for good reason. When the self you thought you knew turns into a thing you cannot recognise, obsessive inward focus seems like the only means of sussing out the switch. It doesn't feel *selfish*: it feels *sensible*.

Depression sufferers may also tend towards introspection. Not-leaving-bed days and too-anxious-to-go-out days and too-numb-to-cry days are claustrophobic because they are days spent in the darkest corners of the mind. But 'selfishness' smacks of greed: not just of self-preoccupation, but of self-satisfaction. On these counts, are depression sufferers culpable? Perhaps they are inward-facing and self-reflective to a fault, but it is not preening self-congratulation: it is a torturous state of jeering self-loathing. Over the course of this project I met people who were struggling with themselves: I met no one selfish.

Abby's story is not tied up with a chocolate box bow, because that is not her truth. She benefits from two conventional treatments – pharmaceutical and psychological – as this was the combination of remedies most commonly reported (and most commonly found helpful) by my interviewees. In this sense, Abby is 'lucky': although many sufferers gain relief through medication, others do not, or they endure side effects

so intolerable that any benefits are eclipsed. While talking therapy is embraced by some, others find it invasive and alien. Just
as no experience of depression is the same as another, experiences of treatment and recovery vary widely. My interviewees
were quick to dismiss the concept of a 'happy ending' as fallacy.
That is not to say that *happiness* – the emotional state we all
experience sometimes – will forever elude them: it is the concept of 'ending' that does not fit. After a long period of despair,
relearning the art of contentment is an ongoing challenge: like
a rusty instrumentalist, one must reawaken muscles and memories that have been lying dormant.

Some of my interviewees even described feeling guilty
about reacquainting themselves with happiness, as if they
were betraying the part of themselves that had struck up a
kinship with misery. Even those whose 'black days' had long
since passed were uncomfortable with the notion that it had
'ended' – perhaps because depression had been a companion,
and to barricade it into the past felt disloyal. Interestingly, those
women who were in the throes of depression at the time of
interview balked at the idea that the condition might never be
'finished': they clung to the hope of total transformation. Those
already established on the path towards recovery were more
mellow: able to appreciate the distance between themselves
and their demons without the need for reassurance that they
could go further.

'When you're in it – when you're in the depression –
you're so unhappy you think you'll only feel better once
you've escaped from it completely. You hate it so much
that you don't want even the shadow of it in your life.
But then you move away from it a little and you realise
you do feel better, and you move further away and you
feel better still, and you go on feeling better the further

away you get. And at that point you start not minding so much that you can still see it behind you, because in a way it's comforting to look back on it. Because if you're looking back on it you're no longer inside it. And you stop thinking, *Can I get further away? Can I get away from it completely?* because you're too busy feeling glad with where you are.'

# What I wish I could tell you about my depression

There may be things I can't do because of my depression. There may be things I can do, despite my depression. There may be things I can't do sometimes but can do at other times. Depression doesn't affect me consistently, predictably or globally.

My depression can make me feel as though I have flu. It gives me headaches, stomach-aches, muscle aches. I ache all over. I'm sorry if I complain a lot about being tired, or if I sleep more than other people. I know it must seem like laziness, but the exhaustion is real and physical.

The fact that I am depressed does not mean you are a bad parent, sibling, relative, friend or partner. Perhaps there have been problems in our relationship, and perhaps those have affected me, as I'm sure they have affected you. But my depression is probably unrelated to anything you did or did not do. Please try not to feel personally responsible for my condition: when you feel guilty, I feel guilty that you are feeling guilty.

You might know other people with depression, and their depression might look different to mine. Please do not try to draw comparisons between us – to distinguish between 'severe' and 'mild' cases. They might be able to work, and I might not; I might hide my depression in public, and they might not. We are different people, and our depression will manifest differently. Not better or worse, or more or less valid – just different.

I spend a lot of time feeling bad about myself. My mind is a cruel, punishing place. I can think of so many ways in which

I am not good enough, and many of them are things I will never be able to change.

My depression rarely pays attention to the calendar, the occasion, the weather. Of course I wish I wasn't depressed at Christmas, or on someone's birthday, or in the summer, or on 'a beautiful morning', but I can't control it. I am not being intentionally ungrateful or obstructive.

Gratitude and depression are not mutually exclusive: my having depression does not mean I am not grateful for the privileges I have in my life, or the people I have around me. I can be grateful for those things and still have depression.

There is no single treatment to cure all cases of depression, but there are many things that might work. Medication, psychological treatments, exercise, a change of career, alternative therapies – they all have huge potential, but none of them is magic.

If I tell you how I am feeling, the best thing you can do is accept what I am telling you as true. I don't need a list of reasons why I shouldn't feel that way – I know these feelings are not rational or logical – and I don't usually want a barrage of practical solutions. The most helpful things are patience and empathy.

Being depressed is lonely. I appreciate people keeping me company, in person or through messages. Even more, I appreciate people still wanting to be close to me after a period when my depression has made me insular and isolated.

# *Yasmine*

'Did you feel on top of the world?'

No. I felt I had swallowed the world.

I felt I had taken the world between two palms – the whole variegated globe of it – and brought it to my mouth. I had peeled back my lips, dropped open my jaw and expanded my throat. My cheeks strained to accommodate the sphere of blue and green and I took it into me – all of it – and it stretched me taut. My cheeks were like two wombs, tight and swollen with the bulk of life. For a moment, when I tried to swallow, I couldn't breathe. The mass of it was suffocating. But then my tongue sank down and my chest opened up and it went into me, and I was a snake bolting prey.

I took in every arid desert and lush forest, and the two melded inside me, and the moisture seeping into the sands was ecstatic. I took in the sacrosanct orb of the moon and its legion of stars. I took in rivers and oceans and teardrops and rain, and the liquid swirled through my veins, salty and clear. Most of all, I took in the sun. The periwinkle peeking of the sun in the morning and the peach-mottled ebb of the sun at dusk. Every sunbeam that had ever shone was inside me, and the glorious heat radiated from my eyes and ears and the tips of my fingers.

I didn't feel on top of the world. I felt that I was the world.

---

I am up very high in the hospital. My bed – tucked into the corner of the bay – is next to a large window, and outside the window the city spools, busy and grey. It is like when you look at a patch of earth or grass, eyes scanning the spot as a whole, and it looks still and unmoving. And then you switch into your other vision, your high definition vision, and you see that within the stillness the ground is seething. Insects scuttle in and around and over one another like lice in thick hair. When you adjust your lenses – lock in your retinae – you see that the city is pulsing with tiny, suited ants. The streets are teeming; the offices bursting; the monuments bustling. I wonder whether anyone has thought of this analogy before. It is, I think, a *brilliant* analogy. An *inspired* analogy. My cluster of senses is so *brilliantly, inspirationally* attuned to the outside world. My high-definition vision is so clear – so precise – that every corner I see is as pointed as a pin, every edge as sharp as a blade. I am the only one who sees in this way. I am so *special*.

The nurse stationed beside my bed is a marvellous mass of coffee-bean flesh. She sits like a solid slab of marble and stares into the middle distance. When she leans over to wrap the blood pressure cuff around my upper arm, her skin smells of coconut. It is a deep, wonderful smell. Her phone is charging next to my bed. Every so often, it illuminates with a message she ignores. I want to read the messages. I want to know more about her. She is mine. In the six-bed bay, no one else has a nurse all of their very own, stationed solidly next to their bed like a sentry. Not the appendicitis in Bed Two or the kidney infection in Bed Five. Just special, *special* me. When I go to the toilet, she gives me a plastic bowl to pee into. I think this is eminently sensible. The straw-yellow fluid is a part of special me. Every part of me must be preserved.

I have always had a nurse of my own, ever since I got here. In 24 hours, I have had four different nurses. *Four!* All for *me!* They have all been solid and strong. They have all worn gold crucifixes around thick, creased necks. They have all talked to me about God. When Nurse Three, Esther, began to talk to me about God this morning, I realised that she *was* God. Of course she was God. The sun was leaking through the big, dirty window behind her and it made the air around her glow. Her hands looked worn, and suddenly I knew it was because, once upon a time, they had sculpted the world. I felt so powerful when I realised Esther was God, because I knew that she was here talking to me because I was meant to be God next. That's how it works, being God. One person does it for as long as they are able, and then they choose a successor. Esther's eyes were wrinkled at the corners, and her dark, oiled hair was greying at the roots, and her feet were flat in their sandals. I could see she was ready to give up the weight of the world, transfer it to another pair of shoulders, and of course the shoulders she chose were mine. God chose me to be God next.

When I realised this, God's words were washing over me like warm bathwater. The lilting, melodic sing-song of her voice made the sound so deliciously soft. The whole situation was so deliciously exciting that I laughed. It bubbled up inside me, tickling my throat, and burbled out, high and pure and tinkling.

'You know, Yasmine, that sometimes, with these problems that you have, sometimes you have to look to God, and ask—'

'Ma ha ha ha ha ha ha ha ha ha ha!'

I could feel myself shining, glimmering, as the light around God began to flow into me, and I trained my eyes to hers, all the better to drink in the glow. My laughter bounced from the walls around us, mingling with God's voice. She stopped talking, and looked at me, and her face was worried, but I know it was only because of the enormity of the situation – the momentous transfer of power. I revelled in the laughter.

'Ma ha ha ha ha ha ha ha ha HA HA HA!'

Esther looked down at her flat feet. I think she was a little sad not to be God any more. She got up slowly and walked out of the bay and returned with two pellets of chalk in a small paper cup. I thought: *This must be what you live on when you are God*; so I swallowed them down. I slept after that. On the seventh day, God slept.

When I woke there was a new nurse at my bedside. I felt muzzy and indistinct, as if I was wrapped in cotton wool. My first sleep as God was a very deep sleep. It is a tiring business, carrying the world on one's shoulders.

'Hello Yasmine. You have had good sleeps. My name is Patience.'

Patience is sitting beside my bed. I wonder what happened to Esther. Sadly, I think she probably died. I'm sure that is what happens when one has been God but is no longer God. Patience is wearing a kaftan patterned with tiny coloured squares. The light outside is dying now, the sun sinking lower and lower above the ant farm, and I realise this must be because I have allowed it to sink. Because it is my sun, and my sky, and my ant farm. I shiver with the deliciousness of it all.

'Are you cold, Yasmine? Would you like another blanket?'

Patience is as soft and sing-song as Esther. I think she is probably one of my angels. I must organise the angels, but for now I am sleepy again. It is six o'clock. A trolley clanks down the corridor outside the bay, and a hairnetted woman loads food onto my bed-tray. There is soft, brown gloop of pasty meat and powdery potato and sugary, wet carrots and sandy crumble submerged in neon custard. I am ravenously hungry. I cannot get the food into me fast enough. It tastes amazing. The salt burns my tongue. The custard is so sweet my mouth aches. I scrape the plate and bowl clean. I want more food.

'Can I have more? Can I have more food?' I ask Patience, anxiety tightening my throat, because I know that I need more food.

'What? You still hungry?'

'Yes. Yes. Can I have more?'

I don't know why Patience is looking so surprised. I am *God*, for God's sake. It's hungry work.

'What you want? Toast?'

'Yes. Toast. I'm very hungry.'

She ambles off, and returns a little later with a plate of white toast and packets of butter and jam and cellophane-wrapped biscuits and a banana. *Thank you, Angel Patience.* I unfold the foil from around the butter and tear back the film lid from the jam, smearing them frantically, unwrapping the biscuits as I swallow the toast, peeling the banana as I crunch through the biscuits, mashing the banana between my teeth and finally feeling almost sated.

'You full up now?'

I don't understand why Angel Patience is behaving as if this is funny. I am very, *very* hungry. I could eat more – I wonder if I have sweets in my bag, loose Chewits or Fruit Pastilles lying at the bottom among receipts and Rizlas – but the hunger is quieter now and I think I can last until nine o'clock, when the hairnet women will bring me tea and more biscuits. I push the bed-tray away, and press the button that will make the bed flat. The clanks and bleeps of the hospital are very loud. I need to make them quieter. But before I can instruct Angel Patience, sleep comes, like anaesthetic, and I am gone.

---

'You've had other suicide attempts, haven't you?'

'No. I know what you're talking about. You're talking about when I was on the tracks.'

'Yes. So when you were on the train tracks you didn't want to die?'

Oh, you really don't understand at all, do you? I wasn't going to *die*.

No one was listening, you see. No one accepted how much power I had. I had power flowing through my veins, every cell of my body bathed in electricity. I crackled when I moved, and every move I made was deeply significant. Every song was written about me. Every quote was a reference to me. Every stranger wanted to talk to me. I was the sun and the world.

No one would listen. They whinged and whined and made my head ache.

'Be *careful*, Yasmine!'

'Slow *down*, Yasmine!'

'*Look* before you cross the *road*, Yasmine!'

Slow *down*? I needed to *speed up*! There was so much to do and to see, and I wanted to do it all, see it all, capture it all and hold it in my hands before gulping it down and making it a part of me. There were so many people who needed me, so many spaces only I could fill, and the 24 hours of the day were pressing in on me from all sides, and there was so much to achieve and not enough time to achieve it. They were the ones with the problem, not me. Why couldn't they see the sparkling, enticing beauty in every corner of the world? How could I not want to do everything, all the time, when everything was *so fantastic*, when *I* was so fantastic?

'Be careful' didn't make sense to me. Why be careful when I was invincible? They behaved as if I could be mown down by a car at any moment – but surely they must have understood that that just wouldn't happen to me? The world couldn't hurt me when I *was* the world! I was titanium, and I listened to 'Titanium', and it was so plainly written about me that I tweeted David Guetta, asking for a private email address, because I needed to thank him personally for having written about me. He didn't reply, but I knew he would reply, eventually, it was just taking a while, and that was fine, because I had *so much else* to be getting on with in the meantime.

No one would listen to me. I needed to find a way to show them that I was unbreakable, and that's why I went down to the tracks. You understand now, don't you? I wasn't going to *die*. The train would have come, vibrating the metal beneath my feet, and I would have closed my eyes and stretched out my arms, and at the last moment – the split second before the nose of the train collided with my nose, knocking me out of the universe – I would have soared up, up, up. Oh. Of course. I should have told you. I thought it was obvious. I can fly.

'I just needed people to listen, you see. I just needed them to understand.'

———

I do not trust the drip in my arm. I have been watching it for the past two hours, and I am sure I can feel every drop hitting my bloodstream. I think they are trying to dilute me, because they have realised just how powerful I am, and they are worried that, with this much power, I could overturn the ward. They're right. I could. But I am *God*. I use my powers for good, not evil. I cannot let them dilute me. The essence of me is concentrated, like neat cordial, and that is what makes me so special.

'Could you take this drip out, please?' I ask my new angel, Angel Miriam, who is sitting, arms folded placidly under the shelf of her bosom.

'The drip? You want it out?'

'Yes please. I would like the drip out.'

'We cannot take the drip out, Yasmine. You need it. It is making you better.'

*Let's not do this, Angel Miriam. Let's not play this game. I've seen through it, game over, the end, so please let's fold up the board and put the lid on the box and get on with our day.*

I smile a very sweet smile at Angel Miriam.

'I will not be diluted, Angel Miriam.'

'What? Why you call me angel, Yasmine?'

*Angel Miriam is so funny! She is such a joker! She is certainly one of my favourite angels.* I laugh, loudly and heartily, and the sound of my laughter among the clanks and bleeps is delicious. 'Ma ha ha ha ha ha ha ha ha HA!'

'Are you OK, Yasmine?'

'Angel Miriam. I am *excellent*.'

*It is true. I am excellent. I am so incredibly charming! I am so deeply lovable! I must get this drip out. I cannot have any of this incredible charm and deep lovability going to waste.*

'I would like the drip out. Now, please.'

'We cannot have it out, Yasmine. You need it for the medicine.'

'Please, Angel Miriam. You need to do as I say. There's a good angel.'

'Yasmine, I cannot let you take it out.'

The tape holding the drip in place is wickedly sticky, and it smarts as I tear it off, plucking out my arm-hairs. I do not want to lose them as they are a part of me and every part of God is sacred, so I lay the tape aside. I will salvage the arm-hairs later. I am about to whip out the needle – no mess, no fuss – when I feel Angel Miriam's warm, strong hand around my wrist and hear her deep, strong voice calling over another angel. In a flash, there is a flock of angels around the bed, a horde of angels, at least a hundred angels, and I think this is a preposterously large fuss to be making about my very reasonable wish to remain undiluted.

'Please, angels,' I reason, spreading my hands in appeal, but there is a sharpness at my skin and the edges of the angels go fuzzy. It is a warm, sleepy feeling. Angel Miriam's hand still clasps my wrist, and I take it between my fingers and bring it to my nose and inhale deeply. Angel Miriam smells of coconut, just as Angel Esther smelled of coconut, and the smell is so wonderfully exotic. I kiss the soft skin, and I am gone.

---

'Are there times when your mood drops? Do you have low periods?'

'Sometimes I get down.'

'Can you tell me more?'

When I am up, it is as if I have swallowed the world. When I am down, it is as if I have been sliced open, had the world wrenched from my belly, and been sewn up with loose, clumsy stitches. I clutch myself, holding my edges together, trying to understand how it can be possible to feel so empty. It is not the emptiness of having nothing inside; it is the emptiness of having *no insides*. A shovel has been taken to my interior and my organs have been hacked out. Layers of internal flesh and fat have been scraped away. When they stitched me back together, they didn't stitch together a person; they stitched together a sagging balloon of skin.

I lie on the tiled bathroom floor. The pain in my stomach is incredible. The pain in my head is worse. The person I was – the person who had swallowed the world – dances at the corner of my consciousness, and she is not me. We are not the same. Everything about her was glowy and inside she held the whole world; everything about me is despicable and there is nothing inside me but stale air. I do not eat. I sip rusty water from the bathroom tap. My tongue grows a thick, stinking layer of yellow fur.

Sometimes, I see armies of black spiders scuttle along the skirting board. There are so many of them they turn the white wood black. They move quickly, in a pack, and I can tell they are evil, but I do not know how to stop them. I do not have the energy to stop them. So I let them rush at me, and when they crawl over my face I do not have the energy to flinch.

'And the highs and lows – do you ever feel like they come together?'

The together times are the scariest times. I have the energy of a high and the mood of a low. I am powered by battery acid, desperately alive and desperate to be dead. I think about suicide constantly. It crouches in every nook and cranny of my mind. *Kill yourself, kill yourself, kill yourself.*

There are a hundred and one things I need to do, and the thought of doing any one of them makes me lividly angry. I need to clean the kitchen. The rubber gloves make my hands clumsy. I *hate* them. I spray cleaning fluid onto my tongue. It tangs. I need to be punished. I cut myself. The blood is bright and I am agitated. The need to clean the kitchen is even greater.

I want to crawl out of my skin. There are too many thoughts in my head, all of them cruel and corrosive. I cannot sit still. I cannot be quiet. I call people I barely know and spit poison I barely understand. People are plotting against me. People have put cameras in my house. People want me dead. I gnaw at my nails, my lips, the skin on the inside of my cheeks, and taste iron. Someone is poisoning me – someone has contaminated my water supply. I need to buy bottled water. I can't find my trainers, I can't find my purse, I can't find my door key, and I need to clean the kitchen. I slide down the wall in the hallway like a wet pancake and pull at my hair until the follicles pop out of my scalp.

54

I lie on my side, curled like a prawn, tracing my fingers over the translucent threads of tissue raised from my arms. The scars are made of thin, smooth skin. They pattern me in beautiful stripes.

I am becoming sane. I can feel it. The bright, loud madness is trickling away. I hate this part. Sanity solidifies inside me like concrete. It holds me to the ground. I cannot soar when I am sane.

There was a man here this morning. He pretended he did not know that I was God. It was terribly funny. When our eyes locked I dissolved into giggles, because it was so terribly funny watching him pretend not to know that I was God. He was wearing a blue ribbon around his neck. It was as if he thought he was a cow. He was a cow and I was not God – ma ha ha ha ha ha ha HA! – what kind of nonsense is that? People pretend not to know that I am God because they want me to think they are talking to me because they are interested in me, and not just because I am God. That's what the man was doing. I appreciated the sentiment. I humoured him.

The man said he was trying to find a bed for me. I told him I was already in bed. I laughed so hard I choked. He leaned back in his chair and waited for me to stop. He said he was trying to find a bed for me in a psychiatric unit. I couldn't think of another joke, though I wanted to make one. I was enjoying the delicious fountain of laughter. He asked if I thought I needed to be in a psychiatric unit. I said no. He asked why. I said I was becoming sane. He asked how it felt to become sane. I said I wanted to block it out, stop it encroaching. He asked why. I said it was because when I am sane I realise all the things I did when I was insane. He asked what kinds of things I meant. I said the kinds of things I was doing before I came into hospital. He asked what kinds of things those were. I didn't want to talk about it, so I forced out a barking cackle – 'Ma ha ha ha ha HA HA HA!'

– and he said we could talk about it another time. Then he left, and I curled back onto my side, horribly tired.

Soon, I will be completely sane. I can feel it. I will be sane, and I will have to care about the money I spent and the people I slept with and the madness I oozed. I might have long, clear weeks of sanity, and I will forget how it felt to be soaring. Or I might sink down to the depths, and resurface with fresh stripes on my arms. I want to hold onto the insanity for these last moments. I want to hold onto the frightening, agonising ecstasy of the episode.

———

'What can you remember from before you came into hospital?'

It was as if I had been turning up the volume on a favourite song, twisting the dial clockwise and feeling the pulse of the bass like a heartbeat. I loved the song, and I loved the beat, and the louder it played the more ecstatic I felt. But I couldn't stop. My hand was possessed. I was turning and turning the volume dial, and the dial had no limit – no sticking point where I could turn no further – and the sound was getting louder and louder and it didn't sound like music any more, it sounded like a roar. And at the same time, my other hand had reached out of its own accord and found other dials and was twisting them clockwise, and colours were so bright I could smell them, and smells were so pungent I could taste them, and tastes were so strong I felt sick.

I needed to run a marathon. There was one happening in two weeks, and I hadn't done any training, but I knew I could run it – I could run it *easily* – but I was confused and frustrated because the website was telling me it was too late to register. The stupid, *stupid* internet robots clearly had no idea who I was, because if they knew who I was they would let me register, because I *had* to run the marathon. I decided I would run

it alone, right now, and I put on my trainers and filled a water
bottle. As I was heading out of the flat, I remembered that I
couldn't run the marathon, not that day, because I was supposed
to be writing my novel. I reckoned I could write 20,000 words
a day, and it was Tuesday, and I wanted the novel finished by
Friday, and if I was going to have it finished by Friday I needed
to start today. So I sat down, and opened a blank document,
and began typing. It wasn't right. My legs were twitching under
the desk and I had to run, I had to run there and then, and I
thought perhaps I could run the marathon, reach the finish and
hammer out my 20,000 words then. So I put the laptop in my
rucksack and set off.

Out on the pavement, the world was so painfully distract-
ing. I needed to talk to every person I passed, but I passed them
too quickly, so I had to keep stopping, doubling back, trying
to find them, because I *needed* to talk to them. I had so many
ideas that I needed to share, ideas that people needed to hear,
because I was wonderful and my ideas were wonderful and to
keep them inside would be to deny the public a small part of
my wonder. I passed a dog, lead looped around the bicycle racks
outside the supermarket, and the fury – the burning, scalding
fury – was so huge it winded me. I was picking at the knotted
lead with clumsy fingers, and the dog was barking so loudly my
eardrums smarted, and a man was there, a big man, an angry
man, and he was shouting 'WHAT ARE YOU DOING?' and I
was shouting 'I'M RESCUING YOUR FUCKING DOG!' and
he was shouting 'MY DOG DOESN'T NEED RESCUING!' and
I was shouting 'YES IT FUCKING DOES. YOU ABANDONED
IT!' and he was shouting 'NO I DIDN'T. I WAS DOING MY
SHOPPING. ARE YOU MAD?' and I thought for a moment I
would kill him. If I had decided to kill him, I would have done
it – I would have done it with one hand – and I wanted to kill
him to show that I *could* kill him. But there were people all

around, and I couldn't afford to go to prison, because in prison they wouldn't let me finish my novel or my marathon. So I spat a wet, bitter ball of saliva at the man's feet, and I pounded away.

Miles from home, I couldn't remember why I was running. I tried to get on the train. I couldn't understand why the barrier wouldn't let me through. I pushed it, hard, and an insane woman in a fake uniform pulled me aside and talked in a fast voice about oysters. She was clearly a lunatic, and I needed to get away, because she could be dangerous, so I ran into the street and withdrew a handful of notes from a cash machine and hailed down a taxi. The taxi driver had terribly evil eyes. They bore into me in the mirror, and I thought I might be in an unlicensed mini cab, and I couldn't think how to check whether I was in an unlicensed mini cab, but I knew that if I was in an unlicensed mini cab I needed to escape because unlicensed mini cabs are where rape happens. I opened the door while it was still moving, and the rapist yelled, and I flung the notes on the seat and ran.

I didn't know I was running home until I arrived at the door. I had no memory of the journey. When I got inside I sat down at the desk and pulled the laptop out of my bag and opened it up, as if I had never left. It was dark, but my face was lit by the glow of the screen. I hammered at the keyboard, churning out words that were *beautiful* and *profound* and bordering on *genius*, and I was almost *disconcerted* by how *talented* I was. The tick of the clock was loud, too loud, much too loud, and I took it down from the wall and put it in the dustbin outside. Time was rubbish. I typed until early in the morning and then, mid-sentence, I decided the novel was too good to keep to myself, and I had better begin circulating it as widely as possible so that Penguin and Harper Collins and Random House could marshal their resources for the big auction. I Googled London's top ten literary agents and sent a group email, which they all said not to do, but I did it anyway, and I didn't send a covering letter or chapter summary or list of top five competing titles because I didn't *need* to. *I was special*.

I was beginning to feel an itch in my teeth, a stiffness in my face, and I wondered whether I might be tired, but I knew I couldn't sleep because there was no time for sleep. I boiled the kettle, dissolved five teaspoons of instant coffee and five teaspoons of sugar in a mug of hot water, downed it, opened twenty tabs on my internet browser and bought things. I bought a very expensive camera, because high-quality photographs were going to be very important for the blog I was going to start, and I bought three vegan cookbooks, because, as God, I didn't think I should be consuming my own creations, and I bought a floor-length silk gown for £400 because I was going to need something to wear to all the awards ceremonies I would soon be attending. I wasn't sure what I would be winning awards for, but I knew I would win them. Just for *being me*.

At some point, within the warped hours of rubbish time, I felt very strongly that I needed to have sex, with lots of people, for a long time, and I lowered myself into the grimy cellars of the internet and looked for prostitutes. I got distracted by a nagging ache in my stomach, and I realised I hadn't eaten in three or four days. Veganism was suddenly trivial, and I was in the supermarket, filling a basket with boxes of chocolates, pots of double cream, blocks of cheese and thickly iced cakes. I bought bottles and bottles of wine. I ate without tasting or feeling or thinking, and then I vomited because the cream curdled with the wine in my stomach and propelled itself out. I was sick and I wanted someone to look after me, so I rang my mother, but it was the middle of the night and she didn't pick up. I convinced myself she had been murdered, so I ran to my parents' house and pounded on the door. They stood over me, un-murdered and unnerved, as I keened on their sofa. I didn't know why I was crying, because I didn't feel sad, and after a while I sat up and wiped my eyes and laughed my delicious laugh – 'Ma ha ha ha ha ha ha HA HA HA!' – and began to tell them about my Big Plans. I was struck, as I spoke, by my eloquence, and I thought they must feel very proud to have me as a daughter. They didn't respond as I wanted them to respond. My father said, 'Yasmine, sweetheart, you're not making any sense,' and I was infuriated that he didn't understand me – that he was so far beneath me – and I left, hurling obscenities into anxious faces.

At home, I wrapped myself in a thick, soft blanket, and felt itchy all over. I raked my nails across my skin, but the itch leapt about my body. I couldn't pin it down. Suddenly I wanted to sleep – I wanted very badly to sleep – and I shrugged off the blanket and lay down on the rug in the living room. The itching on my skin was blistering, burning, and it occurred to me that I was on fire. I was very definitely on fire, and if I didn't put out the fire I would burn to death. So I grabbed hold of the edge of the rug and turned over and over, rolling myself as tight as a pea in a pod. That stifled the flames. I lay for a long time, or a short time, I don't know how much time because time was rubbish and the clock was in the bin. I lay on the floor, rolled up in the rug, but sleep would not come. I saw a shape dart out of the shadows, and I was sure it was a rat – a big, dark rat – and then I saw more, hundreds of them, a battalion of rats, and there were so many of them that I didn't know what to do. The rats outnumbered me, and I was achingly tired and couldn't sleep, and I was so desperate to sleep and escape the rats that I unrolled myself and padded to the bathroom and gulped down tablets until the canister stopped rattling. And then at last I slept, and when I woke the air was buzzing with clanks and bleeps, and there was an angel in a kaftan sitting next to my bed.

---

It comes to me that I am not God. It comes to me in incremental drips. I think, perhaps, that is what has been dripping into me all this time: wet drips of knowledge that I am not God. The wetness dampens my organs. It makes me sad.

There is a man in a grey jumper and blue jeans sitting next to my bed. He is slim and dainty and not an angel. Dots of black speckle his jaw. He sits with one leg hooked over the other, hands folded on his knee. A card dangles from the blue belt around his neck, and there is a picture of him on the card. I know it is him because he has told me his name and that is the name on the card, but the picture looks nothing like him. I think perhaps he is an imposter – an undercover agent – so I should not speak to him. But his face is mild and kind, so I think perhaps he is a saint – one of my saints – so I should tell him everything. But then I remember that I am not God any more. I do not have saints. I think perhaps he is just a doctor. I think perhaps he is just a man.

It strikes me that this is the same man who has been visiting me since I arrived. He has sat in the chair by my bed with his legs crossed. He has asked many questions, and written down many answers. He has scribbled on slips of paper and magicked the paper into the pills I have swallowed. He looks different today. He is smaller and more pulled-together. His voice is closer.

'I wasn't God, was I?'

'Did you think you were God?'

'It was true back then. It *was* true.'

'Does it make you sad to think you might not be God?'

'It was nice to think it. It made me feel special.'

'Do you think you need to be special?'

'I liked being God.'

'Do you find your thoughts are jumping around?'

'It's like frogs in my head.'

'There's a medication that could help with that. It would

help your thoughts settle down. It would help you to focus. Would you try it?'

'I don't like taking a lot of pills. They're bad for you.'

'If they weren't on prescription they might be bad for you. But the medications we prescribe aren't bad for you. They can help you.'

'I'm crazy, aren't I?'

'You have an illness, Yasmine.'

'I've got rats in the attic.'

'You have a problem with your moods.'

'Frogs – I said it, didn't I? I'm mad as a box of frogs.'

'I think you're enjoying playing around with words.'

'I'd like to go to sleep now.'

'That's OK.'

'I'm very tired.'

'I can come back later. You can sleep now.'

'When I wake up will I be God again?'

'You weren't well when you thought you were God, Yasmine. You weren't in a well place.'

'If I can't be God, can I be an angel?'

'I'm going to let you sleep, Yasmine. I'll be back later. We can talk some more then.'

---

'The medications we've been giving you in hospital, Yasmine – by and large, they're the same medications we thought you were taking at home. And yet, when you were at home, things were out of control, weren't they? And since coming into hospital, you've stabilised.'

'Yes.'

'Do you always remember to take your medications at home?'

'Most of the time.'

'When do you take them?'

'When I remember.'

'Do you take them with water?'

'I take them with wine.'

'You can't drink on these medications, Yasmine.'

'Then how can I take them?'

'You can take them with water.'

'Oh.'

'How much are you drinking at the moment?'

'One or two.'

'Glasses?'

'Bottles.'

'I think that's something we should talk about. It will make everything harder, drinking that much. It won't help with the moods.'

'OK. I'm sorry.'

'You don't need to be sorry.'

'OK.'

'Is there anyone at home who could help you remember to take your medication every day?'

'There's no one. It's just me.'

'OK. Is there a friend – anyone at work?'

'I don't have to work. I won the lottery. You know that.'

'Is that true, Yasmine?'

'No.'

'OK.'

'But I work by myself. I run a small business. It's all online. I work from home.'

'OK. So, who do you have to support you? Emotionally, I mean. Family?'

'My mum and dad. They live quite close.'

'OK. Do they know you're here at the moment?'

'No.'

'Could you tell them?'

'No.'

'Why not?'

'They would be upset. They're old. I'm a burden.'

'Don't you think they would be more upset to think of you coping with this alone?'

'No. Maybe.'

'What about friends?'

'There's no one. I lost them all.'

'Can you tell me more?'

'I say things I don't remember saying. Really horrible things. I lie. And I do horrible things. I don't know I'm doing them. It's like a different person. When I'm in that state – when I'm like that – I think I can do whatever I want and everyone will love me regardless. But I can't. They don't.'

'I think it can be hard for other people to understand the big mood swings your condition involves.'

'Yes. Hard.'

'Have you had urges to hurt yourself since you've been in hospital?'

'No.'

'Why do you think that is?'

'I feel safe here.'

'That's good.'

'Yes.'

'Do you think it will be hard to go home?'

'Yes. Hard.'

'What are you worried about?'

'It will all get bad again. I'll be really crazy again. It's so tiring being like that. It wears me out.'

'I can understand that. But things don't have to deteriorate at home. I'm confident we can keep things stable. It will just take hard work.'

'What kind of hard work?'

'Well, you're going to have to take your medication reliably. You will have to stop drinking. Eat well. Exercise. Go to your appointments. All those things.'

'Mmm.'

'How does that sound to you?'

'It sounds like a lot of work. And boring.'

'Yes. It's a lot of work at first. And it's boring.'

'It's not very fair.'

'Can you tell me more?'

'Other people don't have to do all these things just to stay sane. Other people don't have to work this hard. It's so much effort for something other people have without any effort.'

'Yes. That's true. It is unfair in that sense.'

'Will it always be this much work?'

'No. I don't think so. Most people find that, once they've established good habits, it doesn't feel like hard work any more.'

'Is that the truth?'

'Yes.'

'OK.'

'I think we should try to discharge you tomorrow.'

'Really?'

'Does that worry you?'

'It feels soon. But I think it will always feel soon.'

'Yes. I think it's right for you to go home tomorrow. You won't be without support. But we should get started with try-ing to manage you as an outpatient.'

'Am I not going to the unit?'

'Do you remember the conversation we had yesterday? I don't think it would be constructive for you to be admitted to the unit this time. I'm happy with how you've stabilised here. And there might not be a bed in the unit for a week or more, which is too long. We need to get used to managing you as an outpatient long-term. Does that sound right to you?'

'Yes. OK.'

'Do you have any questions?'

'Will I see you again?'

'Yes. I'll come by tomorrow to see you before you leave. We can have another chat then.'

'OK.'

———

'How are you feeling today?'

'OK. A bit worried.'

'That's normal. Have you got someone coming to pick you up?'

'No. There's a bus.'

'Will you be OK?'

'Yes. I'll be fine.'

'Is there someone you can be with for the rest of today?'

'I'm not sure.'

'It might be a good idea. But it's up to you.'

'Yes.'

'Do you have plans for the day?'

'Not really. Nothing big. I need to go shopping. Should probably clean the flat. That kind of stuff.'

'OK. That sounds good.'

'Pretty boring.'

'Boring things are good sometimes. Good to get them done.'

'Yes. I suppose.'

'And you'll go to your appointment at the community service tomorrow?'

'Yes.'

'Good. I think you'll be seeing a support worker. And then a psychiatrist as soon as there's an appointment available.'

'What's a support worker?'

'Usually a nurse or a social worker. Sometimes a healthcare assistant. You can check in with them as often as you need. It's someone to talk to about how things are going.'

'OK.'

'Are there specific things worrying you?'

'Not really. I don't actually feel that worried. I feel sad.'

'Can you tell me more?'

'I don't know. I don't like being this way. It's so tiring and lonely. But there are bits of it I like.'

'What do you like?'

'It's exciting sometimes. The build-up. Before I wind myself too tight and everything gets scary. I feel so warm. I feel so special.'

'Yes.'

'I get sad thinking I won't ever feel that way again.'

'Yes. It's an extreme way to be. The high mood.'

'I have to give it all up, don't I?'

'I wouldn't think of it as giving something up. I would think of it as gaining something different.'

'It feels like giving something up.'

'It's not going to happen overnight, Yasmine. You're still the same person. You still have the same brain.'

'Yes. I suppose.'

'Is there something in particular you feel you're going to lose?'

'Just that feeling, I think. The feeling that I had swallowed the world.'

'Yes. And what did that feel like?'

'Strong. Powerful. Invincible. Bright. Special.'

'It sounds like it was a good feeling.'

'It was a good feeling.'

'Do you think you might be able to find another way of achieving those feelings?'

'I don't know. I don't think so.'

'No?'

'I don't think so.'

'I think so.'

'Do you?'

'Yes. I do.'

'Do you feel those feelings?'

'Sometimes.'

'Oh.'

'A nurse will be here in a moment to give you your medication to take home. I'm going to let you get off.'

'OK.'

'Do you have any questions before I go?'

'No.'

'OK.'

'Thank you.'

'My pleasure. Good luck, Yasmine.'

'Wait.'

'Yes?'

'I wasn't God, was I?'

'I think we talked about this before. You felt that you were God, for a while.'

'Yes. For a while, I did.'

'And that was a good feeling?'

'It was the best feeling. But I wasn't God, was I?'

'I think you felt God-like.'

'I want to feel like God again.'

'I think it's hard to let go of some elements of the high mood, like we talked about. They were extreme positive feelings.'

'But *was I* God?'

'You felt like God.'

'You're not going to give me an answer, are you?'

'I don't think that would be helpful for you.'

'Seems pretty fucking unfair to me.'

'You're finding lots of things unfair at the moment.'

'Lots of things *are* unfair at the moment.'

'That's what you feel.'

'That *is* what I feel.'

'I'm going to have to go now, Yasmine.'

'You *are* going to have to go now, Doctor. Why are you smiling?'

'Sometimes things are just funny. Sometimes you want to smile.'

'Sometimes things are just unfair, too.'

'Yes. And sometimes they're unfair and funny.'

'Maybe.'

'Goodbye, Yasmine.'

'Bye. Thank you.'

'Goodbye, Yasmine.'

---

I had to spit up the world, you know. I had to open up and let it out, because it wasn't mine to hold inside. I choked down chalky pellets and they pulled the world from my gut in a stretched, blue-green ribbon. It was not the same as the lows, when the world was wrenched from my abdomen with swift, surgical precision. It was a slow, dripping loss.

I miss the person who held the world in her stomach. I miss her verve and vibrancy. I miss the purpose with which she tackled tasks, the kaleidoscope lens through which she viewed her surroundings. I miss being God.

This new person, this pills-and-patience, appointments-and-abstinence person – I do not know her. She is small and ashamed. Day after day she faces the consequences of the things the vibrant self chose to do. She occupies my body, but she is not my soul. She is made of disparate, underdeveloped parts. She is not me.

I am supposed to go for a run every morning after a breakfast of slow-release carbohydrates and mindfulness. When I drag myself out of the house, the hard pavement slaps my feet through the worn soles of my trainers. Running while manic was elating; running while 'stable' is gruelling. Porridge and almond butter coagulate in my stomach. I feel very heavy.

Sometimes, I drink a glass of icy white wine in place of dinner. I dip my toe into dangerous waters, taunting the forces I shouldn't miss. *Go on, come back, I want you back. Stop, stay there, keep away. Come closer. Retreat. Come back …*

They tell me that the longer I stay sober and stable, the less like hard work the sober stability will feel. Perhaps, this time, I will loiter in this place long enough to find out. It could be tricky, though. Someone has to be God. I think it has to be me.

> 'But it's just mood swings, isn't it?
> I know loads of people who are probably
> bipolar. I know loads of moody people.'

## 'Swinging': How to Cope with ~~Having Bipolar Disorder~~ Being a Very Moody Person!

### *Coping with ~~Hypomania~~ Excitement!*

It may have been months since you last felt this way. You may have had weeks of clear, cool equilibrium before now. You may have had only days. But *today* – today, something is different. Something warm and slightly electric is running through your veins, like a fizzy drink or charged blood. Isn't it *great?!* Who *doesn't* love excitement?!

Every step you take is urgent. You are filled with an energy that cannot be spent. At work, you type with a machine-gun tap-tap-tap. Colleagues watch you through hooded eyes and you want to snap your fingers in their faces: *Look alive! Keep up! Why are you all moving so slowly?* You want to take the grey world around you and perform mouth-to-mouth resuscitation, filling it with the colour flooding your insides. You want to give the world a shake.

In the morning, you go for a walk that becomes a run. Why walk when you can run? The technicolour cars and parades of shops are so bright they make your eyes ache. The handful of early morning joggers and dog walkers radiate a strange, pure beauty, and you want to take their heads between your two hands and kiss them, firmly, on their beautiful faces.

Never mind that you are encased in glass. Never mind that you cannot invite others in. You are soaring, soaring, soaring. So just *enjoy the ride*.

71

### Coping with ~~Mania~~ Overexcitement!

~~Mania~~ Overexcitement! It's like excitement, but *even better!* Like being a Labrador puppy, really. Except that you can't sleep. Your limbs twitch when you lie down. You are *too alive*. The lack of sleep makes you itch. It makes you brittle as hardened sugar. Oh, and you haven't eaten in five days (or was it six?), but you are *fucking fine*, alright? It's *other people* who are doing it wrong, *wasting time* on *meaningless tasks* when there are *so many problems in the world to be solved*. You say this to your colleagues, slapping your palms on your desk so they smart. You are given the rest of the day off work. Excellent news. More time to solve problems.

You feel weightless. You need to be anchored by heavy, tangible objects. You make extravagant, outlandish purchases online. Expensive? It must be *excellent* quality, and you deserve only the best! You add the heavy electric mixer to the cart. Perhaps you will open a bakery.

Clarity descends. Everything is falling into place. Of course! You feel weightless because you can fly! You can fly because you are superhuman! Your thoughts speed up. Of *course* other people are wary of you! *They know your power*. And another, cold thought: *They are trying to bring you down*. At least, if needs be, you can open the window and take to the skies.

You open the curtains (how long have they been closed for?). The sky is blood red. In the street, every pushchair-bound child and iPhone-chained adolescent has twisted to look at you, and your heart sets up a marching rhythm at your throat. *They have come for you. They have come for you. They are coming.*

~~Mania~~ Overexcitement! What's not to love?!

### Coping with ~~Depression~~ Sadness!

The inevitable crash. It's a real drag. You wake on the floor having slept for fifteen hours. You feel as if you are rotting from the inside out. A stale stench hangs around you. Your mouth is bitter and dry. Perhaps a bottle of liqueur is standing in a sticky, dark pool: a token of the mania that gripped you fifteen hours ago. Perhaps you were enjoying months of stability, then felt yourself slip downwards over the course of the week. Perhaps you find yourself here without rhyme, reason or warning. You curl your knees towards your chest. You wish your mother were here.

In the kitchen, the worktop is coated in a fine film of flour. There is a bowl of curdled sugar and egg. You run your fingers over the £400 food processor you will never use. You wonder what other purchases you might have made; how deep into your overdraft you might have sunk. You pick up your phone, flung to the corner of the room, and trace the cracks in the screen. You read through the texts you sent – a frantically assembled word salad, seething with self-importance and anger. You listen to the voicemail messages – the concerned voices of the first week; the frantic questions of the second week; the silence of the third week. You kicked your way out of the grey, everyday world, and now it doesn't want you back.

Your arms feel leaden. Your fingers are asleep. You feel as if you are walking through glue. You stand at the window for a while, and vaguely remember thinking you could fly. No one watches you. No one sees. You are nothing, nothing, nothing.

### Coping with ~~a Mixed State~~ Confusion!

You are restless with exhaustion, bursting with emptiness, numb with feeling. Everything is topsy-turvy. Before, when you were limp and listless, the spectres swirled behind your lids, the voices soft in your ears: *Swallow the pills, float away. Make a noose, squeeze away.* You were protected by soft apathy.

Now, there is no apathy. Now, there is intention: hunger for hurt. During depression, the menacing grey shapes in the world were cloaked in bulky mist, but now they have been shorn of the fug of exhaustion. Their edges are sharp. Their teeth are pointed.

Their intentions are evil. The world around you is full of faceless enemies, and you are so very frightened.

The hatred is so strong you want to crawl out of your skin. You hate every square centimetre of yourself. You choke down the pills and you curse when you wake in a hospital bed. This is wrong. The world is wrong. You are wrong.

Who doesn't feel confused from time to time?!

> 'That's the thing. It's not just mood
> swings. It's not like that at all.'

I wrote sections of Yasmine's story with white noise playing in my ears. YouTube boasts mammoth tracks – 'CELESTIAL WHITE NOISE: Sleep Better, Reduce Stress, Calm Your Mind, Improve Focus: 10 Hour Ambient Sound' – designed, I suspect, to soothe newborns to sleep in place of the washing machine or hairdryer. When you listen to CELESTIAL WHITE NOISE through earphones, it feels as if there is enormous pressure inside your head: rolling waves of sound that build but never break. The noise is nebulous. You feel it in your teeth. It is some-how threatening. When you turn it off, reality rushes in, flooding the craters and crevices that were previously filled with noise. In some small way, I think perhaps this is how it feels to be Yasmine.

Bipolar disorder is generally understood as extreme mood swings: giddy highs and crushing lows. This conceptualisation is not devoid of truth – bipolar disorder is a mood disorder and does entail mood lability. The misconception lies in the com-mon understanding of bipolar 'highs and lows' – i.e. as variants or exaggerations of the ups and downs we all encounter during the course of day-to-day life. Through my interviews, I came to see that happiness is a lightness in the chest and a brightness in the mind; mania is a wound-too-tight, stretched-too-taught intensity. As we know from Abby, sadness is melancholic grey, where depression is silty black. 'Mood swings' are fluctuations from happiness to sadness – contentment to irritability – that ebb and flow like tides; in bipolar disorder, shifts between states can feel like shifts between people – bewildering swings from one internal world to another.

Yasmine is severely afflicted – and debilitated – by bipolar disorder. During manic, depressive and mixed episodes she experiences psychotic symptoms: hearing, seeing or experi-encing things that do not exist to others. She has grandiose delusions, and her relationship with reality becomes warped.

Psychosis is not present in all cases of bipolar disorder; around a quarter of sufferers I spoke to reported psychotic symptoms. In this respect, I faced a conundrum: to include these experiences, and fuel the perception of bipolar disorder as floridly outlandish, or to leave them by the wayside, and fuel the perception that psychosis is too aberrant to discuss.

My reasons for embodying psychosis in Yasmine were thus: I believe, in contemporary understanding of mental illness, there exists a binary, with 'acceptable' suffering one side and 'unacceptable' on the other. We accept the depression that leads to unwashed clothes and days in bed. We accept the self-mutilation that leads to long sleeves and scarred skin. We accept the anxiety that leads to nibbled nails and the occasional stomach ulcer. These conditions are safe on the one side of the binary, because these sufferers still know up from down, left from right, right from wrong. These sufferers exist within a reality that is, if not the same as our own, within a tolerable margin. They are 'sane'. What of the conditions on the other side of the binary? The people who mutter to themselves in the street; burble with laughter at no one's joke; argue, impassioned, that up is down, left is right, right is wrong and that they can fly? Psychosis is a widely recognised symptom of bipolar disorder, and the more I listened to my interviewees the more determined I became to embody it in Yasmine because, in reality, there is no line between the 'acceptably sane' and the 'unacceptably insane'.

A binary perception of mental illness benefits no one: the 'insane' may find themselves held at arms' length, but the 'sane' may be denied rapid treatment, or accused of melodrama. One is 'not sick enough' right up until one is 'too sick': there is little comfortable middle ground. I was also keen to present my interviewees' complex experiences of sanity itself: some described themselves neither as 'wholly sane' nor 'wholly insane', but flitting between the two. It would be so much more comfortable to think of sanity and insanity as steady states – one is either 'mad' or 'not mad'. If this were the case, one could reassure oneself: 'I am not mad. Other people are mad. I will never become mad.' But it is not so: 'madness' is not a deep, dark cavern to be fallen into, but a winding, twisting street to be stumbled onto and off again. My interviewees were refreshingly candid on this subject: they described episodes of 'insanity'. They did not portray madness as a demon – merely as a temporary state of mind.

Yasmine's story is not everyone's story. Many bipolar sufferers never experience a fully-fledged manic episode, their condition instead characterised by numerous periods of depression and occasional symptoms of hypomania (a milder variant of mania, characterised by elation and hyperactivity, sometimes preceding a full-blown manic episode). Many sufferers are able to hold down successful careers, relationships and social lives, never requiring hospitalisation.

It is also inaccurate to suggest that bipolar sufferers find themselves in a constant state of extreme high or low mood. This *can* be true: in rapid cycling bipolar disorder, the individual experiences four or more manic, hypomanic or depressive episodes in a twelve-month period, and can find that they spend the majority of their time in 'high' and 'low' states. Such patients may swing between highs and lows over the course of a single day, or their state may shift predictably, in line with the changing seasons. In other cases, 'extreme' states occur relatively infrequently, and are interspersed with lengthy periods of stability. Of particular importance, a bipolar sufferer's mood shifts are not *always* the product of their condition: during stable periods, 'normal' mood fluctuations are no different to those experienced by the rest of the population.

It is a common misconception that the 'euphoria' of a manic episode is productive – even desirable. While some aspects of the manic state – and, perhaps more so, the hypomanic state – may be enjoyable initially, moving into a manic episode is like driving a car faster and faster: the vehicle becomes dangerous and impossible to control. During manic states, bipolar sufferers may behave out of character, making decisions that can lead to disaster in their personal, professional and sexual lives. Mania does not result in exhilaration, but devastation. The state of mania itself is exhausting, fraught with insomnia that breeds paranoia, and the 'come down' is excruciating: the horrible, haunting sense of having been hijacked by a technicolour alter ego, hell-bent on destruction. There is a particular cruelty in disorders that entail destructive behaviour over which the individual has little control, and sometimes, after the fact, about which they have little knowledge. My interviewees described surfacing from manic episodes and feeling they had been drugged or abducted: their memories of the past days or weeks were hazy, their desperation to 'undo the damage' palpable. By and large, control over our own behaviour is something we take for granted: bipolar sufferers do not have this privilege. They do not ask to become manic or depressed. They are not given that choice.

A theme that arose again and again during my research was loneliness. Irrespective of status, social situation or specific condition, when my interviewees discussed their experiences, they were discussing times of loneliness. Bipolar disorder breeds loneliness: during manic episodes, sufferers can feel superior to others, and irritability or aggression can destroy relationships that will later be mourned. Depression causes paralysing apathy, preventing its victims from conducting even the most basic of social interactions. During a mixed state, when manic and depressive symptoms cruelly collude, sufferers can feel thrown in different directions, unable to name their needs or accept help. Many of my interviewees felt that bipolar disorder had a significant impact on their relationships – with friends, family and partners – and many voiced hopelessness in reference to the bonds that had broken under the strain of their condition. This is highly relatable. Although, by and large we cannot relate to the *scale* of loneliness brought about by this illness, we all know what it is to feel lonely, and the kernel at the core of the emotion is the same.

The out-of-character actions that can occur during bipolar episodes are not only frightening: they are shattering to self-esteem. For most of us, self-perception is constructed, at least in part, from knowledge of our own actions: 'These are the things I do; these are the things I do not do.' For individuals living with bipolar disorder, the roster of 'I do this; I do not do this' is turned on its head: '*I* don't do it, but the *other* "me" does it.' 'Bipolar' does not mean 'split personality', but some of my interviewees felt they had different selves – or different versions of the same selves – some of whom behaved in ways they found shocking, even abhorrent. For this reason, referring to those *living with* bipolar disorder simply as 'bipolar' is wrong. Sufferers often find their condition draining, devastating and difficult to manage: to be defined by it is decimating.

On the subject of recovery from bipolar disorder, the Depression and Bipolar Support Alliance advises sufferers: 'Recovery happens when your illness stops getting in the way of your life. You decide what recovery means to you.'[14] Recovery is two-fold: there are the multiple, smaller-scale 'recoveries' that take place after individual episodes of depression, mania, hypomania or mixed state, and there is the bigger-picture, ongoing process of 'recovery' from the disorder as a whole. This 'bigger-picture recovery' can be hard to pin down – not least because, in day to day life, it is so often eclipsed by the need for repeated smaller recoveries. A depressive downswing might last two weeks, after which returning to stability might take a further month. Significant episodes of mania and psychosis can last for multiple weeks, requiring years of recovery. Perhaps, then, it is less helpful to separate 'episode recovery' from 'general recovery' than to think of general recovery as a patchwork of episode recoveries. With time, most sufferers gain an understanding of the ways in which depressive and manic episodes can be prevented – usually through taking medication consistently, avoiding drugs and alcohol, eating and sleeping well, and being mindful of factors that might trigger a spiral into either mania or depression. What pay-off, if any, is there for this tiring, relentless vigilance? Although honest when describing the trials of their illness, most asserted that they would not, given the choice, rid themselves of the condition.

'I know everyone probably says this, but it's just part of who I am. I really don't know who I would be without it. It's not easy at all – it can be so tough – but it's me. I don't think I would give up being me for the sake of having an easier life.'

This was mirrored in most of my interviews: although mental illness is excruciating, one would not be without one's condition. This attachment may be exaggerated in bipolar disorder, as it grants an ability to experience intensities of mood, belief and sensation most of us will never know. The lows are agonising, but aspects of the highs can be thrilling. Bipolar disorder is an illness – but one that offers scope for bleaker misery and fiercer joy than is permitted by the 'standard' range of human experience. Yasmine's story ends with simultaneous loss and gain: the loss of the giddy, delusional belief in her own omnipotence in exchange for the gain of increased control, stability and wisdom – a different way of being 'God'.

# What I wish I could tell you about my bipolar disorder

Please don't refer to me as 'bipolar'. It makes me feel as if I'm not a person, only a condition. I *have* bipolar disorder; I *am not* bipolar disorder. There are lots of things about me that are more interesting and important than my illness.

A manic episode is an intense experience – it is not necessarily a *good* experience. There are elements that are thrilling, but many more elements that are scary and uncomfortable. Mania often pushes me away from people I love and usually makes me do things I later regret. It's not something to be envied.

I'm not an 'out of control person'. My bipolar disorder has nothing to do with how disciplined or undisciplined I am.

Sometimes my bipolar disorder makes me believe things that aren't really true or see things that aren't really there. That doesn't mean I can never be trusted. In the moment, my delusions or hallucinations seem completely real to me, but they occur in distinct episodes. Most of the time my grasp on reality is just as strong as yours.

I can still be happy, sad, excited – all the normal emotions – without any influence of mania or depression. Not all my emotions are related to my disorder.

I struggle with loneliness, even when I am surrounded by people. Sometimes I feel trapped in my own head, and that is a very lonely thing.

After a manic episode, I feel as though I have woken up and found that, while I was asleep, another person used my body for bizarre, humiliating activities. Please try not to bring up the things I did when I was manic. It makes me embarrassed.

I can't always control my upset, fear or anger. On some days my brain is hypersensitive, and the smallest stimulation can make me explode. I'm not trying to be melodramatic: my emotions really are that intense.

I know I go 'up and down' a lot, but that doesn't mean that either state is false. When I am up I genuinely feel invigorated and electric, and when I am down I genuinely feel hopeless – sometimes even suicidal. The co-existence of the two extremes doesn't invalidate either one.

Although mania and depression both exist inside me, they never meet. When I am depressed, it is impossible to imagine that I will ever have the energy and verve of mania again, and when I am manic the concept of depression seems alien.

I don't have different personalities. I have different states and different intensities. But I am always me.

# *Georgia*

Who's house are we
going to tomorrow??

**Mais xox**
Not mine, Alfie has scouts

**Charl <3**
Yours G?

Yep sure ☺

**Mais xox**
Thank yoooooooou ☺

**Charl <3**
Is your laptop fixed

Yes haha

**Charl <3**
Dinner

**Mais xox**
☹

Same ☹

**Charl <3**
Bye

**Mais xox**
Be good

Don't die

---

A greyscale horizon: winter-ravaged trees claw at a barren sky.
*'We cut and kill flowers*
*Because we think they're beautiful*
*We cut and kill ourselves*
*Because we think we're not …'*

A pencil-and-paper girl, mouth obscured by a swipe of charcoal.

*'Don't get too close*
*It's dark inside …'*

A wan face, features crumpling again and again on an automated loop.

*'The girl who seemed unbreakable, broke*
*She dropped a fake smile and whispered to herself,*
*"I can't do this any more …"'*

Letters carved into skin, blood spilling like ink.

*'I'm not OK …'*

The laptop is open on Charley's knee, her finger tapping the down key, hungry eyes sucking in the ghoulish posts. Maisie rests her head on Charley's shoulder, the string of her greying friendship necklace clamped between teeth. Her pink cheeks and glazed eyes make her look feverish, and I gently untuck her hair from her shirt collar, blowing cool air onto her neck. She doesn't move. When I have to look at the screen – when Charley nudges and points – I make my eyes blur so the pictures swim murkily together. The loud, proud misery of the black-and-white images makes me feel dirty.

'Can we do something else now?'

I lift the sweaty scarf of hair from the back of my own neck, but no one whistles cold air onto my skin. The room is stuffy and smells strongly of us. My English book is rucked inside the sheets, uncapped pen leaking blots of blue. I always mean to do my homework, but something happens to time when the bedroom door is shut and the curtains are closed. Time is sucked away in a vacuum of us. I look at my worksheets and I write the date and I read the assessment objectives, but my attention flits back to the two heads, nestled together above the laptop screen, and I am drawn to them like a moth to light. I need to be with them, moving and seeing and breathing in time.

Back at the beginning, back in Year Seven, I had Maths with Charley but not with Maisie, and English with Maisie but not with Charley, and Maisie and Charley had Science together but I was in the other half of the register. So we didn't become friends that quickly. We trickled together from different class-rooms at breaktime and lunchtime, and chatted about teachers and television, and then at some point we were bound together by something stronger than cement. I don't know when or why. The friendship squeezed us together, like a noose pulled tighter and tighter.

Now, Maisie texts from my doorstep at 6.30 each morning, and I creep out like a spirit, and we yawn our way to the 6.45 bus. Charley lives on the other side of the high street, so she meets us in the form room at 7.00. Our eyes are puffy as pink marshmallows, and by fifth period I want to put my head on my textbook and fall asleep, but it is worth it. From 7.00 until 8.30 each morning it is just us, alone in the form room, and that is the best thing in the world. At 3.30 we ditch the bus and walk, stretching out the fifteen-minute journey like bubblegum: an hour, two hours, three hours. We dawdle indirectly home, alter-nating licks on a sherbet-dipped lollipop that burns our mouths raw. One afternoon, mid-winter, we sat on the wall outside Maisie's house for so long that when we stood the backs of our skirts were frozen solid. We laughed then, bodies convulsing and converging around one another, the warmth of infatuation melting the ice on our clothes. We fell in love with each other that winter, when we were thirteen and completely grown-up. Then, as spring brewed, we fell in love with suffering.

I would never describe Charley as happy, and she would never want me to. She is snippy and sarky and confident in an off-hand, don't-care sort of way, but her face is always frowning.

Even when she laughs, it sounds frowny, like there is something wrong inside that she only lets out through a wrinkled forehead and a not-right laugh. The first time Charley came round for tea in Year Eight, we sat in the lounge for a while, squashed together in the armchair next to Mum's sofa. Mum chatted to Charley, and my face prickled red hot, and once we got up to my bedroom I mumbled without knowing what to say.

'She has to lie down. She's not well. She's got stuff wrong with her. Like, with her bones. They're really achy. That's why she's lying down now, in the middle of the afternoon.'

Charley shrugged in a don't-care sort of way, and we flopped on my bed and played with Snapchat filters. When Charley left I kissed Mum on the forehead, and inside I apologised for apologising for her.

'Did you like Charley?'

'Mmm. Interesting girl. Seems a bit troubled.'

*Troubled.* What a desperately, painfully romantic thing to be.

Maisie isn't frowny – Maisie is a space cadet. Maisie is wispy, as if she were made of candyfloss or communion wafer or something else that dissolves on your tongue, and her hair is so straight it is like there's a weight tied to each strand, dragging it down towards the ground. Maisie is barely even there at all, and certainly not there with enough conviction to determine our direction as a threesome. It was always going to be Charley who sent us down the track we followed. Charley and her frowning forehead and her not-laughing laugh and her Troubles.

---

**Charl <3**
Are you coming to mine tomorrow?

Yessssss

**Mais xox**
My mum says I have to be home by 6 ☹

6???

**Mais xox**
Ikr ☹

**Charl <3**
Ffs can't you stay later?

**Mais xox**
I can't my grans coming over ☹

**Mais xox**
Will you come to mine on Saturday??

> Yes for sure! We'll
> have all day then!

**Charl <3**
Maybe

**Mais xox**
Please come Charl ...

**Charl <3**
Got to go

**Mais xox**
Ok ...

> Bye. <3

When Charley shuts her bedroom door and rolls up her sleeve to show us the red line bisecting her arm, I ask, 'What's that?' and I hate how high and tight my voice sounds. It is the sort of scratch you would get from being clawed by a cat or snagged by a bramble. Except that it is determinedly, unfalteringly straight. And it is right across her right wrist.

I slip off my shoes and join her on the bed, and Maisie does the same because Maisie always does the same.

'Cut, stupid.'

'How'd it happen?'

'Safety pin.' She traces it with a finger and winces an exaggerated wince. If we hadn't been there, she wouldn't have winced.

'Did you ... was it ...?'

89

She nods gravely, and our eyes meet. And she doesn't say anything with her mouth, but with her eyes she says: *Jump*.

I don't want to jump. I want to keep my feet on the ground. But I want Charley; this is just how much she costs. So with my eyes I ask: *How high?*

It is cold and grey and February, and 8.30pm by the time I get home from Charley's. I dump my stuff in the hallway and creep through to the lounge where Mum is lying on the sofa, asleep. The drumbeat of *EastEnders* thumps from the TV. I go into the kitchen, stretch up on tiptoe to open the medicine cupboard, and pour two grey tablets and one green-and-white tablet into my hand; I put them in an egg cup, pour a glass of water and put both on the low table next to Mum, ready for when she wakes up. I lift her crutches from the floor and lean them against the arm of the sofa, so she can reach them. Then I slip from the room like a helpful burglar.

**Charl <3**
Have u done it yet?

No …

**Charl <3**
U don't have to G. I just need to.

I wish I could help
Charl …

**Charl <3**
No one can :/

Luv u <3

**Charl <3**
Speak later xx

Please stay safe xxx

**Charl <3**
I'm always safe.

I peel off my tights and jumper and skirt and flop them over the radiator. The fleecy fabric of my pyjamas is soft and soothing. I reach into my skirt pocket and take the pin into my waiting fist; then I walk through to the bathroom, lock the door, and sit on the lowered toilet seat. I roll my sleeve up to my elbow, unclasp the pin with one deft flick of my fingers, and I rotate my arm so my palm is facing upwards. I notice how delicate, smooth and untainted the skin of my wrist looks; then I dig the pin in and tear straight across. The pain is so sharp that tears bite at my eyes. My toes curl. It must be the second worst pain I have ever felt. The first is when I broke my arm falling off the climbing frame in Year Three, but this is nearly that bad. I am certain when I look down I will see a ghastly, gaping wound leaking blood into the palm of my hand, and I wonder how I will get to A&E and back without Mum noticing.

The two-inch scrape looks like a fine, pink thread, speckled with blood like spittle. I feel so disappointed it is like I have swallowed a sack of rocks. I take a picture on my phone because otherwise there's no point. It looks slightly more impressive once I've applied a black-and-white filter, and I feel slightly better. I wipe the blood away with a piece of toilet paper. Two five-pence pieces of red. I put the picture on our group chat, and the tiny circle of Charley's profile picture appears, so I know she's seen it. Maisie was last active 34 minutes ago. I've won.

**You sent a picture to GCM <3**

**Charl <3**
??

:/

**Charl <3**
Do you feel better now?

Yeah. Alot better.

91

**Charl <3**
Just put a plaster on it, make sure
your mum doesn't see

> She doesn't see
> much lol

**Charl <3**
Lucky.

Before, I never knew what bound Charley and Maisie and me together. It was stronger than cement. Now I know. We have to stick together because we're all Troubled, and now the Troubles have been unleashed, demanding to be tattooed on our skin. After school we share hushed, intimate minutes, sitting on Charley's bed, sleeves hiked up to our elbows, running our fingers over the shiny silver strings of cuts past, the raised gashes of cuts present, the smooth canvas for cuts yet to come. Our arms are striped with lines of angst, and the more lines we acquire the more I love and fear Charley. I fear she will kill herself, and I don't know whether I would be more traumatised by losing a friend or losing the competition. If Charley kills herself I will have to kill myself too, and I think Charley knows that if I kill myself she will have to kill herself too. We don't worry about Maisie; Maisie is too wispy and not-really-there to kill herself. I don't think Charley or I really wants to die, so when we crush our bodies together in a goodbye hug I am not surprised when she whispers, 'Bye. Be good. Don't die.' And I am not surprised when I whisper it back.

Charley is the worst cutter. The hierarchy is Charley, then me, then Maisie, and our harmonious co-existence rests on the upkeep of that hierarchy. Charley is the leader; I am close behind; Maisie is just filler. It is Charley who discovers that, if you get hold of a very tiny screwdriver, you can loosen the metal casing of one of the standard-issue pencil sharpeners that sit in pots at the back of the classrooms, and can pluck out the tiny silver blade. A real *blade*. So much better than the unglamorous point of a safety pin. We deplete the school's pencil sharpener supply so quickly they put a notice in assembly about 'the importance of respecting school property'. We keep pencil sharpener blades in our bags, in our pockets, between our phones and their cases. When I run my finger along the edge of the blade in my pocket during Maths, it is as soothing as a hug.

It is Charley who discovers the murky depths of Tumblr. Page after page of pornographic suffering. She drinks it in, eyes shining, mouth twitching, bent over her laptop after school. Romantic pictures of frosty, leaf-shorn trees form the background for brooding poetry quotes. *'Miles to go before I sleep.'* Grotesque, *surely-that-can't-be-real-can-it?* images of wan girls, lips sewn together with big, clumsy stitches and pulled into haunting leers, words branding their foreheads: *I'm fine.* Searching 'self-harm' on Tumblr is like stepping into a world where all the colour has been drained away. The people in charge of the internet try to block it, but it's all still there if you know where to look. Before you're allowed to see the search results, a little message pops up asking if 'everything is OK' and giving you the number for the Samaritans. The first time we read that message we laughed and laughed, because of course everything wasn't OK; in fact everything was so not-OK we had lost track of what had even made everything not-OK in the first place. We laughed so hard I almost felt the cold in my bones thaw.

Today we are at Maisie's, slug-like on our stomachs, bedclothes curled around us. When I move, crisp packets crackle. The laptop is open in front of Charley. I am so close I can see the individual acne scars on her cheeks. Maisie is on her other side, shirt and jumper ridden up above a sliver of back-skin. Every so often, Charley draws our attention to something on the screen: *Look at that. Look at that pain. Isn't that incredible?* And we nod and murmur, and when I blink I see pain projected onto the black of my eyelids. I rest my head on Charley's shoulder and breathe in the smell of sweat, and salt and vinegar, and suffering. The cheap polyester of Charley's school jumper grates against my cheek. *This is love, isn't it? I am in love with Charley. I am in love with our friendship and with belonging. But I got here too late. I fell in love with Charley too late to stop her falling in love with hurting.*

———

> Have u seen
> the weather forecast??

**Charl <3**
Ikr. 28 degrees on Thursday. :o

> Ffs. Gonna be
> soooooo hot at school ☹

**Charl <3**
Ikr. Gonna be so bad with jumpers …

> Argh. Ffs.

**Charl <3**
Well not like there's anything we can do about it lol.

> No. See you in 15.
> On bus with M.

**Charl <3**
See you xox

By the time spring has bled into summer, everyone is bleeding. School is awash with copycat cutters. Wearing a jumper in the sweltering summer classroom is a statement. When I sit next to another girl wearing a jumper, she always rolls up her sleeves in faux-absent-mindedness and flashes me a battalion of super-ficial scars. She wants to impress me because I am (nearly) the top, and that makes my stomach lurch with pride. Sometimes, I respond in kind. It is a macabre game of you-show-me-yours-and-I'll-show-you-mine, and I know that mine will be better because mine are better than anyone's (except Charley's).

At some point between spring and summer, cutting stopped being something I *had* to do and became something I *wanted* to do. The spiky pain lost its spikes. Now, it doesn't really hurt at all. It feels like a puppy mouthing me. It is a predictable, companionable sort of pain, and I am the one stopping and starting it. I don't just cut for Charley any more – sometimes I don't even tell her when I've done it. I cut for me. It grounds me, and seeing the blood come out makes me feel I am being purified. Sometimes, when I cut, I think of all my Troubles. When I was little, when Mum could walk and drive, I would scream when she left me and my sister Lily in the car to pay for petrol or get money from the cash machine. Once, I managed to get out of the car and run across the main road to reach her, and I knew it was naughty but I had to be with Mum. After that, a woman called Tara came to the house to talk to me, and she said that my feelings were like a volcano, and when I did things like run across main roads it was the volcano erupting. She gave me a purple pen and it was the best present I'd ever had. I'm not sure if cutting makes those memories hurt less, but I'm not sure how much those memories really hurt in the first place. But sometimes I think of them, and then I cut, and then I don't think about them any more. I just think about the blade and the blood.

When school breaks up for the summer, Charley and Maisie and I are elated. Six whole weeks with no commitments but each other. On the last half-day before the holidays we go to Maisie's house in the afternoon and sit in her garden and eat ice lollies covered in hundreds and thousands and plan whose house we are going to go to each day for the next six weeks. Knowing I'll be on the Isle of Wight for an *entire weekend* mid-August terrifies me: what will they do without me? What will I miss? I almost ask Mum if I can stay at home by myself, but I don't want to upset her. She is spending more and more time on the sofa, and I am having to be more and more grown-up and responsible, for her and for Lily. I know I ought to be grown-up and responsible about the Isle of Wight too.

> What time shall I
> come over tomorrow?

**Charl <3**
Anytime

> Shall I come as soon as I've
> dropped Lily? Like 9.30?

**Charl <3**
Sure

> Aghhh can't wait!!!! <3

**Charl <3**
Yeah

> U ok??

**Charl <3**
Sure

> I'm really sorry about
> the isle of white ☹

**Charl <3**
Its ok.

> I would way rather
> stay here and see u

**Charl <3**
Its fine. Maisie will still be here.

> :(

The summer days settle into a rhythm. When I get up I make breakfast for Mum and Lily, lay out Mum's pills for the day and make sure she has everything she needs within reach. Then I

walk Lily round to a friend's house, and then I am free. I meet
Maisie on the corner of her road and we share bags of sweets
on the walk to Charley's, or I meet Charley outside the post
office and we share bags of sweets on the walk to Maisie's,
or I meet Maisie and Charley in the park and we share bags
of sweets on the walk back to mine. There are always sweets:
rainbow-coloured wine gums and fruit gums and hard gums,
and we chew them greedily as if filling ourselves with colour
in readiness for a day that will be uniformly black and grey.
In the bedroom, we close the curtains and kick off our shoes
and empty the blades from our pockets into the middle. We
don't cut when we're together. It's a rule. I don't know why.
Then Maisie chooses the DVD and I put it into the DVD player,
and Charley starts up the laptop, and the colour seeps from
the room. We work our way through self-destruction-themed
films: *Painful Secrets*; *Cyberbully*; *Sharing the Secret*; *Wristcutters*;
*The Virgin Suicides*. We've seen *Girl, Interrupted* so many times we
can recite whole scenes from memory. Charley refreshes and
re-refreshes her Tumblr homepage, the first to see every new
post that pops up, and the room is lit only by the glow of two
screens. Maisie often puts her head on my lap, and I stroke her
straight hair away from her face. Sometimes we all lie on our
backs, side by side, so close we breathe as one. It is strange to
feel so warm and safe when all around us is darkness and danger.

The paracetamol thing starts soon after I get back from the Isle
of Wight. We are standing in the kitchen at my house, waiting
for a pizza to warm in the oven, and I am opening Mum's medicine cupboard to do her afternoon tablets.

'What's that?'

'What's what?'

'That.'

Charley reaches up and takes down one of the big bottles of 100 paracetamol I collect for Mum from the friendly man in the pharmacy, who wouldn't normally give out prescriptions to under-18s, but he knows Mum and knows that I am very grown-up and responsible.

'Paracetamol.'

'Can we have it?'

'Have you got a headache?'

'No.'

There are five bottles still up there – enough that no one will notice one missing – and I've been away for the weekend and need to stay in favour.

'Yeah. If you want.'

The timer pings and we divide the pizza between three plates and go back up to my room. There is a glint in Charley's eyes, and when we are sitting back on the bed she deftly twizzles the childproof cap from the top of the bottle and pours out a handful of bullet-shaped tablets.

'How many shall we take?'

Maisie looks at me, and I look at Charley, and Charley and I look at one another for a long moment.

*Jump.*

*How high?*

We don't take many that afternoon – five or six each. They are big in my throat and hard to swallow and I feel sorry for Mum, choking down so many each day. I tell myself that I'm just empathising with her – just being a good, grown-up, responsible daughter. That's all. Maisie keeps coughing and bringing them back up. The handful of bullets disappears into Charley like dust into a vacuum. For the rest of the afternoon we sit in silence and half-watch *Skins* and half-wonder whether this is the end. At 6.00 we are all still alive, and Charley and Maisie have to go home for tea. We hug each other extra tight and whisper hot against each other's cheeks. 'Bye. Be good. Don't die.'

Once they have left I go downstairs and put a frozen lasagne in the oven, then walk round the corner to collect Lily. On the way home, she tells me that she and Emily have been building a kingdom for their fruit-scented, animal-shaped rubbers. It sounds sort of fun. We eat tea on our laps in the lounge and watch *Grand Designs*. After tea I go upstairs and have a shower and put on my pyjamas, and when I go into my bedroom the bottle of paracetamol is still standing, uncapped on my bedside table. And I think, *I don't feel so good.* I upend the bottle and tip out a couple of pills and swish them down with stale water from my school water bottle. *Now I feel better.* Then I climb into bed and turn off the light, and when I plug my phone into its charger the screen illuminates with a message from Charley.

> Charl <3
> Be good. Don't die.

On the first day of Year Ten I leave the house in a flurry and a shirt I ironed the night before, thinking the start of a new school year deserves some small ceremony. I am ten minutes late: when I glance over my shoulder I see the bus coming up behind me, and I have to run to catch it. The exertion brings a chalky residue to my throat. I hawk it up and spit white onto the pavement, and the bus driver gives me a dirty look as I tap my pass to the reader. My mouth tastes of bile and paracetamol.

I haven't been taking many. When I woke up the morning after the first time, I was half-surprised to be alive and half-distracted by a nagging twinge in the back of my head. I shook out two tablets, considered them, then added another two. I swilled them down and wished I'd only taken two, then wished I'd taken more, then wished I hadn't taken any at all, then reached into the music box on my side table and withdrew an emergency blade and cut, lying on my back, my arm above my head. It felt strange – decadent? – to cut lying down, arm above my head.

> **Charl <3**
> Can u bring those pills to mine tomorrow??

> > Not sure … Don't want mum to notice …

> **Charl <3**
> She won't notice tho

> > Lol true.

> **Charl <3**
> Bring them yeah?

> > We shouldn't take like loads

> **Charl <3**
> Why not?

> > Isn't it like really dangerous?

> **Charl <3**
> Yeah lol
> Do u care??

> > I'll bring them. See u tomorrow. Luv u xox

> **Charl <3**
> Thanks <3

Charley treats the pills like a game she wants me to play by myself. She lies on the bed, poking me with her foot, voice sing-song yet snide. 'Bet you can't do twelve. Bet you can't do fifteen. Bet you can't do twenty.' Twenty is the limit. The day I did twenty I felt sick and strange, and after an hour I vomited white chalk all over the duvet and we had to change the cover without Mum or Lily noticing. Once the fresh cover was on, Charley let me lie with my head in her lap and she stroked my hair and it felt nice. She never pushes me past twenty. Something sinister lies on the other side of twenty.

When Maisie and I get to school Charley is already there, waiting outside the door. When we hug, Charley holds me tighter than usual, and her face looks drawn. We sit in the corner of the new form room, Charley on the windowsill, Maisie and me on the table underneath, and she rolls up the sleeve of her jumper. I look at her arm and taste sour in my mouth. The underside of Charley's arm is still covered in the familiar cross hatch of pink lines, but the swarthier skin on the top – untouched before now – is raw and blotchy. Sores eat up palm-sized patches of tissue. Clear fluid has seeped into the fabric of her shirt sleeve. Maisie makes a sound like a small, scared mouse. I swallow down acid.

'What did you do?'

'Bleach. I boiled it. Then poured it ...' she says, looking down at her blistered arm with blank eyes. I wonder whether she is in shock. I wonder whether I should call a teacher or an ambulance. I wonder whether it would be worse for Charley to die or for Charley to hate me. Then she looks up, her gaze meeting mine. One eyebrow twitches infinitesimally upwards.

*Jump?*

I look at her, and try to will empathy into my eyes, but suddenly I can't find it in me. I am dulled.

*No.*

The rest of the day is a poor imitation of the hours of summer when we couldn't get enough of each other. I tell myself it's just a bore to be back at school. That's all. Nothing's changed. But when we are at Charley's in the afternoon I pretend to get a text from Mum telling me I need to collect Lily early, and I leave before the end of the third episode of *13 Reasons Why*.

We've seen it before. We've seen them all before. I don't want to be there anymore. When I get home the house is quiet, and I go straight to my room and pick up the bottle of paracetamol and pour some out into my hand and then pour them back and screw on the cap. I go into the lounge and sit down next to Mum, who is just waking from her afternoon sleep in front of *Cash in the Attic*. She sits up and I soften against her, head on her shoulder and then in her lap. The couple on screen earn enough money at auction to build a dressage enclosure in the garden for their daughter and her pony. They are very pleased. Their daughter and her pony are even more pleased. Mum strokes my hair. It feels nice.

Are u ok??

**Charl <3**
Yeah why

I'm worried about u :(

**Charl <3**
Don't be

I care about u Charl.
I'm worried your really
hurting yourself

**Charl <3**
Yeah and
U do it too
I like doing it

I'm really tired

**Charl <3**
Is that it?

What do u mean?

**Charl <3**
Lol

What??
Charley??

**Charl <3 was last active 1 minute ago**

**Charl <3 was last active 3 minutes ago**
**Charl <3 was last active 16 minutes ago**

The next day I am determined to push down the sickly-scared feeling that rises in my throat when I think about Charley's mangled arm. If being her friend means joining her in the dark, Troubled place where she corrodes her skin, I'll do it. I'll do it in a heartbeat. I need Charley, and she needs me. When I see the 6.45 bus swinging towards my stop I stick out an arm, but Maisie's seat is empty. I can see it through the window. I duck my head, embarrassed, and the driver jerks away.

Where are you? Am
at bus stop xox

The 7.00 bus comes and there is still no Maisie. I am starting to feel antsy. I stand at the bus stop for an hour and a half. For an hour and a half I watch as suited businessmen and cosy mothers with buggies and buzzy schoolchildren come and go, and as every bus pulls up to the stop my pulse bangs in my ears, and as every window reveals an empty Maisie-seat – or no Maisie in the Maisie-seat – it drops down into my toes. My thumbs go stiff from pounding the buttons of my phone.

Mais, where are
u??? xox
Is everything ok? xx
Mais please reply? x
What's going on??

At 8.15 I see Lily, hoving into sight at the top of the street, aiming for the 8.20 bus to her primary school, and when she sees me her face lifts into a smile, like a sunbeam framed by mousy brown hair. She breaks into a little run to get to me faster, and when she arrives I grab her elbow so hard she squeals. I yank her onto the bus and don't speak for the entire journey, even when she tries to tell me more about Fruity Animal Rubber Kingdom.

When I get to the form room it is seething with noise and bodies and giggling, gabbling girls. Charley is sitting in her place at the back, Maisie is sitting in her place at the front, and I crash down my bag in my place in the middle. My throat burns and my eyes prickle because everything is wrong. We sit in silence as Miss takes the register. It is a pointy, cold silence that jostles between us at our desks, falling into step beside us on the way to Geography. Charley takes History, not Geography, so we don't see her during first period, and I put all my energy into thawing Maisie. *It can't be that hard. I haven't done anything wrong. OK, it was a mistake to go home early yesterday. It was stupid. I shouldn't have done it. But they can't really be angry with me over it, can they? They can't **stay** angry with me over it. This is **Maisie**. Maisie is made of cotton wool and indecision. Maisie couldn't stay angry with anyone.* But in Geography, Maisie's Charley impression is faultless: the set jaw; the determined forwards gaze; the cold, hard quiet.

At morning break Maisie goes to the toilet, so I am first back to the form room. I hoist myself onto the desk in our usual corner and know that things will be alright. When I see Charley through the glass panel of the door I beam at her, hoping to convey: *I'm so glad to see you. I'm so sorry I was shit yesterday. I really want to make it up to you. I really care about you, Charley.* She stalks into the room, slow and purposeful, her gaze unwavering. I feel my smile freeze on my face, my cheeks turn to plaster. The classroom is a pulse of bodies, but the air is still between Charley and me. She comes very close – so close I can see the freckles that, from a distance, make her skin look tanned, and the patches where her hair is raggedy after I cut it last week. Her rucksack is slung from one shoulder, and she rests her weight to that side. The words that drawl from her mouth are so familiar I could say them myself, but they sound foreign now. Normally, they are words we dress in the garments of care and concern, wrapping them around one another like a protective enchantment or soft blanket. Now, they sound scratchy and sneering. As Charley swings her bag to the other shoulder and turns her back, the words burrow deep into my ears and dig their claws into my brain. I can't catch my breath.

'Bye. Be good. Don't die.'

---

**Charl <3 is active now**

> Whats going on
> Charl??
>
> Shall I come to
> yours after school
> tomorrow??
>
> Are u cross with me??
>
> Ffs Charley please just
> say something even if
> your cross with me
>
> I don't get what I did
> wrong but whatever it
> was I'm really sorry

**Charl <3 is active now**

When Charley wants something to happen, Charley makes it happen. Usually, when Charley wants something to happen, it involves blades and Troubles and her own body. When Charley wants to hurt herself, Charley hurts herself, and the parents sitting with their mouths pressed shut in front of the television and the teachers sitting with their ears pressed shut in the staff room and the friends sitting with their eyes pressed shut can't stop her. Nothing can stop her. Before now, I never knew that the thing Charley wanted to happen could involve silence and sniggers and someone else's suffering. When Charley wants to hurt someone, she hurts them, and the grovelling texts trailing rows of kisses and the pleading eyes trailing tracks of tears and the desperate appeals trailing choked words can't stop her. Nothing can stop her. In Year Ten, Charley wants to hurt me, and Charley makes it happen.

In Year Ten, I learn that the loneliest thing is to be lonely in a place where you never used to be lonely. If you never have friends, you never know what you're missing. You never know what it's like to have someone to save a seat for and someone who saves a seat for you, and you never know that sherbet lollipops taste better when someone else has licked them first, because then you're not just tasting the sweetness of the sugar but the sweetness of knowing that you're close enough to someone to share their *spit*. Ex-friends hurt more than never-friends. Charley hops from being a friend to an ex-friend – Maisie following her like a snotty toddler – with such rapidity she makes it seem as if the two states were side by side all along. But they weren't side by side. Not for me. The chasm between life Then and Now is gaping. Cruelly, it is only really Now that I understand the perfection of Then: how much of a love affair the three of us had. It feels funny that what bound us together was suffering, because Now makes me realise that Then wasn't suffering at all. Then was playful, mysterious, arousing and glittery. Now isn't like that. Now, everything is dull.

At home after school, knowing that Charley and Maisie will be curled up on the bed where I belong, I don't fill myself with paracetamol. The halo of excitement surrounding the rattling bottle feels too much like Charley, and that feels too much like falling apart. I still cut, and I don't know why that feels any less like Charley than the paracetamol. Maybe it doesn't. Maybe it feels like my last means of being close to her. Once the first few weeks of Now have established that Then isn't coming back,

I establish some ground rules of my own. I cut twice in the morning on the right wrist, and twice in the evening on the left wrist. A cut in the morning for Charley, a cut in the morning for Maisie; a cut in the evening for Charley, a cut in the evening for Maisie. Two neat, perpendicular lines for every morning and evening I mourn my two people. I should feel gloriously, deliciously Troubled, but I feel nothing. Then, cutting was a kick and a buzz and a squirm of excitement. Now, like everything else, it is dull. I hike my sleeves up when Charley and Maisie are nearby, but I am not really cutting for them. I am cutting for me. Charley would be proud, but I don't have Charley any more, I only have me. And I want to cut.

I sink into silence. Sometimes, like when your teacher sets it as a condition for work, silence can mean only talking loud enough for the person next to you to hear. Sometimes, like when your Mum accuses you of it, silence can mean only talking when you need or want something. Now, silence means *silence*. It means not talking to anyone all day, and not breathing loudly, and not moving loudly. I am invisible. Sometimes in my head I yell, wanting someone at school or at home or in between to hear me and see me and lift me up and hold me in warm, safe arms. But no one hears, because I am silent. And no one sees, because I am invisible.

Being invisible means it is not hard to stop going to school. One morning I wake up and realise I can't sit through the silent bus ride and silent lessons and silent break time and lunchtime and all-the-time. I slip out of bed and across to my desk, and I write Mum a note saying that I can't go to school that day, and I go back to bed and don't go to school for three months.

I feel red and black. Hot-red; burning-red; danger-warning-STOP-red. Empty-black; nothing-black; tar-soot-badness-black. Redness and blackness and silence everywhere except in my head, where everything is loud and rasping.

*You could go and get the paracetamol bottle from the cupboard and neck the lot. How many are there left in the old bottle? Your bottle? Fifty? You could open a new one. Swallow a hundred. Fill yourself up with poison. Go on. Go on. I dare you. Go on. Do it. Or you could go out, get the bus to the shopping centre and walk through Primark and Marks & Spencer and come out the other side and go into the multi-storey car park and get the lift up to the top and wind your way through the parked cars and go to the edge and step off. Fall down and down and down. Go on. I double dare you. Go on. Do it. Or you could get the rope from the garage, the one that Mum used to use for Scouts, and tie it like Charley showed you off Tumblr, back when you were a real person, and loop it round the curtain rail and climb up on a chair and jump and snap your neck like uncooked spaghetti. You could, you know. Go on. I double, triple dare you. Go on. DO IT.*

I would do it, if it weren't for the dullness. I don't have the energy for a dramatic feat of pill-scoffing. I'm too tired to leave my bed to catch the bus. My crumbly brain can't remember how to tie a noose. Day by day, I am saved from suicide not by hope, but by fatigue. It is torturous and tedious and not at all Tumblr.

I exist between sixteen walls. Bedroom. Kitchen. Lounge. Bathroom. Mum's morning meds. Bed. Toilet. Bed. Mum's afternoon meds. Bed. Mum's evening meds. Toilet. Bed. No shower. No toothbrush. Little food. Television on my laptop – perversely, comedy panel shows. The laughter of the Studio Audience makes my ears prickle and my chest hurt, and I don't know whether it is a balm or a torment. Laying Mum's meds beside her bed one morning and tiptoeing out, I hear her stir behind me. I stop. She whispers, 'Sweetheart. Can I help?' I squeeze my voice into dull submission and croak, 'No.' We go back to sleep in our separate bedrooms, consumed by the worries in our separate heads. Except, more and more, it is not just worries filling my head. More and more, my mind is a mangle of nightmares and hatred and black, evil thoughts. No longer content with planning my own death, I imagine Charley's and Maisie's too. Charley's demise is a given: she cuts too deep, nicks a vein and exsanguinates oozily all over her crisp white duvet cover, redness framing her like a target. Maisie simply fades away, a higgledy-piggledy collection of bones and skin. After all, Maisie was never really quite there at all. Their imagined deaths curl me into a knot of terror. I put my hands over my ears. I screw my face up tight.

*Shut up shut up shut up SHUT UP!*

Even when my eyes and ears are covered, I can still see them. I can still hear them. Charley and her slashed wrists, groaning softly. Maisie and her broken body, crumbling and creaking. Me and my tired liver or my shattered bones or my breathless lungs. Me and my silence. Standing at the top of the stairs, my limbs are heavy and my head is swimming. Pushing the cool wood of the lounge door with flat palms, I find Mum awake and looking surprised. The TV is turned off – the TV is never turned off. My mouth is dry and I am shaking, and Mum is looking really scared. Feelings bubble into words that bubble up and out of my mouth: 'Please help. Please help me.'

———

It feels strange to be at the bus stop at 8.00. I never get the bus before 8.30 any more; college doesn't start until 9.00. None of the usual faces are here to greet me. The 8.30 bus is seething with schoolkids, but at 8.00 there are only a few. The rest are grown-ups – proper adults, going to proper, adult jobs. It is peaceful. The bus is busy but not full, and I pick my way past a pushchair to the empty seats at the back.

She is sitting on the left, and for a second it looks wrong because she always sits on the right. But, of course, she doesn't – not any more. Or, at least, she might, but I wouldn't know, because I get the 8.30 bus these days, and – although I didn't know it before today – she gets the 8.00. But it is undoubtedly her, and in the same moment that I realise this, she raises her head and sees that I am undoubtedly me. The bus lurches forwards and I lurch into the decision to sit down beside her.

'Hi, Maisie.'

'Hi.'

Not much about Maisie has changed in a year. She is still plain and pale and somehow not-really-there, though her face stands out a lot more now that she applies her make-up with a shovel. Dying her hair a blonder blonde has made it look slightly less wispy, but it still hangs around her face in long, straight ribbons. We've not spoken since school, but you don't have to speak to people to know what they're doing. From Facebook, I know that Maisie got Bs and Cs in her GCSEs, then went on holiday to Zante with her Mum and little brother, then stayed on at the school sixth form to do A levels in Art and Sociology and something else. From rumours, I know that she was hardly at school at all during that first term of sixth form. Someone heard that she went into a psychiatric unit for obsessive compulsive disorder; someone heard that she had glandular fever; someone heard that Maisie tells a lot of lies.

As well as knowing that I never came back to school after what happened (except for exams, which I sat in a different room to everyone else), from Facebook she will know that I moved to the college in town for sixth form. She will know that, before the move, I went on holiday to Cornwall with my auntie and three cousins, and that during the first term of sixth form I was in the school production of *Carousel*. From rumours, she might know that during the first term of sixth form I had a brief relationship with one of the boys in *Carousel*, and that Lily and I had to live with our Nana for two months at the beginning of the year after Mum had a fall and went into hospital.

There is a lot about me that Maisie won't know – from Facebook or from rumours. She won't know that after what happened Mum took me to the doctor, and the doctor sent me to a counsellor called Pam who told me I was floating through life, numb, because I had got used to feelings hurting so much I couldn't bear to feel them any more. She won't know that after Mum's fall and the time we spent at Nana's there were lots of meetings about us and we got taken to some groups for Young Carers and now a woman called Paula comes to the house every day to do Mum's meds and help her walk, so me and Lily don't have so many jobs any more. She won't know that Paula isn't my favourite person, but she's OK. She won't know that in Cornwall we spent all day every day outside, playing rounders and swingball, and drinking apple juice from tall glass bottles. When I lay on the grass and looked up at the sky Lily flopped down and put her head on my stomach. It was the first time in months I had really felt a feeling, and that feeling was freedom.

On the bus, we speak in muted, meaningless words. I think we both wish we hadn't got on the same bus. It is all too close and too raw. Charley crouches between us, invisible and unacknowledged. I expect we know the same amount about Charley. Like Maisie, she stayed at school for sixth form, but wasn't in any of Maisie's classes – I think she took Biology, Psychology and Maths. She didn't stay for much of the first term, and this term she hasn't come back. No one really knows why. Some people say she was sectioned. Others say they see her in the park, 'off the rails', drinking and smoking with friends they don't recognise. I hope maybe she's just moved away. We don't say it, but I think Maisie and I both miss her, and each other, and us.

We get close to the stop outside school, and I stand up to let Maisie squeeze past. I could hug her, but I don't, then I wish I had. But I don't think she wants to be hugged. The bus slows to a stop and she joins the queue of people jostling to get off.

'Let's meet up sometime, yeah?' she mumbles, not looking at me.

'Yeah, let's.'

We both know we won't, because we both know we don't really want to. But saying it is a comfort, because we can pretend that the world that has sprung up between us isn't really there, and that we are fourteen again.

Maisie spills off the bus in a crowd, head down, bag handles looped over her shoulder. I watch her back as she walks down the street, then glimpse her face as the bus pulls level with her, and then she is behind me. I probably won't see her again. I get the 8.30 bus these days.

I face forward and remember eleven-year-old Maisie, and eleven-year-old Charley, and the tight, knotty love we had.

*Bye. Be good. Don't die.*

'But some people self-harm in such a visible way.
If they're so keen for people to see, it must be
attention-seeking. There can't be much behind it.'

## 'Not Much Behind It!': The Ultimate Guide to Attracting Attention for No Good Reason!

1.  Do you feel overwhelmed by the stress of school? The looming exams, hurtling deadlines and unreachable standards? Do you need to apply the brakes?

    You could approach a sympathetic teacher and express your woes. A problem shared is a problem halved! *But could you guarantee they would care? Could you guarantee they would care* **enough**? You could limit the academic burden, conveniently 'forgetting'/'losing'/'not managing' assignments that require excessive effort. You can't worry about grades if you don't care about grades! *But slackers are dime-a-dozen – is that really the way you want to go?*

    *Score the smooth skin of your forearm with red, angry slashes.* In the moment of bloodletting, the school–work–exam woes are crowded out, replaced by a taunting mantra: *I am not sure. I am not safe. I am not well.* And if a concerned staff member catches sight of the scars, peeking from an upturned shirt sleeve? You've got their attention! It's all for attention! *Isn't it?*

2.  Is your home is an unhappy cloister of lowered eyes and raised voices? Do you feel so full of rage you could scream; so full of tears you could drown? Are there siblings who clamour and crowd; parents who cannot hear and will not see; doors that sigh and slam? Do you feel trapped between four walls? Do you need to escape?

You could request a family meeting – lay out your issues calmly and rationally. Communicate to ameliorate! *But you've tried talking it out before. Nobody listens. Nobody cares.* So you shout and scream and bash around. Grab your phone and a stolen £10 note. Bang the front door behind you with such force the doorframe jangles. Return late at night, fuzzy with 90p cider. Climb into bed, your back to the room, your back to the questions. *But are you solving the problem or just escaping it? You need to progress, not stagnate …*

Lock the bathroom door. Turn on the shower. Watch as rusty tracks run into your hands. The stinging pain muffles the home–anger–suffocation woes, and there is only the wheedling voice: *Remember, you are not sure. Remember, you are not safe. Remember, you are not well.* And if a suspicious parent catches sight of the scars, poking from long-sleeved pyjamas? You've got their attention! It's all for attention! *Isn't it?*

3. Do you stand in front of the mirror, appraising the bulges and bumps of your body? Do you feel lumpen and plain? If it's not too big, it's too small; if it's not too small, it's the wrong shape; if it's not the wrong shape, it's the wrong size; and back to the start. Do you feel trapped inside a too-small skin? Do you need to relieve the pressure?

You could take decisive action – join a gym, eliminate simple carbohydrates, establish a five-step skincare routine. *But 'lifestyle changes' take weeks to make a difference: you need relief right now.* So sell the mirror for £15 at a car boot sale and use the money for better things – worrying about your looks is a waste of time! *But you do worry, and the worry will not be shifted by any amount of empowered self-talk. The worry drives you crazy. You're going to snap …*

*Pinch the flesh with angry fingers. Squeeze so hard you brand yourself with nail-prints. Mark your breasts and abdomen with sharp* little *nicks*. Through gritted teeth you mutter the only words you know to be true: *I am not sure. I am not safe. I am not well.* And if an alarmed friend catches sight of the scars, lurking between low-slung skirt and naval-skimming T-shirt? You've got their attention! It's all for attention! *Isn't it?*

4. From the classroom to the shopping centre, do you hear the whispers whistling in your ears? Do messages leave your phone before thoughts leave your head? Have you said or sent or posted something wrong? It is there, forever, on The Cloud. Do you struggle to keep up with the relentless buzz of communication? Do you need a pocket of silence?

   You could implement a week-long Technology Detox – in today's constantly communicating world, there's nothing like some time offline to refresh and relax; it's like taking a holiday without leaving your living room! *But what will people say about you behind your back? It's not safe to be away from it …* You could face the snide silences and tight, abbreviated clusters of consonants head on. Shrug off the unliked Instagram posts and tweets, the unshared Facebook articles. *But you can't stop the sting of rejection, can you?*

   *Find a dark, dingy corner of the internet where strangers speak in sharp, shadowed graphics. Find a league of lost souls whose arms and legs and torsos are patchworked with fading red lines. Find a place where suffering is celebrated, where no one is sure and no one is safe and no one is well.* And if an interfering adult comes across your posts, left illuminating the screen in a rare moment of carelessness? You've got their attention! It's all for attention! *Isn't it?*

5. Do you see yourself from the outside, sprouting like a bean in a tightening shell? Do you see yourself traipsing through the shopping centre, surrounded by clones? Do you feel yourself from the inside: small and scared and desperately wanting the

world to stop spinning? Do you cower behind the façade of normality? Do you need to externalise the internal maelstrom?

You could talk – *but what would you say?* Yes, you could act – *but what would you do?*

*Slash yourself; mark yourself; hurt yourself. Hope that someone sees. Pray that someone hears the words you cannot say: 'I am not sure. I am not safe. I am not well.'*

> 'That's the thing. It's not just attention-seeking.
> It's not like that at all.'

Georgia landed in my lap in a whirl of sinister teenage sub-culture, and her inclusion here is testament to the power and proliferation of stories of this type. While each of the other characters suffers from a diagnosable mental health condition, Georgia occupies an interesting hinterland. Self-harm is considered a 'standalone' behaviour, not a core pathology in itself, and while self-harm in young women is associated with depression and anxiety,[15] studies of 'normal' populations often find self-harm prevalence as high as 25 per cent.[16] How should we conceptualise deliberate self-injury: as a coping strategy, practised by the mentally well and unwell alike? If so, should Georgia's story really be here, alongside depictions of 'true' mental illness? Does self-harm ever *really* present in isolation, or is it always the result of a larger disorder? At points in her story, one could argue that Georgia shows signs of depression, a personality disorder, and even psychosis. However, this chapter is dedicated to the discussion of self-harm first and foremost, in acknowledgement of the frequency with which it was reported by my interviewees, and the complexity of the emotions it betrayed.

Georgia's story has an intense social component. While talking to her doppelgangers, my own memories of single-sex education roared up in a wave of heady, oestrogen-thick reminiscence: the air rattling with rumours; the unspoken hier-archies; the desperation to be special. Reading it back, there are moments when Georgia's story seems so sinister – so haunt-ingly *dark* – I find myself edging towards disbelief. Surely *that* didn't really happen. Surely it wasn't actually like *that*. But then I cast back to my own adolescence: the cryptic Facebook statuses begging for concern; the mysterious seduction of suf-fering; the idolisation of TV characters whose *issues* made them irresistible. Beautiful, broken girls. That *is* what it's really like. These things *do* really happen.

In writing Georgia, I was aware that I was, perhaps, playing into the hands of a cliché: the angsty teenager, motivated to self-destruct by petty social squabbles and a desire to be noticed. But in telling Georgia's story, I hope to illuminate the intricate maze of adolescent experience, which is all too often condensed to 'attention-seeking' by the unsympathetic. Georgia turns to self-injury due not to boredom, but to confusion, loneliness and desperation for purpose. The self-harming teenage girl is a well-known character, but she is usually wan, 'troubled', and two dimensional; the irritation we may feel towards her stems from our lack of insight into her background. Although the majority of those I interviewed were adults, most who were currently struggling with self-harm had begun injuring themselves during adolescence. This provides a useful origin point, deserving of further exploration. (It does not, as many seem to think, invalidate their suffering.) Yes, Georgia is a tangle of teenage pain, and culturally we have arrived at an expectation of pain throughout adolescence – but there is a difference between normal, growing pain and extreme, unwell pain. Georgia's experiences are no less serious, valid or worthy of compassion because of the age at which they occur.

Georgia's story explores a particular corner of self-harm subculture (and it can be a subculture of sorts): she becomes enmeshed in a world where self-mutilation is communal, social and implicitly related to status. Although this is not a unique scenario – no character in this book is based on one person – it is by no means representative of all self-harm stories. The act of self-injury can be private, even shameful; the scars it leaves may be assiduously concealed. However, given the prevalence of shame in relation to mental illness, I was interested to explore the opposite scenario: situations in which people gain perverse pride from their suffering. In this context, self-harm is doubly seductive: used as an attempt to relieve uncomfortable emotions, and to impress peers. Stopping seems an impossible prospect, as it would entail the loss of both a crutch and a badge of honour. Again, the experience of self-harm as a source of pride should not be taken as license to discount its seriousness, or assume sufferers to be selfish or manipulative. If anything, it is an indictment of a society that values success and individuality above all else, such that being 'the best' is paramount, be it attaining the highest exam results, gaining entrance to the most prestigious university or cutting the deepest.

Through Georgia, I was also keen to present a theme that arose again and again during my interviews: the intensity of female teenage friendships. Many of my interviewees recalled the love affairs into which they entered with early adolescent friends as being as intense as – although entirely different to – romantic attraction. When such relationships are at the centre of a life, turbulence within those relationships can destabilise that life. There is, of course, a difference between tumultuous teenage years, characterised by changeable moods and intense friendships, and a period of frank mental illness – and this is why I found stories like Georgia's so captivating. What begins as mimicry of a Queen Bee's self-harm spirals into months of profound depression and suicidal thoughts that border on delusions. Georgia faces strains at home, at school and within herself, which might have been dealt with through healthy coping mechanisms – but she is presented with self-harm as both a ready-made solution and non-negotiable condition of friendship. Georgia's friendships are so central to her sense of self that this condition appears rational, and self-mutilation grows from an obligation into a compulsion into an obsession. This reflects the 'conspiracy of circumstances' so common to stories of mental illness development: predisposing factors interact with precipitating factors, such that while one person may become unwell in response to a given experience, another might emerge unscathed.

The infatuation with pain that a handful of my interviewees described was often fuelled by the media they consumed: sinister sites that lure in fractured people and churn out shattered people, all the while purporting to bolster and heal. In dingy corners of the web, misery is revered as a sacred state, with self-harm a prominent feature of discussions, posts and images. The majority of these sites do not actively promote self-injury – graphic images of slashed wrists are accompanied by melancholy quotes, not 'how to' tips, and are often interspersed with posts geared towards recovery – but there is a ghoulish respect for suffering among online devotees. Faceless users speak candidly – *boastingly?* – about the sheer number of professionals involved in their 'highly complex' case. In their online biographies, they list name, nationality, and number of hospitalisations. A hop, skip and jump away, on the 'anorexiarecovery' hashtag, this information is complemented by 'lowest ever weight' and 'number of times tube fed'. Some pictures are snapped hurriedly – hospital wristbands, bandaged arms, stitched skin – while others are posed with obvious care – jutting bones, drops of blood on white enamel, lifeless eyes. Concerned comments come in floods, and one can imagine the figure in the pictures, sucking them in like smoke, fighting to feel filled up but finding themselves emptier than ever.

If pain is paraded, rather than hidden away, is it attention-seeking? Just as 'selfish' implies self-interest and self-congratulation, 'attention-seeking' pejoratively implies a desire for *undeserved, unnecessary* attention. It brings to mind greed, immaturity and impatience, suggesting manipulation and an inappropriate desire to be coddled and adored. Georgia is less an embodiment of attention-*seeking* than attention-*needing*: she harbours a deep, *justified* need to be noticed, acknowledged and supported. Of course, it would be infinitely healthier to articulate that need verbally, but many of my interviewees felt that the gravitas of their problems would not be understood if they tried to speak them. They did not have words big enough or strong enough to voice their feelings, but feared that even their insufficient words would be interpreted as melodramatic. Self-harm is a bold, line-in-the sand scream, far more difficult to ignore than tears or texts. In this light, the 'it's just attention-seeking, so it's not serious' argument is perplexing. Choosing to elicit attention through self-injury is unusual and extreme: if one is willing to go to such lengths, it suggests a need that is urgent, profound *and serious*.

Of course, the 'function' of self-harm extends well beyond articulating un-articulable needs. My interviewees showed me that relationships with self-harm are as varied and nuanced as relationships with friends or partners. For some, the act of physically hurting the body was highly significant: women felt they needed to be punished for some form of inadequacy, and found relief in committing their self-hatred to skin. For others, it was an anaesthesia of sorts, with the act of harming providing release from tension that would otherwise build to unbearable intensity. A small subset reported that they were only able to give and receive care in the context of self-injury: while in day-to-day life they felt unable to treat themselves gently, they were able to deal with their wounds with tenderness. It was a small positive interaction with the body.

Just as it would be impossible to present a character who embodies all motives for self-harm, I could not realistically capture every method. Georgia cuts herself, as this was the most common behaviour reported during my interviews, but self-injury can present in many guises – from burning to overdosing. Although, in some instances, the line between intent to *harm* oneself and to *kill* oneself might appear blurred, the majority of my interviewees were quick to clarify that their self-injury did not reflect a wish to die. Some found that self-harm had become incorporated into their lives as a means of remaining on an even keel: a release valve, preventing emotions from building to a point at which suicide might be contemplated. Others acknowledged that, at times of self-injury, they were highly distressed, but that this did not correlate with a wish to end their lives. Those who had, on one or more occasions, self-harmed in a life-threatening way often reported feeling ambivalent: they were aware that their actions could cause death, and this was neither a motivation nor a deterrent. They experienced a dull, 'what will be will be' apathy.

To a certain extent, Georgia's recovery hinges on the passing of time; however, self-harm can begin in adolescence and persist into adulthood, or present for the first time in middle age. For many of my interviewees, a combination of therapeutic intervention and ageing was referenced as the cornerstone of 'recovery', and this is embodied in Georgia. Some spoke in the rhetoric of addiction, noting that, once they were able to break the habit of hurting themselves, it became easier and easier to turn elsewhere in times of crisis. They were candid about the wrench of recovery:

'The problem is, self-harm works. So you don't want to stop doing it, because it really works. You feel really resentful when people tell you that you have to find another way of dealing with your emotions, because you already have your way, and it's totally effective.'

'Totally effective' was not a unanimous description of the behaviour – most acknowledged that, like a drug, self-harm provided instantaneous relief followed by a building desire to repeat the process – but the majority admitted that, at first, it is counterintuitive and infuriating to be expected to move away from a tried and tested mechanism for distress relief.

'Recovery' from self-harm is complicated by its concep-tualisation as a coping strategy, with some suggesting that recovery should not involve *elimination* but *moderation*. Certain researchers argue that hospitalised psychiatric patients should not be banned from self-injuring, but allowed to do so in a safe, measured way (e.g. using sterile equipment provided by the facility).[17] Patients should still be treated with medication and psychological therapy, with the aim of diminishing the urge to self-injure – but the act of self-injury should not be embargoed. This approach to self-harm treatment is, of course, controver-sial: are professionals minimising the risks to patients' health, or assisting them in harming themselves? Speaking to the *Guardian* in 2009, when treatment programmes allowing 'safe self-harm' were being pioneered, Ian Hulatt, mental health advisor for the Royal College of Nursing, said: 'It is a very complex and confus-ing issue, but then, so is the phenomenon of someone hurting themselves to feel better.'[18]

Is the concept of recovery from self-harm a useful one? Or can there be a healthy life into which self-harm is incorporated as form of stress relief (like smoking or drinking alcohol)? By and large, those women I spoke to who considered themselves recovered no longer self-harmed, or did so infrequently. There was general consensus that, while self-harm can be part of a *high-functioning* life, it has little place in a *happy* life, largely because it keeps one subtly separated from the rest of the world, with a corner of the mind preoccupied by the urge to cut, to hurt, to injure. In this, self-harm 'recovery' has much in com-mon with recovery from any other mental illness: it is a process of opening up the dark – but precious – inner world to the light, and of realising that its dingy corners are far less enticing than they might have appeared in the rush and whirl of early flirtations with suffering.

# What I wish I could tell you about my self-harm

Self-harm can serve so many purposes. Sometimes I do it to punish myself, because I feel like a bad person. Sometimes I find it soothing, like lancing a boil. Sometimes the physical pain distracts me from upsetting memories. It is hard to pin down a single motivation or function.

I may self-harm in a very visible way. Sometimes this is because when I am hurting myself I don't think about the marks it will leave and where those marks will be. Sometimes I want people to see that I am struggling. Yes, it would be better to articulate that struggle, but words are dismissed more easily than scars. Self-harm might seem desperate, but I feel desperate.

Please don't call me attention-seeking. I'm not a noisy child.

Some forms of self-harm are invisible. These are no less valid than obvious cuts or burns.

Most of the time, self-harm is not a suicide attempt. I might self-harm regularly, but never consider suicide.

Self-harm can be addictive. It can feel like an itch I need to scratch or an urge I need to act on. I might not have self-harmed in months or years, but when I am in an emotional situation it may still be my dominant impulse.

If you learn I am self-harming, the most helpful thing you can do is ask: 'What can I do to help?' Being asked 'why?' is overwhelming, because I don't have a coherent answer. I might not know why I am doing it, or it might be too hard to explain.

I know self-harm can seem bewildering and aberrant, and your immediate reaction might be panic. If you can, please try not to let your fear manifest as anger or accusation. If I think I have upset someone, the urge to hurt myself is intensified.

If you're worried about me, and we have a trusting relationship, it's fine to ask if I am OK. I might find it hard to be honest straightaway, but it will remind me that you want to listen when I am ready to talk.

# *Freya*

**Absence**
Today at 7.23

Hi Gavin,

I'm really sorry but I don't think I'm going to be able to come in today. I've woken up feeling really unwell and I think I might have a temperature. I'm going to try to get a doctor's appointment this morning and hopefully I'll be back tomorrow.

Apologies for the inconvenience,
Freya.
Sent from my iPhone

I clasp my knees tight to my chest, and bite down until the joint is branded with ridged purple marks. Sweat is collecting under my breasts, and suddenly I feel very bare. It seems indecent, emailing from my work account, while cocooned in a chrysalis of duvet and unwashed sheets. I feel as if Gavin is peering out from the phone screen, nose wrinkling as he takes in my grubby state.

I delete 'Sent from my iPhone', then retype it, then delete it again. If I really had woken disoriented by fever, would I be lucid enough to drag myself to my desk and my laptop, or would I be sending this from my phone, as I am doing? I retype 'Sent from my iPhone', and eye the blue of 'Send' in the top right-hand corner. My jaw clenches like a tight fist, and my fingernails pattern the soft skin of my forearms with moon-shaped marks. A CBT book stares accusatorily from the shelf, but my thoughts are too loud and skittering to make room for its chirpy advice.

**Finding ways of escaping engagements might ease anxiety in the short term, but over time this will only fuel the fear. The best way of tackling an anxiety-provoking situation is to face it head on – running away this time will only make it more tempting to run away again next time!**

*The office is so hot and noisy and crowded. There isn't a corner of space where no one can see me. I am on show all the time. There are people who see every mistake I make. There are people who watch me. There are crowds of people who make the air thick with noise and body heat. Everyone wishes I wasn't there. Everyone hates me.*

I grit my teeth so tight an ice pick of pain shoots up to my temples. The tension that has wrapped itself around my lungs grips tighter, and every muscle, tendon and ligament in my body aches. A fine film of moisture chills my forehead. Every thump of my heart is a gag pushing my stomach closer to my throat, and the nausea is suffocating.

**The day always seems much more frightening when it is stretching out ahead of you. In the mornings, try to get up, get washed and get dressed without allowing your mind to fixate on worries. Once you're ready for the day, the day will be ready for you!**

*I can't do anything. I need to stay here. I can only be safe here.*

**Try to rationalise your anxieties. Are you *really* in danger? Is anything *really* threatening you? Or is the threat imagined?**

*It's a bad world out there. Anything could happen. I could make more mistakes. I could make a fool of myself. I could get hurt. I could get sick. Anything could happen.*

**If you feel yourself panicking, look at your surroundings. List what you can see. Identify the colours. Ground yourself in your environment.**

*Four walls. Four walls closing in. One bed. One bed tethering me between sticky sheets. One laptop. One laptop full of work I haven't done. One shirt. One shirt that will pinch under my arms and make me feel I am in a cage.*

**Try to notice one pleasant thing as soon as you wake up. Is the sun shining? Can you hear birds singing? Are the clouds an interesting shape?**

*Close the curtains. Keep them closed. I need to make a burrow. I need to make a cave. Shut everything out. Shut the world out.*

**Break your day down into manageable steps. Once you're up and dressed, what do you need to do next? Have breakfast? How are you getting to work? Concentrate on getting to the train station, or the bus stop, or into your car. Don't think about the day stretching ahead – divide it into small, achievable tasks.**

*Can't get out of bed. Mustn't get out of bed. Buses crash. Trains collide. Cars spin off roads. My chest is tight. I can't manage a whole day at work. My chest is too tight. My heart is beating too fast. If I get to the train station, I've committed to getting on the train, and if I get on the train, I've committed to going to work. I can't go to work today. I'm not well. I can't manage.*

**If you're having a hard day, try to speak to a friend. Let them know your anxiety is high. Ask if you can check in with them on your lunch break. Plan in some contact with a familiar person – even if it's only short.**

*No one can know. No one can know I'm like this. I need to close myself in. I need to shut myself away.*

**Remember, most people are far more understanding than you think!**

*They hate me. Everyone hates me.*

When my thumb connects with the blue of 'Send' and the email wings its way to Gavin's iPhone, it is as if I have found a ledge to cling to: a lip of cool, solid stone that stops me plummeting down, down, down. I blow out a shuddery breath; my lungs sigh like punctured tires. The guilt will come soon, low and gnawing and yawning – *What have I done? How could I? How COULD I?* – but for a moment I gulp down the cool relief like water after a drought. Tension peels from my organs like dried glue.

Now that I have committed to my escape, the other emails come easily, trickling from my fingers.

To: margaret.walsh@gbgassociates.org
From: freya.hart@gbgassociates.org

**Absence**
Today at 7.34

Hi Margaret,

I'm so so sorry but I'm not going to be in today – think I have that bug that's going around. The notes for the meeting are saved to my desktop – file called 'Meeting 28/06/17'. My password is FH235. Could you by any chance print them and have a look through, and bring up anything you think's worth mentioning? They're probably rubbish so don't worry if you don't want to raise any of it! So so sorry to drop you in it like this. Promise I'll make it up to you!

Freya x
Sent from my iPhone

-----------

130

To: charlotte.king@gmail.com
From: freyah@gmail.com

**Sorry!!**
Today at 7.36

Hey Lottie, I'm sooooo sorry but can I rain check for tonight?? I've woken up feeling like death and think I'm just going to go back to bed, so I won't be in town this evening as won't be going to work (and probably not up to drinks anyway – might try to get some antibiotics from the dr). I really really want to see you though, can we do sometime next week? I'm pretty free, just let me know when works for you.

Loads of love, please don't hate me!! Freya xx
Sent from my iPhone

Please don't hate me. Please don't hate me. *Please don't hate me.* It's all I want to say to any of them. It's all I want to say to anyone.

*They will hate me, though. Of course they'll hate me. I'm USELESS. Skipping work again? I'm a SLACKER. They KNOW that. Everyone talks about it. Behind my back. 'I'm amazed Freya still has a job – she's barely ever here!' 'Stomach bug? Again?! Pull the other one! She's just lazy.'*

As I type my apologetic emails, I feel the raised eyebrows and pursed lips of the boss and colleagues and friends who hold my flimsy excuses up to the light, peering through the holes. I hate lying, but my life is constructed from airy untruths. I lie like I breathe, as if in order to live I must inhale oxygen and exhale lies. The guilty lies I spit hide guiltier secrets.

*I couldn't tell the truth. The truth is too pathetic.*

Yesterday, at 4.45, I was at my desk but needed to be away from my desk. I had been making stupid mistakes all day. I printed a twenty-page document, then remembered we were supposed to be going paperless. I left a garbled message on a client's answerphone, then spotted the note on the file: '... do not use voicemail ...' I sent an email invitation to an event 'starting at 7.00', then realised it started at 6.00. And when Gavin cheerfully brandished the document in his chubby hand, joking, 'Which little environment-hating scumbag is responsible for this?' I giggled nervously with the others, and twisted my fingers so hard I heard them crack, and trained my eyes to the desk until he sighed and dumped it in the recycling bin. And when the neat line of innocuous type jolted into my field of vision – 'Please do not use client's voicemail. If client is unavailable, please call back later.' – I felt terror and nausea rise in my throat, and I didn't call back later, and I knew I wouldn't call back at all. And when I re-checked the time of the event and had my error confirmed, I pulled at my hair until long strands wrapped themselves around my palm, and I didn't email again with the right time.

*No one else makes mistakes. Why am I so useless? I can't admit what I've done. Everyone will hate me. I have to escape.*

It was 4.45 and I wasn't supposed to leave until 5.30, but suddenly I was hot, too hot to think, too hot to breathe, and I thought I might be sick.

*If I'm sick in the office, I'll never be able to go back. Everyone will know how disgusting I am. Everyone will hate me.*

A neon red sign was illuminated at the front of my skull – 'ESCAPE! ESCAPE! ESCAPE!' – so I turned off my computer without saving my work and grabbed my bag from underneath the desk and when I passed Ruth she muttered, 'Off early again, Freya?'

*See? She already hates me. She already thinks I'm a slacker.*

When I pushed open the glass doors of the building I felt light-headed with relief. In that moment, it didn't matter that

I had left early for the second time that week, or that my shoes had clip-clopped across the floor to a soundtrack of tuts and sighs. All that mattered was that I had escaped, because if I hadn't escaped then—

**Nothing untoward will happened. It's only a feeling. It's only anxiety. Anxiety builds and then diminishes. It doesn't last forever.**

*—I would have died. The walls would have closed in and my heart would have exploded from my chest and I would have expired, and it would have been noisy and messy and inelegant, and worse than the dying – far worse than the dying – would have been the hatred. Everyone would have hated me for the noise and the mess and the inelegance, and the inability, even in death, to do anything – ANYTHING – right.*

When I walked home it was pleasantly cool, and I felt pleasantly light and free from nausea, and I went to bed pleasantly calm and purposeful. Okay, it hadn't been a good day. So what? Everyone has bad days. Before I fell asleep, I planned the next day: an irreproachably good day. When I arrived in the office the next morning, the first thing I would do would be to make Ruth a cup of tea, maybe take her a biscuit – I'd buy some biscuits on the way in, some posh ones, ones with dark chocolate on top – and apologise for having left in a hurry the previous day. 'I just realised I was late for an important meeting across the road, you see,' I would say, 'and I had a bit of a panic.' I would be self-deprecating about it. 'Honestly, Ruth, you know me – me and my anxious ways!'

*When you lie you always tell as much of the truth as you can. She'll guess. She'll know.*

Then I would go to Gavin, and ask if I had missed anything through leaving early *in order to go to my very important doctor's appointment*, and ask if there was anything he needed me to do, and offer to make him a cup of coffee. And then I would sit – calmly, purposefully – at my desk, and ring the no-voicemail-please client, and apologise with heartfelt sincerity for the answerphone error, and then I would log on to my email, and send a message with the correct time of the upcoming event. I would salvage my document from the recycling bin when no one was looking, and work calmly and purposefully through the To Do list—

**If you feel tasks piling on top of you, write them down! Crossing things off a list gives a real sense of achievement, and is a good way to manage a workload that might otherwise seem daunting!**

—and I would eat my sandwich at my desk at lunchtime, like you're supposed to when you're committed and diligent, and I would stay until at least 5.30, possibly 6.00, and by the time I left I would feel proud of my hard day's work.

Darkness does strange things to pristine plans. When viewed by the clear light of Future, my plans are ideal: neat, satisfying, and laughingly achievable. Somehow, when they pass through the dark, night-time tunnel and emerge as Present, they are morphed and distorted. The tunnel's walls are coated with tarry black paint that rubs off on my light, bright intentions and turns tiny tasks into missions.

*They hate me. They hate me. They hate me.*

This morning, I woke at 6.00, the other side of the tunnel. My throat had been packed tight with cotton wool. The bedroom was full of sinister shapes. Every muscle, every square inch of skin, felt tight on my body. In the dewy light, I watched the clock hands race round to 6.15, 6.30, 6.45, and with every flickering minute I felt the lid of a coffin lower.

I sent the emails at 7.30. Was that too efficient? If I had really been awake all night with a fever, would I have been up to sending emails first thing in the morning?

*They're sent now. There's nothing I can do. I just have to wait for people to hate me.*

I curl onto my side, phone clutched in my hand. Outside, the sky is lightening, and I wish it wouldn't. Soon the street will be full of the chatter of children going to school and mothers going to toddler groups and real people going to real jobs, and I will still be in bed. The sweat has evaporated from my forehead, and the skin is dry and cool. I am not ill.

*I am just lazy.*

I wish I was ill.

*I am just useless.*

I hold my phone close to my face and tap an app with bright colours at its rounded corners. In this game, you have to connect as many dots as possible in 30 moves. When you connect four dots in a square the phone buzzes, and the buzzing makes me feel good. I want to play the game until the pattern of yellow and blue and red and green and purple dots is tattooed onto the backs of my eyelids, so I can still see the game when I close my eyes. As long as I am playing the game, everything is OK. Nothing unexpected happens in the game. I play over and over and over again. If I score over 120, everything will be OK. If I score over 150, everything will be OK. I'll stop as soon as I've scored over 200. I'll stop in ten more minutes. I'll stop as soon as I stop feeling sick.

*Don't make me stop. I need to play the game.*

When I close the game, I see a tiny white '2' encircled in red above the Mail icon, and the elastic band of tension that the game has loosened pulls taut again. It constricts around my throat. When I go to my inbox, there is one email from Lottie, and one from Gavin.

To: freyah@gmail.com
From: charlotte.king@gmail.com

**Re: Sorry!!**
Today at 8.42

Aww no worries babes! You poor thing, that sounds rough! There is definitely something going round. No problem at all about tonight, let's do next week for sure. I'm free Tuesday and Wednesday after 6.00. Either of those suit you?

Rest up and take good care of yourself Frey!
Lots of love xx

Her kindness reaches through my lies, caressing me with undeserved warmth, and I feel small and shamed.

To: freya.hart@gbgassociates.org
From: gavin.shepherd@gbgassociates.org

**Re: Absence**
Today at 8.49

Dear Freya,

I'm sorry you are unwell today. Would it be possible to speak on the phone?

Yours,
Gavin.

If Lottie's message poked at me with a fingernail, Gavin's slashes me in two. Anger radiates from the words on the screen.

*He hates me. He hates me. HE HATES ME.*

The tightness in my throat is back, and the room feels stuffy and airless. I feel as if there are a hundred snakes writhing inside me, tangling around one another, and I know I am going to be sick.

*Speak on the phone?* **Speak** *on the* **phone***? I know what that means. He's so angry. He's so, so angry. Why didn't I just go to work?*

I cannot be in bed any more. I stand, but I am suspended, statue-like. I don't know what to do. I can't even cross the landing to the bathroom, because that would be a decision, and I can't make a decision. The beige carpet comes towards me as I crouch down to the floor, back against the wood of the bed frame. I drag my fingernails across my scalp. I want to rake off the skin.

**When anxiety takes hold, try to ground yourself. Count backwards from ten. Breathe right down to the bottom of your ribcage. Remember, there is nothing** *physically* **wrong with you. This is a feeling, and feelings pass.**

*I'm really not well. I'm really seriously not well. I can't speak on the phone. There is no way I can speak on the phone. I have to escape. I HAVE TO ESCAPE.*

To: gavin.shepherd@gbgassociates.org
From: freya.hart@gbgassociates.org

**Re: Absence**
Today at 9.13

Hi Gavin,

I'm really sorry but I'm not feeling up to speaking on the phone. I've actually lost my voice! Is there anything I can help you with via email?

My infrastructure of lies is so tall and so fragile. I add to it all the time, and the more I lie the flimsier the lies become. The lies at the bottom are made of cardboard and superglue, but the ones at the top – the lies just under my feet – are made of cloud and clingfilm.

*'I've lost my voice'? 'I've **lost** my voice'? Why don't I just say, 'I resign'? 'Goodbye, Gavin — I am clearly too incompetent to work for you. I am not even competent enough to lie convincingly in order to get out of working for you. I hope you find a nice, honest, competent replacement. I hope one day you manage to stop hating me.'*

To: freya.hart@gbgassociates.org
From: gavin.shepherd@gbgassociates.org

**Re: Absence**
Today at 9.21

Dear Freya,

No worries. It was just a question about the meeting today – but Margaret tells me you have already been in touch with her about it.

Hope you feel better soon.

Yours,
Gavin.

I wish he had poked a finger through my lie-world. I wish he had taken a swipe at the barely-there-at-all top layers of the charade, because if the top layers fell apart then, flimsy as they are, their combined weight would topple the middle layers – the more robust, newspaper-and-Sellotape lies – and those would crash down upon the bottom layers, the core lies, the cardboard-and-glue lies, and then I would be broken into bits from the fall but at least I would be on solid ground. Gavin is too kind. He leaves the lies as they are; he leaves me balancing on the swaying tower of invention. He does not tell me he hates me. *Even though he does hate me.*

Later, when I am lost in a loop of Five Low Sugar Desserts Using Bananas and Seven Easy No-Churn Ice Creams—

*As long as I am watching videos I am safe. I don't have to think about anything else when I am watching videos. On this app, one video follows straight on from another video. That is good. I need there to be no time in between videos. I need the videos to fill up my mind.*

—Margaret emails.

To: freya.hart@gbgassociates.org
From: margaret.walsh@gbgassociates.org

**Re: Absence**
Today at 11.56

Dear Freya,

So sorry to hear you are not feeling well. Thanks for your notes – they were very thorough and helped a lot with the meeting. I will feedback to you tomorrow – a couple of things to be actioned, but only when you're back on your feet.

We miss you here and hope you will be back soon. It is Angela's birthday. We will save you a slice of cake!

BW,
Margaret

Sometimes, I feel as if I am pressed against a thick pane of glass, watching the world unfurl. On my side of the glass, things are soft and safe and slow; on the other side, things are bright and fast and colourful. On the other side of the glass there are people, talking loudly and moving quickly. On my side there is only me. Bed and internet and emails happen on my side; voices and birthdays and cake happen on the other side. Sometimes, I press myself so hard against the glass that my breath leaves mist on its surface. Sometimes, I want to be there, in the real world, like a real person, not in my soft, safe prison. But my glassy fears are thick and immovable. I am terribly lonely.

To: carl.morton@gbgassociates.org
From: freya.hart@gbgassociates.org

**Sorry!**
Today at 11.54

Hi Carl,

I'm so so sorry I wasn't at the meeting this morning!

*Look, Carl, I never really wanted to go to the meeting. I don't like
the fact that, once everyone has arrived, someone – usually Jamie
– closes the heavy meeting room door. Once the meeting room door
has been closed, I know I can't escape without everyone staring,
and I start to sweat. The big meeting room feels like a very small
meeting room when it is full of bodies and the door is closed.
But I was going to come this morning, because I knew you were
speaking, and I was worried that if I didn't come and hear you speak
you might hate me.*

*I didn't 'miss the meeting', Carl. I know it started at 9.30 this
morning, because I checked the email twice and screenshotted
it on my phone and checked the screenshot a few more times. It
takes me an hour to get to the office if there are hold-ups, so I left
my house at 7.30, just to be on the safe side. I had to wait round the
corner from the office for almost an hour. I walked up and down
the street. If I just stood still, I was afraid someone might see me,
and might ask me why I was loitering like a lost dog, and I wouldn't
know what to say. So I walked up and down, pretending to be going
somewhere, not going anywhere.*

*I went into the office building at 9.00, but still didn't want anyone
to see me, because if someone saw me they would probably ask
why I had arrived so early for the meeting and I wouldn't know
what to say. I went to the toilets and put my feet up against the
door so no one would know there was anyone in the cubicle. I don't
know why I did that, Carl. The door was locked, so it was probably
more conspicuous that there were no feet on the floor, but still I
pretended not to be there.*

*I didn't want to go to the meeting room bang on 9.30, because I knew no one else would arrive bang on 9.30, so if I went to the meeting room at 9.30 it would be just the two of us, just you and me, alone in the meeting room, and we would have to make small talk and I'm no good at talk, whatever the size. I went to the meeting room at 9.30. The door was closed and there was no one in the corridor, heading towards the meeting room. I wasn't sure whether or not I could hear voices through the door, and I didn't want to stand outside, trying to decide whether or not I could hear voices through the door, because if I did that I was worried someone might come down the corridor, see me, and say, 'Freya, what on earth are you doing, hovering outside the meeting room?' and I wouldn't know what to say because I couldn't explain why I was hovering outside the meeting room.*

*Carl, I'm sure you will say I should have just opened the door and gone into the meeting room. But the thing is, Carl, there were probably people already in the meeting room – maybe lots of people – and I knew that if I opened the door and went in a gang of faces would turn to stare at me. Everyone would be looking at me, Carl. They would be looking at me and thinking I was late and lazy and inept and disgusting.*

*So I'm sure you understand that, really, I had no option but to scurry back to the train station and go home. I wasn't due into work today anyway – I was only coming in for the meeting. I know, Carl. I should have come to the meeting. Not-coming to the meeting took up my entire morning anyway. But everyone would have stared at me, Carl. They would have hated me.*

I'm so sorry but I only realised when I was on the train that I had arranged to see a client this morning at 10.00, and I didn't really feel I could cancel at the last minute! So sorry not to have heard you speak! I'll be there next time!

Freya.

----------

To: alliestenning@hotmail.co.uk
From: freyah@gmail.com

**Sorry!!**
Today at 18.48

Hey Allie,

I'm so so sorry but I don't think I'll be able to make it to dinner tonight!

*Look, Allie, I have no way of knowing what you're planning to cook. It could be that you're planning something unthreatening, like spaghetti with no sauce, or a packet of digestive biscuits, but somehow I doubt it. I am fairly sure that, if I come to dinner, you will present me with a plate of fish or chicken, or something involving rice, and how can I knowingly walk into that kind of death trap?*

*I know I agreed to come to dinner, but back when the dinner was in the future it seemed a manageable prospect. I'm supposed to do things like arrange to see friends for dinner, and I'm actually very good at the arranging part. But now that the dinner has shuffled its way out of the future and into the present, I have realised there is no way I can do it.*

*What if you served me undercooked chicken or reheated rice or just-past-its-sell-by-date fish, Allie? I would have to eat it, because I couldn't be rude in case it made you hate me, but then what would happen? As soon as I swallowed, the grimy bacteria would burrow into my gut, pummelling my insides with small fists. I would feel the contaminants writhing inside, and I would start to feel sick. You know what happens if you have food poisoning, Allie? You can't stop it. You just throw up.*

*I'm doing you a favour, really, Allie. Because IMAGINE if I threw up at your house. Imagine how disgusting that would be – how disgusting you would think I was. I don't want you to think I'm disgusting, Allie. I can't let you think that.*

My sister is staying at the moment and sadly she's really not well! So I think I had better stay here and look after her, poor thing! Could we reschedule, maybe for next week or the week after?

So so sorry again Al, I was really looking forward to it!
Freya xx

----------

To: mark_m@gmail.com
From: freyah@gmail.com

**Sorry!!!**
Today at 19.02

Hi Mark,

I'm SO sorry for SUCH short notice but I don't think I can come to the play tonight after all!

*Right, so here's the deal. I just had to get off my train, Mark. It was hot, and the air was so dense it didn't fit down my windpipe. I couldn't get any air into my lungs. There were so many people, packed tight as anchovies, and I felt we were being heated and heated and eventually we would explode. The smell of bodies was nauseating, and I could feel grime collecting on my skin; other people's germs streaming through my pores. I thought I was going to faint, Mark. The sweat coated my face in a sheen.*

*I sat on the platform for a while. I watched the minutes blip by on my phone. I watched it get too late for me to make it to the theatre on time, and once it was too late for me to make it to the theatre on time I felt relieved. I couldn't have come, Mark. There would have been so many people – so many people you knew and I didn't, so many people I should have charmed and impressed. I can't charm or impress anyone, Mark. There's a stain on my dress. I look a state.*

*It's great that there's Wi-Fi on the underground these days. I don't even have to go up to street level to send this. I'll probably sit here for a little while longer, watching the tubes pass, waiting for one with plenty of free seats. I need to get home and shower. I need to get the grime off my skin. But first I need to find a tube with enough empty space that I won't have to breathe in anyone else's used air. I might be sitting here for an hour. I'll wait as long I need to.*

I've just got off the phone to my Mum and apparently my Grandad has just been taken into hospital! Nothing too serious I don't think, but I really feel I should go and be with him – my Mum is out of the country at the moment and I don't want him to be by himself!

Really hope you enjoy the play, so so sorry again for the short notice!

Freya x

---

'How have things been since we last met, Freya?'

*Things have not been good, Andrew.*
    'Erm … Pretty good. Yeah. Not too bad.'

'Good. Good. That's great. So, when we met last week, I think we discussed some … some of those "challenges" you were going to have a go at, if you remember?'

'Yeah, yeah I remember.'

'So what's been happening with that? Did you manage to arrange anything?'

*Andrew, I am sensationally proficient at arranging things. You would be stunned by my ability to arrange.*
    'Yeah, yeah, quite a lot actually. I mean, a few things. My friend Allie – I've been saying I'll have dinner with her for ages – so I finally set that up for Tuesday. And then on Thursday this guy I know from work – Mark – invited me to a play he and some of his friends were going to. So I said yes to that too …'

'Excellent! It sounds like you've worked really hard!'

*Oh, Andrew.*

'So talk me through what happened with the challenges. Let's start with – did you say it was a dinner? On Tuesday? Let's start with dinner on Tuesday. How did that go?'

'Well … I …'

*I didn't go, Andrew. I realised I hadn't remembered to tell her that I'm a vegetarian, which I'm not, but if I tell people I'm a vegetarian they are less likely to feed me poisonous food. But I hadn't remembered to pretend to Allie that I am a vegetarian, and once I remembered that I hadn't remembered, it was two o'clock and I was due there at seven and I didn't want to call and risk her being angry that I hadn't pretended sooner. I had no way of guaranteeing that she washes her pots and pans properly and cooks her food properly, and it's no reflection on her — Allie's great, I really like Allie — but if I went to dinner with her I would almost definitely get sick and then it wouldn't matter whether I liked her or not because she certainly wouldn't like me any more. If I got sick, she would hate me.*

'So I felt very anxious beforehand …'

'Yeah. And can you say what the anxiety was about?'

'I was worried about what she might be cooking. I was worried I might get food poisoning.'

'Yeah. OK. And what did you do to bring down the anxiety?'

*I invented a sister and pretended she was sick. I wriggled out of the arrangement like I wriggle out of every arrangement I make.*

'Well, I sort of … I basically just … I just cancelled, really.'

'Oh. Oh. So, you didn't end up going to dinner?'

*I stayed at home and ate cream crackers and worried about Allie hating me for cancelling.*

'No.'

'OK. And that was because … you were worried that if you went to dinner you might have to eat something that hadn't been prepared safely? And it might make you unwell?'

*Andrew, please don't put it so delicately. I don't worry about being 'unwell'. I worry about hacking and gagging and spewing barely digested food across the table. I worry about the smell and the mess and the looks on the faces.*

'Yeah. I was worried I would be unwell.'

'OK. So, can we … Is it OK if we have a bit of a think about what you might have done differently? So that you might have been able to go to dinner?'

*I don't want to do that, Andrew.*
    'Sure.'

'OK. We did a sheet about this, didn't we? I don't think I have a copy on me … I don't suppose you do?'

*I hate it when I'm not prepared. I wish you would give me some warning, Andrew. I'm normally very neat and organised. I would have brought the sheet if you had told me to.*
    'No. Sorry.'

'That's fine, that's fine. No problem. I'm sure we can remember most of the strategies. What can you think of off the top of your head?'

'I think … I could have written down the things I was worried about. And thought about whether they were actually things I needed to worry about, or whether they were just anxiety?'

'Great. Yeah, that would have been a great thing to do. What else?'

'I could have done that … breathing thing. With the counting.'

'Yes, great, the breathing exercise. Fantastic. What else?'

'I could have rung Allie. And let her know I was feeling anxious about the meal. So that she could support me.'

'Fantastic. That would have been an excellent thing to do.'

'Yeah. That's all I can think of.'

'No, that's fine, that's great, we've got three really good strategies there. So, and I'm pushing you here, Freya, but do you think you can try to tell me why you didn't use any of those strategies on Tuesday?'

*OK, Andrew, I'm sure there are many benefits to breathing deeply and reaching out to friends and committing worries to paper. I'm sure those strategies are very powerful indeed. But they are not going to do the one thing I need them to do, and that is to stop me being sick. I could use all the strategies in the world, but there would still be the possibility that, in a rush, Allie might take the chicken out of the pan too soon and give me salmonella. It's like you're telling me, 'A bomb has been planted in a train carriage. You have to choose a carriage at random and get on the train. Worried? Write the worry down. Breathe deeply. Phone a friend. It's all fine, now, isn't it?' It is very much not all fine. I won't get on the train at all, because that is the only way I can know for sure that I will be safe.*

'I just didn't think.'

'OK. Right. So perhaps the strategies weren't at the forefront of your mind?'

*Andrew, the strategies were not ANYWHERE in my mind. There was no space. My whole head was full of grotesque, high-definition images of bugs and vomit and sneering.*

'Yeah. I just didn't really think of them.'

'OK, well, that's good. That means we know what to work on. And what happened with the ... did you say it was a play? What happened with the play on Thursday?'

*Don't make me say it, Andrew. We both know what happened. Don't make me look you in the disappointed eye.*

'I didn't really ... I didn't make it to that either.'

'OK. And was it the same sort of problem? The same sorts of worries?'

*No, Andrew. That was obviously an entirely different set of worries. I worried about collapsing on the train, and, if by some miracle that didn't happen, about arriving at the theatre dirty and smelly from the train, and about being too socially inept to hold a conversation. People would have thought I was disgusting. They would have hated me. It was an entirely different set of worries.*

'Er, yeah. Mainly just the same type of thing.'

*When I was on the train, thoughts batted the sides of my skull like wasps. I was so full of thoughts there was no room for air.*

'I just didn't really think.'

'OK. So there's something here about knowing what the strategies are, and knowing how to use them, but not remembering to use them in the moment? So that, in the moment, it seems preferable to escape, rather than use the strategies?'

*You're not hearing me, Andrew. There is no point in my remembering the strategies. The strategies are there to make me feel better. Escaping is there to save my life.*

'Yeah. That's it.'

'OK. So I'm thinking: how can we make sure the strategies are right there, in your head, when you need them? Yeah?'

'Yeah.'

'What about … Well, I mean, there are lots of things you could do. You might be a really visual person – perhaps you could list your strategies and put the list somewhere easily visible? On the fridge, maybe? Somewhere you'll always see it? You could make it colourful, so it stands out.'

*I'm twenty-fucking-four, Andrew.*

'Or you could record yourself talking through the strategies, like that guided meditation we did the other day. You might be more of a listener than a ... look-er?'

*I am definitely not a looker, Andrew. I do not need to be reminded.*
   'I think writing them down would be fine. I can do that.'

'OK, great. So where are we going to put the list?'

*Come on, Andrew. 'We' are not going to put it anywhere, are we? The idea is that I will put it somewhere, and even that will not happen.*
   'Probably just the fridge. Like you said.'

'Great. And do you think that might give you that last push you need? To follow through with some of these really great plans you're making?'

*Don't do this, Andrew. Don't give me the pity praise. I know you're disappointed in me. I would have cancelled this session if I hadn't cancelled the last two, because I knew I would have to look at your soft, disappointed face, and I knew I would feel how I feel right now. I feel so useless, Andrew. I feel so small.*
   'Yeah. I think that will be good. That will be helpful.'

'Great. So, we're running out of time. Is there anything else you wanted to discuss?'

*Yes, Andrew. I have actually been wondering whether we might conduct all future therapy via email. You see, Andrew, having to come here every week – yes, I know in reality it's only every other week, but in theory it is every week and that is what counts – it really makes me anxious. I don't like the closed door of the therapy room. I don't like the expectation of progress. I like you, Andrew – I do like you – but I think I might like you even more if I never had to see you in person. I think I would like therapy a whole lot more if I could conduct it the way I choose to conduct most areas of my life – from behind a screen. How about it, Andy?*

'No. I think that's it. Thanks for seeing me. And I'm sorry. For not ... you know ... managing stuff.'

'Don't apologise, Freya. It's a process. You're doing really well.'

*Don't be nice to me, Andrew. Don't pretend not to hate me.*

———

In my bedroom, it is warm and stuffy. Earlier, outside, I sat on the sun-baked patio and smoked a cigarette. I don't know why I did it. It burned my chest. It made me feel very grown up. I thought that, if someone looked out of one of the upstairs windows – the tall, skinny guy from the flat above, or his girlfriend with the tiny tattoo of a cactus at the crook of her arm – they might think I looked quite cool, sitting on the patio, smoking my cigarette. They might think I smoked a lot of cigarettes, sitting on the patio. I wouldn't mind them thinking that.

I have been four weeks without the once-weekly hour of Andrew. In two more weeks, I will have been without Andrew for the same amount of time I was with Andrew. I was gifted six precious sessions (of which I attended three) in which to address the fear that had paralysed me for 24 hours a day, seven days a week, 52 weeks a year for as many years as I could remember. Six hours (three hours) in an airless room with a pasty psychologist-in-training who told me to write 'deep breathing' on a piece of paper and stick it to my fridge, and suggested that I address my phobia of big groups of people by attending a course of evening therapy with a big group of people. I was cocky and callous and ungrateful. I spent most of the six (three) allocated hours watching sweat beads collect on Andrew's top lip and internally sneering at his therapeutic interventions. I held him at arms' length, packing the space between us with superiority and derision, and by the time I relented and removed the ballast he had gone. I squandered my time on curled lips and raised eyebrows, repeating 'No one can help me!' so loudly it drowned out the words of someone who was trying to help me. When I realised what I was doing, and that it was too late to undo it, I felt so small and so petty. Because Andrew was young and possibly ineffective, and six sessions (three sessions) was scant and possibly insufficient, but I was arrogant and definitely disengaged, and that was the biggest barrier of all.

*I hate my anxiety. I cling to my anxiety.*

It came to me in the first post-Andrew week, when I was tapping out another apologetic email, loathing the words on the phone screen.

*I hate the cage that traps me, and I channel that hatred into galvanising its bars. I beat at the pane of glass separating me from the Real World, and I stop beating to apply triple glazing. I cry, 'I'm imprisoned! I can't escape!', and I sit still as a statue, eyes closed, refusing to look for a door or window.*

I went to Andrew because I wanted help. I sat with Andrew and pushed away his help. I finished seeing Andrew, and raged that I had not been helped.

In the second post-Andrew week, I left my job. I clambered out of the tight commitment and left it behind like a snake shedding skin. It scudded along behind me for a few paces, the understanding emails snapping at my heels with pointed kindness, and then it fluttered to rest with the others. If I look behind me, I see a path littered with abandoned jobs; forgotten activities; discarded friends. They coat the ground like carpet. The one constant in my life is the lack of constancy: in my urge to escape, to re-start, to recreate, I break things down and smash things up. I don't serve out notice periods – that's not the way I work. I up and leave. I leave others in the lurch. *I leave destruction where I tread.*

When Mum rang and asked how work was, I told her it was fine. I will lie for a few weeks, steeling myself, and then I will tell her the truth. I will tell her over tea in a Marks & Spencer café. She will sigh. I will cry. The hairnetted staff will avoid our table. I will apologise, over and over again, my voice wet and blubbery. She will look at me with old, tired eyes. *I leave destruction where I tread.*

In the third post-Andrew week, I spread my Andrew sheets on the kitchen table, papering over the bills I had no means of paying. I looked at the charts and graphs and tables and bit back the scorn that heated my throat. I read through the challenges I had not completed; the strategies I had not used; the techniques I had not tried. *The only way to change is to change.*

It is going to be terribly boring, this languorous meander towards sanity. I can tell. Already, it feels like wading through sand. Every step makes my legs ache. Every step takes an age. Behind my heels, the ground is hard and dry. If I turned and ran in the opposite direction, the relief would make the muscles of my legs sing. It would be so deliciously easy to run backwards, but all the destinations – the small and big and in-between places I want to reach – are in front, separated from me by the runway of sand. I have to stop running backwards. I have to do the things I don't want to do and face the things I don't want to face and use my strategies, and it is going to be terribly hard work, and terribly dull work, but perhaps the more work I do the less terribly lonely I will feel.

I didn't smoke inside, but the scent of smoke has travelled into the bedroom on my clothes. I like the smell. It is a defiant, don't-care smell. I have to care about the smell, because I have to care about the grumpy landlord, but I like the ribbons of don't-care trapped between the fibres of my shirt. I can hold them close, breathe them in, and make the don't-care a part of me.

This flat won't be home for much longer. It is eating up money I don't have. When I cry to Mum over tea in a Marks &

Spencer café, I will tell her that I need to move back in with her and Dad. They won't be surprised. I lasted six months this time, which is more than last time, though less than the time before that. Perhaps this disaster is more of a disaster than the last disaster, though less of a disaster than the disaster before that.

*I am a disaster.*

I am lucky to have people who pick up the pieces when I fall apart. But it is hard to feel lucky when one has fallen apart.

I lean over my desk, lift the latch on the small, finger-marked window, and push it open. The air outside is quenching.

To: alliestenning@hotmail.co.uk
From: freyah@gmail.com

**Tonight**
Today at 18.54

Hi Allie, I'm so sorry but I'm having a bit of a nightmare day.

*I don't want to go to dinner. I don't want to risk uncooked poultry and food poisoning and stilted conversation and embarrassment. I don't want anyone to hate me. I want to close the curtains and curl up in bed and play the game on my phone.*

Nothing major but I'm running a bit late. I just need to have a quick shower and change, and then I'll be right over. Probably about 7.30?

Can't wait to see you. Freya x

The only way to change is to change. *The only way to change is to change.*

───────

'But, it's just worrying, isn't it? It's normal to worry.'

## 'Worry Disease': How to Grow a Perfectly Healthy Anxie-Tree™!

### Step One: Planting the Seeds

Lay out the cratered bed of your body, open and exposed, and sprinkle it with nagging, half-formed hang-ups. Sew the body with as wide a range of seeds as possible, and see which take root. The best seeds are small and spiky, with limitless potential for growth. Specific seed-types we recommend include:

- **Social Anxie-Tree™ seeds**: What if no one likes me? What if I make a fool of myself? What if people laugh at me?

- **Health Anxie-Tree™ seeds**: What if I contract some hideous disease from unclean plates or hands or air? What if I am ill right now? What if I die?

- **Agoraphobia seeds**: How can I leave the house? The world is too loud and huge and overwhelming. If I leave the house I will have a panic attack. I need to stay where I am sheltered and safe.

- **Emetophobia seeds**: I think I'm going to be sick. There are so many things that could make me sick. Food poisoning, viruses, motion, allergies ... If I am sick in front of anyone, they will be disgusted. I have to protect myself from sickness.

- **Generalised Anxie-Tree™ Disorder seeds**: I worry all the time. There is nothing that does not make me worry. I can never relax. A looming dread sits at the bottom of my gut. I am locked inside my worries.

Bury the seeds deep in the body. Push them into the crevices of the brain. For successful Anxie-Tree™ growing, it is essential that the worry is allowed to take root in every part of the self. Plant carefully: every seed has the potential to flourish into a debilitating neurosis!

Once all the seeds have been sewn, seal yourself up, and proceed with daily activities. During this phase, you can expect to feel perpetually uneasy – it's a great sign that the seeds are firmly embedded!

### Step Two: Tending to the Seeds

The most effective way to nourish your seeds is to *think* about them, constantly and repetitively. At this stage, it is normal to find that you are drawn to one seed more than others: your mind will naturally gravitate towards a specific preoccupation. You are unconsciously selecting your own personal Anxie-Tree™!

Remember, the way to encourage your seeds to sprout is to devote a *spectacular* level of time, thought and energy to them. Find a helpful phrase to turn over in your mind. We can recommend:

- Everyone hates me.
- Everyone is staring at me.
- If I get sick, everyone will think I am disgusting.
- I am going to have a panic attack if I do [X].
- I can't breathe.

### Step Three: Growth of the Anxie-Tree™

Hoorah! Your time and dedication have led to the budding of your very own Anxie-Tree™! At this stage, you should find that tending is less a chore than an obsession. Your mind will return to the Anxie-Tree™ no matter how hard you try to pull it elsewhere. You will find the Anxie-Tree™ endlessly engaging. It will feel like a love affair. This is perfectly *normal* and *healthy*!

An excellent way to ensure Anxie-Tree™ health is to begin to adapt your life to suit its demands.

Perhaps you are growing a Social Anxie-Tree™? Refuse all invitations to parties, dinners, drinks – refuse to spend time with all but a select circle of people. If you do attend such functions, hide from others. Sit in the toilets. Sit in your car. *They're all looking at you. They're all laughing at you. They all hate you.* Hear that? Way to go! It's the voice of your Anxie-Tree™!

What about a Health Anxie-Tree™? Begin to scrutinise your body intently. Notice every lump and bump and fold of skin. Keep a look out for rashes, swellings, aches and pains, including anything that isn't *currently* a rash, swelling, ache or pain but looks like it could develop into one. Get to know the quickest route to your doctor's surgery – you'll be needing it!

If you have a Generalised Anxie-Tree™ putting down roots, you need to be hyper-vigilant, constantly alert to danger. *What danger*, you ask? Every danger. There is danger everywhere. Nothing is safe. Do you feel that – the patter of your heart, thrumming at 150 beats-per-minute? Get used to it. Get used to the dry mouth and nibbled nails and sleepless nights. It is all *perfectly healthy!*

### Step Four: Enjoying your Anxie-Tree™

Congratulations! You are now the proud host of a flourishing Anxie-Tree™!

Please note: you should feel *immeasurably worse* than you felt before the growth of the Anxie-Tree™. This is perfectly healthy! The Anxie-Tree™ lives off your energy. Every breath and meal you take goes directly to – you guessed it – the Anxie-Tree™!

Your life has become very small. Perhaps you have stopped spending time with those whose company you once enjoyed. Perhaps you continue to spend time with them, but feel absent, engaged only with the Anxie-Tree™. An Anxie-Tree™ is a life partner!

If you try to tell others about your Anxie-Tree™, they will likely tell you they have one of their own. This will comfort you. You will press them for more. They will tell you they get worried sometimes, about work or exams or how they look. You will notice the 'sometimes' and wilt, because your Anxie-Tree™ is not just for sometimes: it's for life!

Do not be alarmed by the physical symptoms wracking your body. The relentless nausea, the ticks and twitches, the seizing muscles, the headaches. It's hard work maintaining a healthy Anxie-Tree™. If you feel yourself crumbling, you know you're doing it right!

You will find that, if you voice the Anxie-Tree™'s concerns, the advice you receive will be largely unhelpful.

'But there's nothing to worry about!'
'Have you tried breathing deeply?'
'You'll feel better if you just do it!'
'Have you tried thinking rationally?'

They're all so *silly*, aren't they?! They underestimate your Anxie-Tree™. They think you just have *worries* – tiny, unfertilised little seeds – that could be shaken off with a deep breath or a spot of mind-over-matter. But no, you have progressed so far beyond that! Your Anxie-Tree™ has a life of its own; it is wrapped around you, squeezing the breath from your lungs, speeding your heart and setting up a relentless prattle: *I am not safe I am not safe I am not safe*. Everywhere you go, the Anxie-Tree™ goes too! Everything you do – or, more likely, *don't* do – the Anxie-Tree™ does too! The Anxie-Tree™ has sucked you dry! The Anxie-Tree™ has made your world dark and cruel.

> 'That's the thing. It's not just worrying.
> It's not like that at all.'

Anxiety shares its core symptom with a normal human tendency: we do *not* all have anxiety, but we *do* all worry. As explored through Abby, equating healthy behaviour and unhealthy pathology is not just reductive, but inaccurate. The anxiety described during my interviews was more than an exaggerated worry response: it was a torment, grasping onto anything and everything in its path. An anxiety sufferer might worry about an upcoming exam, but also about whether they will reach the exam hall before everyone else and not know what to do; whether they will reach the exam hall after everyone else and not know where to go; whether their mother is not replying to their text because she has been in a car accident; whether their headache is a brain tumour; whether anyone will be there when they die. Anxiety is unrelenting in its determination to erode contentment, feeding on its host like a leech.

By and large, the anxiety characteristic of generalised anxiety disorder goes beyond the heart-pounding, fight-flight-freeze of discrete 'attacks': it is an omnipresent cloud of dread. There need be no 'dreadful event' on the horizon: the dread is faceless and inexplicable. Some of my interviewees described it as a sense of impending doom, a feeling that the world was a threatening place, or a sense that everyone they encountered was angry with them. For most, the dread was an ever-present undercurrent, but it ebbed and flowed – at times suffocating, at other times surmountable. Changeability is a prominent feature of the illness: on good days, sufferers might be able to accomplish tasks and honour engagements with relative ease, but on bad days the requirements of 'normal life' feel impossible. The upside of this pattern is that the horror of the bad days can cast the good days in warm light: most interviewees had a heightened gratitude for times when they could function without angst. However, the inconsistency can leave sufferers feeling as judged for *being able* to cope as for being *unable* to cope: *You could manage these things yesterday – why is it so hard today? If you're fine one day and not fine the next, aren't you just picking and choosing when to struggle according to when it suits you? You say you were too anxious to meet yesterday, but you're fine again today? How can that be?*

For many people with anxiety, side-stepping commitments provides short-term relief from unease. This is not a question of 'opting out' or 'taking the easy route': when they call in sick to work, there is little doubt that they *are* too sick to work. The phenomenal mental anguish associated with high anxiety is as debilitating as flu or gastritis, and removing the immediate pressure of bundling oneself into clothes and shoes and catching a train can be the only means of achieving some small reprieve. However, repeated escaping of engagements trails a problem of its own: the guilt associated with 'unreliability'. My interviewees repeatedly described themselves as flaky, sometimes based on genuine experience – exasperated friends ('You *always* flake on us!') or end-of-the-tether bosses ('Your repeated absences are becoming a problem.').

This is difficult to square: friends who repeatedly cancel arrangements or professionals who take unscheduled leave *do* present a problem, practically and emotionally. It would be unreasonable to suggest that anxiety sufferers should never be the subject of frustrations. However, frustrations might be minimised if the other party understood the desperation of their friend/colleague – the suffocating paralysis of their panic. Many people with anxiety have an elevated, excessive respect for others' opinions, and are desperate to remain in favour. They fail to behave as they 'should' only when anxiety *forbids* them from doing so – and, in such situations, they are their own harshest critic. Anxiety doles out guilt in spades.

Like Yasmine, Freya is a lonely character, trapped in internal solitude even in the midst of external company. The loneliness of anxiety can have clear causes: one might choose solitude for fear that socialising will invite rejection, judgment or suffocation; one's unreliability might lead to a tapering of invitations. However, this is not a universal pattern – some form intense attachments to certain friends or family members and seek out their company constantly, relying on the safe, solid 'other' for anchorage. Whether superficially solitary or not, people with anxiety often feel alone 'on the inside', separated from the rest of the world by their preoccupations. They are pressed against a window, yearning for the warmth of the world through the glass.

My interviewees described complex relationships with their anxiety: most resented the limitations imposed by the condition, and were embarrassed by how 'odd' and 'abnormal' they felt. However, they did *have* a relationship with the condition, and in many cases the relationship was devoted. The hungry dominance of the disorder means that, as it gains in power and strength, life is increasingly moulded around it, until anxiety dictates every action, thought and feeling. The notion of shedding it can be terrifying, as it feels a part of the identity. Anxiety also masquerades as an indispensable right-hand man, offering protection against rejection/failure/sickness: its eradication equates to the loss of both a friend and a shield. This is why, when it comes to treatment, many find themselves in a strange bind: they seek out professional help, desperate for relief, but resist implementing the advised 'strategies'. Worksheets, breathing exercises and cognitive behavioural techniques are designed to alleviate tension, but – in the mind of the sufferer – anxiety rituals are designed for *survival*. From the outside, resisting anxious behaviour *just once* seems easy – but the neurotic voice is sharp and powerful: *It only takes once for the fear to come true.*

Perhaps, then, recovery is a question of taking that risk? The fear *might* come true – *but it might not*. I spoke to many sufferers who had undergone successful therapy (often, although not always, cognitive behavioural in style), and whose recoveries were characterised by plain 'hard work': repeated analysis of irrational thoughts, and challenges to the restrictions anxiety prescribes. For others, recovery occurred outside the supportive structure of professional treatment, aided by transitions that 'shook up' the routine in which anxiety had thrived (new relationships, careers or school changes etc.). My interviewees painted a picture of recovery as tough, counterintuitive and highly uncomfortable, but enormously rewarding. In fact, rewards can be reaped long before 'full recovery' (if such a thing exists) is achieved: when one has been accustomed to imprisonment in the anxiety cell, even an incremental loosening of the chains grants precious breathing space. The ending to Freya's story is imperfect but reflects the 'pockets of contentment' for which my interviewees felt so grateful, after years of brittle unease.

## What I wish I could tell you about my anxiety

You might be surprised by the range of things that make me anxious. It can include responding to text messages or emails, and sometimes even reading text messages or emails. I worry that every message I receive is going to be upsetting or hurtful, and I worry that any message I send could be 'wrong' in some way. If you find me difficult to contact, it may be because my anxiety is high. I am not deliberately ignoring you.

I know I often make plans then back out at the last minute. I always want to stick to the arrangement, but sometimes I panic and feel I can't. I don't cancel plans because I can't be bothered to go through with them: I do it because I feel there is no other option.

Sometimes, when I need to get out of doing something, I do tell lies. I feel ashamed that I lie so much, and I lie because I'm ashamed of the real reason why I am cancelling: because of my anxiety. It feels much more acceptable to pretend I am ill or having to deal with some family emergency than to let you know how intense the anxiety is.

I can't just 'stop worrying'. When my brain goes into an anxious spin, 'mind over matter' doesn't feel possible.

I often worry about small, insignificant, almost non-existent things. It is rarely helpful to tell me that there is 'nothing to worry about'.

If I tell you I can't do something because of my anxiety, please accept it – don't try to force me because you believe I can handle it if I 'just try hard enough'. I know myself and I know my condition, so I know when something is not going to work for me. Being forced to do things makes me feel trapped, and that makes my anxiety a lot worse.

When my anxiety is very high, it can make me feel insane. I feel helpless and paralysed. It is a horrible way to feel.

I am really grateful when you try to accommodate my anxiety in plans. This might be telling me about arrangements in great detail, making sure there are opportunities for me to leave if I need to, or asking if there is anything you can do to make things easier for me. I know it is a lot of effort, but it makes a huge difference to me.

Please don't tell me to breathe deeply. That won't magic my anxiety away.

I am not being deliberately difficult or trying to make things hard for other people. A lot of my anxiety centres around what others think of me, so it is never my intention to cause inconvenience or exasperation.

I really appreciate it when you continue to spend time with me and invite me out, even when I repeatedly make excuses or cancel on you. Unconditional acceptance and loyalty is very rare, but very special. No matter how much I seem to isolate myself, I still want friends.

# *Beth*

## Production: Beth
## Scene One: 'I Love It Here'

[*Camera pans down the corridor of generic student halls. Close-up on generic white door. Number 14.*]

[*BETH opens door. She is pink-cheeked, dark-haired, plump. She looks nervous. She talks too quickly.*]

### Beth
Hi! Come in, come in!

[*Enter BETH's room. It is spotless. BETH takes a seat on a chair in the centre. A plate of biscuits sits on a small table in front.*]

### Beth
Sorry about the mess. Please have a biscuit. No, no, I don't want one. I never really eat during the day. I never seem to get hungry.

[*Close-up: BETH's face. For rest of segment, we film BETH alone. Her speech is a monologue.*]

### Beth
Well, hi. I'm Beth. This is my university room. I've been living here for about … Well, six months now, I suppose. I go back home for the holidays. My parents? Oh, yeah, well my Mum does checkout, and my Dad was a fireman, but he's been off for a while. Yeah, with his back. Yeah, he does. Disabled living allowance.

[*She gives a small, tight laugh.*]

They say I'm losing my accent now that I've come down south. They say I've started talking all posh. I don't know.

What? Oh, yes. It's fantastic here. It's one of the best
universities in the world. I really love it. What?

[*Her brow furrows. She nibbles her lower lip.*]

I suppose maybe sometimes. Yeah, maybe sometimes I feel I
don't fit in. I mean, there are things about me that are a bit …
I don't know. Wrong. I'm … I'm … I don't really look the right
way. I'm not really … like … thin. Or something. But it's fine,
it's really good here. I really love it here. I do. I promise.

[*BETH is flushing. She appears flustered. She runs out of words, eyes
darting anxiously from the camera to her lap to the plate of biscuits.
She knots her fingers, nails digging into her knuckles. In a sudden,
quick, compulsive movement, she takes a biscuit from the plate; puts
it in her mouth whole; chews; swallows. She looks up to the camera,
eyes wide and skittish, as if hoping it won't have caught her.*]

**Beth**
Sorry. I … I … Sorry. I'm so sorry. I … I love it here.
I'm so lucky. I'm so in control. I … Do you
think you could …? Can I start again?

**CUT**

---

This waiting room is like a Halloween party of painfully unim-
aginative guests. No horns atop headbands, no billowing white
sheets, no seductive cats or nurses. This party is attended solely
by skeletons. These are hungry-eyed young women, whose
cheekbones protrude like cliffs from the plateaus of faces. Their
arms and legs form a forest of spindly branches, knees and
elbows bulging like knots. Their stomachs sink towards their
spines, organs compressed by the wasted habitat, and yet still
they bobble around, driven by nervous energy. Enormous heads
balance on reed-like necks. Bodies bend like stalks. They look
like daffodils.

Some of the daffodils drink from bottles of water they look too frail to lift, crossing and un-crossing their legs, bladders protesting at the influx of gallons and gallons of scale-weight; some pace the perimeter of the room, faces contorted with concentration – '650, 651, 652, 653 … Can't sit down, can't be lazy, can't be FAT …' Some massage swollen jaws, frantically trying to hide the evidence of last night's purge. They are blonde-haired, brown-haired, fair-skinned, dark-skinned skeletons, whose bones ripple proudly beneath sagging jeans and bagging jumpers. Bundles of crumbling, starving bones.

I sit in the corner of the waiting room, desperately trying to disappear. I am not a daffodil. I am a shrub. I feel obscenely, indecently fleshy. My breasts are so swollen the straps of my bra cut into my shoulders – and everyone else is lithely androgynous. My thighs spread across my seat like treacle, threatening to spill off the sides – and everyone else bounds, gazelle-like, on wrist-sized twigs. My face is so bloated my eyes have to squint to see through the fat threatening to squash their slits together – and everyone else is gazing out through deep-set, glistening orbs. I fold my arms across my chest, and then across my stomach, and then across my shame, and pretend I am not the elephant in the room.

When the neat-looking psychiatrist appears at the door, six pairs of starving eyes flick up, empty and alert. My gaze is slow and turgid. He calls my name like a question, and I burn. *Now they know who I am.* I heft myself up and across the room, feeling the added weight of six sneering glances. *Now they have a name to put to the face of this absurd, abhorrent fraud.* I follow the psychiatrist up a flight of stairs and into a small, nondescript room, and by the time I sit down in the armchair opposite his I am puffing. I sip tepid water from a water bottle, and then worry he might think I am imitating the actual sick people down in the waiting room. I screw the lid back on. There is a desk at one end of the room, piles of papers stacked on its smooth wooden surface, and beside it stands a set of scales. I look at the scales, and my stomach twists in horror.

*Oh god. Oh god oh god oh god oh god. I can't be weighed. I can't ever be weighed. I'll break the machine. He'll laugh at me. He'll conduct an on-the-spot demonstration of my obesity, inviting three of his downstairs skeletons to stand on one another's shoulders and wobble onto the scales, their combined weight still not matching mine …*

'So, Elizabeth, you were referred here by …' He riffles papers officiously, reading a line or two and nodding. 'Oh, I see. Yes, I see. You *self-referred* …'

He says, 'you self-referred' as if he were saying, 'you stripped naked and flung yourself down outside the clinic, beating your fists on the ground until one of our poor, perplexed receptionists relented and gave you an appointment.'

'Yes. Well, I … I did go to the GP. And asked about … you know … the food stuff. But she … I don't think she … Well, I thought this might be … The place to come?'

'Of course. Quite. And you believe yourself to be suffering from … bulimia?'

'Well … I mean, it's … it's sort of like that … except kind of like … without the throwing up?'

I squirm in my seat, the red in my cheeks deepening as familiar shame washes over me. *What?? You don't even throw up?? Call yourself sick?? I mean, we struggle to take those slacker bulimics seriously around here, but at least they put in some EFFORT! At least they TRY to do the right thing! Here you are, expecting help when you don't even make yourself SICK?!*

*It's not for lack of trying,* I want to say. *I can't count the number of times I've knelt on the bathroom floor, hunched over the toilet bowl, arm halfway down my throat, desperately trying to get something out. I do try — honestly, I do. But I think there must be something wrong with me — you know, like, anatomically? Because it just doesn't work. I gag and wretch and claw around in there, but nothing comes up. I'm really sorry. I know I ought to try harder. I know I ought to do more to make it work — put in more effort. But I suppose I don't like trying, truth be told. It hurts my throat. I know. Pathetic. I know. Sorry.*

'Ri-i-i-i-ght,' he says, drawing out the single syllable like elastic.

'So it's more like ... Well, just the eating part. Without the sick.'

'Ah. So, we're talking about some sort of binge eating problem?'

'Yes. That.'

'OK. And, how many times would you say you're bingeing at the moment? In an average week?'

*I can't say the real number. No way. Maybe I should ... halve it? Quarter it?*

   'Probably ... two days a week?'

   *A third. That's a fair fraction. A solid third. Very slightly less than a solid third.*

'And, on these days, you binge just the once?'

*What do you mean? When I say two days, I mean two DAYS. The binges last all day. They are continuous. It is eating from when I wake up to when I go to sleep.*

   'Erm, yep. Once.'

'OK. Right. And, during these binges, what sort of foods do you tend to eat?'

*Fuck fuck fuck fuck fuck. I can't tell him. They feel so dirty, those food-words. I CANNOT say them.*

   'Just kind of anything really. I guess.'

'Ri-i-i-i-i-ght. And ... Do you use any compensatory behaviours? Any means of avoiding weight gain from your binges?'

*I wish you'd just say it. I wish you'd just say: 'Well, I'm looking at you sitting there fatly in that seat, and I can see you don't do much to avoid weight gain, or if you do then the things you do clearly don't work, so I'm fascinated to hear whether you are aware of this or whether you are labouring under the delusion that you are somehow taking steps to make yourself slightly less grotesque than you really are.'*

'No. Not really. Not much.'

'Elizabeth, I wonder if you might be able to tell me what you were hoping our service could offer you?'

*You didn't need to say it like THAT. I KNOW I'm ridiculous. I KNOW I'm a fake. I KNOW I don't belong here and I KNOW you don't want to help. I'm fat, but I'm not stupid.*

'I mean ... I'm not sure, really. I looked on the website and I saw there's a day programme here? Like, day treatment? With meals and therapy groups and stuff? Obviously not for right now, because I've got finals, but maybe ... they'll be finished soon, so I could start afterwards?'

'Ah, I see. Well. It's true we have our day treatment programme – intensive treatment programme, we call it – but we normally reserve places on that programme for our most unwell patients. They're very limited, you see. The places. So we do have to give priority to those who ... whose eating disorders are most *severe*, in terms of their physical state, if you see what I mean ...'

*Just say it. Just say 'thin'. Why dress it up like this? 'We only take the very thinnest.' That's what it comes down to, isn't it?*

'Oh, yes, of course, no, that makes total sense, absolutely ... I didn't mean ... Of course I know I'm not ... I'm so sorry ...'

'We do have patients who come here for outpatient treatment. One-to-one therapy with one of our clinicians. And, for some of our patients, there can also be medical monitoring. Of course, that probably wouldn't be such a priority with you—'

*No, of course not. Because, after all, there's nothing really wrong with me, is there?*

'—but we also have a registered dietician who sees patients for meal-planning, nutrition education … That sort of thing. Of course, in our service she does primarily work with those who need to increase their weight: formulating high-calorie diets and such—'

*I've been amazingly successful in formulating one of those for myself.*

'—but I'm sure she also has experience of working with people who … Well … I'm sure she wouldn't be averse to formulating a weight-*reduction* plan, if that was …'

'Oh, right. I guess. I mean, thanks, that sounds like it could be helpful.'

'Good. Excellent. Unfortunately, our service is quite over-subscribed at the moment – it usually is, to be honest – and, as with the day programme, we do have to give priority to those most in need of treatment …'

*I wish you would send me away. I wish you would tell me, straightfor-wardly, that I'm not sick enough. Not sick at all. Just undisciplined. Greedy. Lazy. A horrible person. I really think I would choose that over this awful, humiliating pity.*

'Yes. Of course. Thanks. It's really kind of you.'

'Not at all. So, I imagine we would be looking at a wait time of around six months – possibly nine, but six if we're lucky.'

*I'll email after the session and say I want to be taken off the waiting list. I won't still be here in six months. I will have eaten myself to death.*

'Oh. Cool. Thanks. It's really good of you. I really appreciate it.'

*Oh well. At least you didn't ask to weigh me.*

'Not at all. I hope the big exams go well! Finals, eh? Such a privilege. Best years of my life. All downhill from there – make the most of it while you can, I say!'

*There's no more hill to go down. To get lower I would have to burrow into the ground.*

'Mmm. Yes. It's great. So much fun. So lucky. Well, thanks for seeing me. I'm sure you need to … I'll just—'

*—go and continue the slow suicide.*

'Oh, Elizabeth? One more thing – sorry, little bit awkward I know, but before you leave would you mind just hopping on the scales for me? Let me have a quick check of your weight?'

---

### Production: Beth
### Scene Two: 'A Kind of Problem'

[*Camera pans down the corridor of generic student halls. Close-up on generic white door. Number 11.*]

[*BETH opens door. She appears panicked. She is flushed. She tugs at her clothes. She is chewing. She retreats into the bedroom – camera follows. This room is messier than the last. On the small table in front of BETH's chair sit two plates of biscuits, both half empty. There are crumbs on the floor. BETH hastily tips the contents of one plate onto the other, pushing the first plate under her chair. She moves the biscuits around the plate. A couple fall onto the carpet.*]

172

### Beth

I'm so sorry, I didn't – no, no, it's fine. Sorry, I didn't have any lunch, or any breakfast, and I just … I don't normally … I'm sorry about the mess. Please, have a biscuit. I haven't … I don't think I've touched all of them … No, no, I won't have one, thank you, I never eat during the day. It's fine. I'm fine.

[*She attempts to compose herself. Sits up straighter. Forces a smile. There is biscuit between her teeth.*]

### Beth

OK, well, hi, I'm Beth. I've been— Sorry, but, I was just wondering: can you cut that bit out? The bit where – you know – when you came in, and I … sorry, it doesn't matter. I'll carry on. Hi, I'm Beth, and I've been here for two years. Longer, actually. Two and a half. I've only been in this room for the past few months though. It's my third-year room. Yeah. So, I love it here. Mmm. Maybe. Maybe a bit hard. I love it though. I'm so lucky. If I'd stayed at home, I'd probably have ended up as a cashier or something, but I didn't, I came here, and it's one of the best universities in the world, and …

[*She is getting out of breath. Moisture glistens on her forehead.*]

### Beth

Um, what? Do I …? Um. I don't know. I guess maybe. Sometimes. Sometimes I feel a bit … not good enough. Because I'm not … thin. Sorry. That's shallow, isn't it? I suppose it's just … sometimes I get this feeling of being empty and desperate, and then I feel like I have to eat and eat and eat to get rid of it. Except the eating never gets rid of it, it just makes it worse, because it makes me fatter and fatter, and I've been reading a bit about it and I thought maybe I might have a kind of problem – a kind of disorder, to do with the eating – because it's starting to take over my life, the eating, or thinking about eating, or hating myself because I can't stop eating, and – the control – it's slipping, and I …

[*She catches herself mid-sentence. Her eyes bulge.*]

**Beth**

Oh, god, I'm so sorry. I don't know what I'm saying. I don't know where that came from. Should I ...? Would it be better if I started again? No, I ... I don't really want to ... Please? Can I start again?

## CUT

---

On the 1st of May, things will change. The 1st of May is a day *made* for change – it has change written all over it, the 1st of May does. Brand new month, brand new me, brand new everything. 'May' probably comes from Latin or something, and I bet its original meaning is 'change'. Yup. On the 1st of May, things will change.

(On the 1st of May, things do not change.)

When I am 22, things will change. There is *nothing* like a new age for helping you become a new person. It makes perfect sense that the past year has been so awful. I've been an *odd-numbered age* all this time! I'm surprised things haven't been *worse!* I've been *21!* An appalling age! But 22 – oh, what an *age!* It's so even and matching and *fresh.* It just *oozes* Brand New Me. When I am 22, I'll never binge again. It'll be simple. Yup. When I am 22, things will change.

(When I am 22, things do not change.)

When I move, things will change. It's no wonder everything has crumbled since I've been living here – it's so *suffocating.* So incredibly *limiting.* So full of old habits, old memories. How on earth would I ever have been able to get on top of the bingeing *here?* No! It was always going to be impossible. When I move, I'll be able to take control. Yup. When I move, things will change.

(When I move, things do not change.)

The Stunning, LGBTQ+ Friendly, Vegetarian Friendly, Newly Renovated Two Bed Flat in the Perfect Location with Excellent Local Amenities is bland. I live with Fun Sociable Becka from the flatmate advert. It soon becomes clear that, aside from the first two letters of our names, we share very little. Becka sleeps late in the mornings, her lanky body tangled around her girlfriend in the bedroom that smells of dry shampoo and cigarette smoke, and she gets back from her gigs late at night, guitar slung low across her torso. I get up early, creeping across to the kitchen to make tea, bundling myself out of the house and into the office before the cleaners have finished hoovering. I get home after Becka has left. Sometimes, if I round the corner and see her bike chained up by the bins, I skulk in the car park of the bar across the road until she emerges, disengages the bike lock in a clanking rattle, and whizzes away. I get home after Becka has left, when there is no one in the flat to see me haul my shopping up the stairs and through the door and into my room and – over the course of the evening – into my mouth.

The decision comes daily. I leave the office at five, gratefully clicking closed the tabs I barely understand and waving goodbye to the colleagues I barely know. At the end of the main road there is a junction: left takes me straight home, through a warren of residential streets; right takes me down the high road, past the snapping jaws of brightly-lit supermarket-funhouses that suck me in with promises of fullness-and-fulfilment bound in crackly cellophane. Every day, walking down the main road, I feel strong: purposeful. *No. Not today. Today will be a good day. Today I will ignore the siren call of the supermarket, with its neatly packaged pieces of oblivion, and its stacks of sweet, short-term solutions, and its offer of instantaneous comfort. Today I will turn left.*

Every day, as I near the junction, I feel tension creep from my toes to my fingers to my face. I feel it wriggle up, under my skin, burrowing into every fleshy fibre. My mind splits, the two halves pulling me in opposite directions. The good part floats serenely to the left, weaving its way through the rows of houses and parked cars, delivering me to my door light and virtuous. The bad part veers off, across the zebra crossing, past the emptying cafes and along the aisles of the supermarket until my bags are heavy and my purse is light. There is – underneath the superficial tussle between left and right, right and wrong – an inevitability to it. Every day, as I approach the junction, I know how it will go. I will go right, and it will be anything but right, but I will still do it. Bingeing is terrifying – control-evadingly, stomach-stretchingly, nausea-inducingly *terrifying* – but the alternative is worse. Emptiness. Time. Feelings. If I am not bingeing, I must face up to the wreck I have become through bingeing. If I am bingeing, I am speeding up my own demise, but can close my eyes as I do it. If I didn't binge, I would have to live, and I don't want to live. Not really. So I turn right.

In the supermarket, people mill around, leisurely, as I grab the same things from the same shelves as always, eyes trained on the floor. I glance into people's baskets and envy the normalcy of their pints of milk and bags of carrots. Nice, normal food for nice, normal people. They are doing everything right. My basket is a festival of shiny, scrunchy badness. Bad food for a bad person. I stuff it into myself in a tortured stupor of self-care and self-harm. Back at the flat, sitting on my bedroom floor, biting and chewing and swallowing in a frenzy, I am comforting and clawing at myself with every mouthful. I wish I had turned left and chosen clean simplicity. *I am weak, and I am greedy, and I am out of control.*

One evening, clutching an unfamiliar nubbin of resolve, I turn left and wind my way back to the flat, hands devoid of bags and eyes devoid of secrets. I kick off my shoes, shrug off my coat, and pad into the kitchen, mind buzzing: *Feed me feed me feed me feed me FEED ME.* I stand, paralysed, in front of the cupboard next to the sink, scrutinising each box and packet with miserable indecision. *What should I eat? How much should I eat? Should I eat now? Which has fewer calories – pasta or rice? Shall I be vegetarian this month or not? Would it not be simpler to throw in the towel and eat the lot? Everything in every cupboard? Everything in the kitchen?* I shake thoughts from my head and rice into a saucepan. I'll decide what to eat with the rice once I've calmed down. In my bedroom, I pull my laptop from its hiding place under a pile of clothes. The room is a tip: dirty laundry in every corner, dirty plates on every surface, dirty shoes abandoned by the bed, clods of crusty mud around them. It is always like this when the bingeing is bad, as if the mess of my eating must be mirrored by mess elsewhere. The mess feels fitting, when the bingeing is bad: *Why shouldn't I be surrounded by dirt? I'm a dirty person.* The harder I try to banish the dirt from my public life – the more effort I pour into the calm, clean, competent façade – the more aggressively it invades my private spaces.

Today, though, it is different. *I will not binge today.* If I can get through today, I can get through tomorrow and the next day and the day after that, and before I know it I will have weeks of binge-free time under my (rapidly loosening) belt. Today, that feels possible. My laptop remains unopened. Stomach fizzing with hunger and excitement, I pick up a crumpled T-shirt from the bed and fold it, working my way through all the clothes I can reach before moving on to those strewn across the rest of the room. It is calming – the gentle fall of the fabric on my lap, the repetitive act of arranging the garments into neat squares. Once the clothes are safely tucked away in my chest of drawers, I address the humdrum clutter on the floor: the books that belong on the bookshelf; the make-up that belongs in the make-up bag; the socks that belong in the laundry basket. I clatter the dirty dishes together in a pile and carry them through to the kitchen, breathing in an acrid stench when I swing open the door. The gas flame still licks at the cremated rice. The water has evaporated away, and the grains have clumped together in a charred mass. I turn off the stove and snap on the extractor fan, desperate to avoid the scream of the smoke alarm. A jet of cold water makes the pan sizzle, and I sink, noodle-boned, to the floor.

The rice is ruined and that means my dinner is ruined and that means my day is ruined and that means my new start is ruined and that means my life is ruined. It's *all* ruined. I am wailing so volubly that Becka comes flying from her room, one eye framed in dark make-up. I didn't know she was here. I was so wrapped up in *today is different* and *I will not binge* and *the start of a brand-new life* I didn't notice her bike still chained to the railings outside.

'Beth? Beth, what's up? What happened?'

The sobs are wracking and there is no room for speech. Becka puts a hand on my shoulder and I squirm away. I don't want her to be sucked into my dirt.

'Beth? What's going on? Beth, talk to me. You're scaring me, Beth …'

Fear tightens the edges of her voice, and her concern makes me cry harder. Eventually, drawing in a great, gasping breath, I howl, 'I *burnt* it!'

'Burnt what?'

'I *burnt* it! I'm so *stupid*! I *burnt* it!'

'Beth, what did you burn?'

'The *rice!*'

'The *rice?*'

'*Yes!* The *rice!* I burnt it! All of it! I can't do *anything right!*'

'You burnt some rice?'

'*Yes!* And now I have nothing to *eat!*'

'But can't you cook some more?'

'*YOU DON'T UNDERSTAND!*'

I wrench my face from my hands, glaring at Becka and her stupid suggestions with furious pink eyes. She looks at me with a mixture of confusion and fear. She shakes her head and raises her eyebrows. Confusion, fear and revulsion. Whatever flimsy friendship Becka and I once shared is broken. Her face writhes and twists like a half-naked pole dancer. I make and break friendships like other people make and break promises. I can't have friends. I am too busy having an eating disorder.

When Becka leaves, the loud sobs do not return. The tears that pool on the tiles are soundless puddles of salt.

I have moved. I am 22. It is the first day of the month.

Nothing has changed.

---

### Production: Beth
### Scene Three: 'I Just Can't Stop'

*[Camera pans up along the corridor of a small, shabby flat. Boxes and bags line the hallway.]*

*[Close-up – a door. It is ajar.]*

*[The door opens to BETH, sitting in the middle of the room, on the floor. The room is chaotically untidy. She is surrounded by plate after plate of biscuit remnants. Crumbs and shards litter the carpet around her. She is hunched over, hands moving quickly from plate to mouth, chewing and swallowing determinedly. Her hair falls over her face.]*

*[When BETH speaks, it is without looking up. Her voice is a dull monotone. Her words come between mouthfuls. She does not stop eating. Her speech is indistinct.]*

**Beth**
Hi. I'm Beth. Sorry. It's messy. I can still talk. I just can't stop eating. I have to carry on eating.

[*Camera sweeps round, down to BETH's level. We see her face. It is puffy and drawn. Her expression is glazed. She talks as if hypnotised. She never looks up from the food in her lap.*]

**Beth** [*robotically*]
Do have a biscuit. If you want. No thanks. Not for me. I never …

[*She swallows thickly, still intent on her eating frenzy. She directs her speech to no one in particular.*]

**Beth**
I'm always hungry, you know? Even when I've eaten so much I can hardly see, I'm still hungry. It never goes away. The hunger – it's like a monster inside me. It's like it isn't a part of me. I've been eating for hours. I can feel the food stacked up to my eyes. I'm so hungry. I'm still so hungry.

[*BETH adds her empty plate to a small pile of empty plates sitting to her left. She pulls the next plate towards her, cramming two biscuits into her mouth at once.*]

**Beth**
I think about it all the time. 'It'. I don't know what I mean when I say that. I think about food all the time. I think about eating all the time. I think about my body all the time. I did an online quiz thing the other day – one of those 'diagnose yourself' ones – and it asked how much time I spent thinking about food and my body. The most they offered was 'every day'. They didn't have anything that fitted for me. They should have had 'every second of every minute of every hour of every day'.

[*Her eating speeds up. It is frantic.*]

**Beth**
I rang my mum yesterday. She couldn't understand why I was crying. I tried to tell her. I said, 'eating disorder', and she said, 'But you're not thin?'

[*BETH pauses, mid-mouthful. She gags very slightly.
It seems to take great effort to swallow.*]

**Beth**
It really hurts now. I'm going to have to stop.

[*Her eyes bulge. She places a hand gingerly on
her stomach. She is clearly in pain.*]

**Beth** [*whispering*]
I hate stopping. That's when the thoughts come in. I can't hear
them when I'm chewing. It makes everything peaceful.

[*BETH's expression does not change, but her eyes fill.
Tears descend sluggishly down her cheeks. When she
speaks, her voice is quieter. She sounds broken.*]

**Beth**
It's so stupid, isn't it? It's just food. It should be so easy: eat when
you're hungry; stop when you're full. It should be the easiest
thing in the world. But what about when eating *is* my world?
What about when eating is the first thing I think of when I
wake up, and the last thing I think of before I go to sleep, and
all I think of in between? What about when I comfort myself
by eating, and hurt myself by eating, and numb myself by eating,
and feel alive by eating? What about when I'm *always hungry?*

[*She looks up for the first time, into the camera, as if asking the question
directly to the audience. Her face is full and padded, but she looks
hollow. She looks malnourished. When she speaks, it is a whisper.*]

**Beth**
Please. Can I start again?

## CUT

---

## Production: Beth
## Scene Four: Narrow

*[Camera pans up along the corridor of a small, shabby flat.
It is neat but lived-in. Close-up on wooden door.]*

*[When BETH opens the door, she smiles shyly. She
has no shoes on. Her eyes are clear.]*

### Beth
Hi. Come in. I tidied.

*[She swings the door wide. The room is small – cosy.
A double bed is covered in a patchwork quilt. BETH sits
on the bed, curling her feet underneath her.]*

### Beth

Sit down, sit down. Can I get you a drink? I've just
made myself a tea. Would you like a tea?

*[She rises, going over to a shelf in the corner where the kettle stands and
retrieves her mug. She brings it back to the bed, along with a large red tin.]*

### Beth

Would you like a biscuit? I'm going to have a biscuit.
I like to have one at this time in the morning.

*[BETH removes a biscuit from the tin, then replaces the lid. She dips it in
her tea, and eats it slowly. She doesn't appear to be in any rush to talk.]*

### Beth

Hi. I'm Beth. This is where I live. Oh, getting on for a year now?
Yeah. I like it. To be honest, it was a relief to get away from
university. Yes, everyone says it's one of the best in the country,
but that wasn't always a good thing. Not for me. To be honest,
being there always felt like trying to cram myself into a box I was
never going to fit into. I was never going to be that shape. It was
a very narrow box. And I'm not … I suppose I'm not narrow.

182

[*She grins. Her nose wrinkles. She wraps her hands
around her mug. She is still smiling, but her eyes are
cloudy. There is soft sadness in her words.*]

### Beth

Last time you came to talk to me … I can't not mention it. I
meant to call to explain. But I was just so embarrassed. I couldn't
believe you had seen me like that. I felt like the most repulsive
thing on the planet. I felt totally, utterly abhorrent. I hated
myself. And I knew that, if I had called you, I would only have
cried. The *self-loathing*. It was enough to make me cry. I tried so
hard to push it down with all that food. Stuffing myself until my
insides felt numb – but it just made me feel worse. I lost track
of whether I was eating to hug myself or hurt myself. It was a
comfort, but also an attack. I think a part of me wanted to eat
myself to death. And a part of me really thought I would.

[*She is silent for a moment, tracing the pattern on her mug with
a fingertip. She glances up, giving a small, complicated smile.*]

### Beth

It's not that things are fine now. I don't even really know what
'fine' would look like. How it would feel. At the moment
things are still hard sometimes. Often. It can be so tempting
to side-step out of life. At some point, eating became my way
of doing that. What? No. I don't know why. I wish I did.

[*BETH looks out of the window. It is as if she
has forgotten the cameras are there.*]

### Beth

The other day, I met up with a friend from school. She lives
around here. Crazy coincidence. We went out for dinner. I hadn't
been out for dinner in months. I'm usually too busy pretending
not to eat, then secretly eating everything I can see. We drank
a lot of white wine. It gave me a pain in my stomach. I loved it.
Afterwards, I would normally have gone to the supermarket and

bought more food and eaten it all, because in my mind I'd eaten a meal so I might as well eat the world. But I was tired that evening. I wanted to come home. I wasn't hungry any more. I was full up.

[*Camera closes in on BETH's face.*
*She looks into the lens, smiling ruefully.*]

**Beth**
I think that's all, really. What?

[*She chuckles, eyes crinkling.*]

**Beth**
No. Not this time. I don't want to start again.

**CUT**

———

'But it's just over-eating, isn't it? It's just being greedy.'

## The Binge: Your Seven-Step Guide to Garden Variety Greed!

### Step One – The Thought

It worms its way into your ear. Its tone is high and wheedling, as syrupy sweet as the treats it projects, tantalisingly, onto the screen of your mind.

*Why not do it?*

The thought doesn't discriminate. It can be triggered by the most emotive or anodyne of incidents. You have a stressful meeting. You do badly on a piece of schoolwork. You realise you have an empty day ahead of you, yawningly unfilled. You pass a stranger eating something you yourself would like to be eating. You realise it is a Sunday, or an odd-numbered day, or the last day of a month.

*Why not do it?*

### Step Two – Consideration

The thought makes you itch. You feel the itch in every pore of your skin, every cell of your body. *Want, want, want, need, need, need.* Your jaw clenches and relaxes, saliva building in anticipation.

You shake yourself. You bite down hard on your tongue. You will not let it happen. You cannot let it happen. You imagine the waking-up-the-day-after feeling. The bitter, lived-in carpet of your mouth. The groaning ache of your gut. The smell. It cannot happen again.

And yet ...

### Step Three – Bargaining

*The thing is, if it doesn't happen today, it will just happen tomorrow, won't it?*

The thought is mincing up and down at the edge of your sanity, trilling out a sing-song, sugar-sweet, hop-and-skip spool of seductive, persuasive evil.

*Wouldn't it be better to get it over and done with today? Because, after all, if you do it today, you know you'll never do it again, don't you? You'll do it one more time, then never again! Today will be the last hurrah! And won't that be a relief? To be free of it? To be liberated from this awful millstone? If you do it today – one last time today – you'll never have to do it again. But if you don't do it today – if you don't get this urge out of your system, once and for all – who knows whether you'll ever be free? Do you really want to take that risk? The only sensible course of action here – the only logical, reasonable decision – is to do it. Do it today. Do it now.*

*After all, you've had a terrible day, and you need a way to calm yourself.*

*After all, life feels like too much at the moment, and you need a way to escape.*

*After all, you're a wretched, horrible person, and you need a way to prove it to the world.*

*After all, it's the last day of the month, and tomorrow you can start afresh.*

*After all, I could say whatever I wanted, couldn't I? We both know what's going to happen.*

### Step Four – Preparation

You're on a mission, now.

*Make sure no one knows. Make sure no one works out your game.*

You know where everything is. You could draw a floor plan of the supermarket from memory. In, out, aisle to aisle, fill the basket until it starts to tug your arm from its socket. Things in crisp, colourful packets are good. Money doesn't matter. You wouldn't spend £50 on a T-shirt or a pair of earrings, but £50 on food? Easy. You don't even question it.

*This is not something you want. This is something you need.*

You don't look at anyone. This is important. You don't look at the nice, normal customers doing nice, normal shopping.

*Remember, they are human, you are not. You're an animal now. You're an animal on a mission.*

You might have to go to lots of different supermarkets to get all the different things you need.

*Remember, if you don't get all the different things you need, you won't have done it properly, and if you don't do it properly you'll have to do it again. And the whole reason you're doing it is so you can stop doing it. Remember?*

You might have to stand in a queue at a fast food restaurant and order enough food to feed a family. You might have to tap a few buttons on your phone and summon enough food to feed a family. By the end of your preparations, you are armed with enough food to feed four families. Four families-worth of food will somehow have to fit into one person.

*What did I tell you? You're not a person.*

### Step Five – Resignation

The withdrawal from the outside world can be minimal, partial or complete, depending on the day. Perhaps you remain present in body, going to work or school like an ungainly puppet animated by a dozy puppeteer. Perhaps you leave early, pleading sickness or emergency – pleading anything other than the need to plaster your insides with food. Perhaps you give yourself over entirely to the demands of the internal seductress, cancelling plans – calling in sick – locking the door and closing the curtains. Perhaps you take hold of the four corners of your world and tug, tug, tug, until your universe is reduced to you, and your food, and your apathy.

### Step Six – Execution

*Find yourself a burrow. A place where no one can see you. Find a door that locks. It doesn't matter if it's a bathroom. It doesn't matter if it's a cupboard.*

*Bite, chew and swallow.*

*Remember how you felt that life was too big – too overwhelming? Now, life is small. Life is tiny. Life has been reduced to a triad of actions. Biting. Chewing. Swallowing. Let the food blur into a bland, beige bulk. The food doesn't matter. What matters is spiriting it from outside to inside. What matters is filling yourself.*

*Bite, chew and swallow.*

You adjust your position as the food goes in. Sitting up becomes difficult, after a while.

*That's a sign you're doing it right. It should hurt your stomach to be held in a vertical position. Go ahead – lie down. You've come this far – why not take the debauchery even further?*

The pain is crunching and biting and all-consuming, but that doesn't stop your crunching and biting and consuming.

*You've got to carry on. You've got to carry on until everything that was outside has been taken inside. You've got to get it done.*

*Bite, chew and swallow.*

It's difficult to eat while crying, but not impossible. The mucus mingles with the food in your throat, and it is nauseating, but you do not stop eating. It is mind over matter; mind over body.

*If you start to gag, try not to worry. You might need to throw up. Why not? More room in your stomach that way.*

*Bite, chew and swallow.*

### Step Seven – Aftermath

At some point, you pass out. You do not faint.

*Fainting is for bone-and-tissue, daffodil-headed eating disorder sufferers. Fainting is not for animals.*

You do not faint – but nor do you sleep. Sleep is warm and cosy, like gradual submersion in bathwater. You do not sink into slumber – you fall out of consciousness. One moment you are swallowing hard against the snake of pain writhing up from your gut – the next you are gone. You fall from the world.

You wake on the floor, surrounded by detritus. There may or may not be vomit in the sink. Your mouth may or may not be full of half-chewed food. You may or may not have six missed calls from your workplace, asking why you are not at your desk. You may or may not be crying.

You have probably not managed to eat all the food you were supposed to eat. There are leftovers, which – given a few hours – will turn from nauseating to tempting. You open the packets, pour the contents into a black bag, and coat them in bleach. That way at least if you try to claw the precious morsels back, eating them might kill you.

*You can dream.*

You look in the mirror. It is the final torture: the final self-abuse, designed to trigger enough revulsion to propel you from turgid sub-human to squeaky-clean superhuman. If that change could be fuelled by disgust alone, it would happen now. The swollen convection of your stomach rises like a mountain from dimpled flesh. The fat enrobing you hangs, saggy, like bulky winter clothes. Your eyes are sunken and slit. Can you eat your way to blindness?

*Wouldn't that be a relief?*

> **'That's the thing. It's not just overeating.**
> **It's not like that at all.'**

Although they all fall under the umbrella term 'eating disorders', it is important to clarify the general distinctions between the pathologies discussed below. Beth suffers from binge eating disorder (BED), characterised by discrete periods during which she feels compelled to consume large amounts of food. Eating binges also occur in bulimia nervosa, but are followed by 'compensatory behaviours': most commonly forced vomiting, but sometimes laxative abuse, excessive exercise or fasting. Anorexia nervosa sufferers may binge on occasion, but their condition is hallmarked by prolonged food restriction and maintenance of a low weight. Of course, there are many other forms of eating disorder, and the subjective experience of any eating disorder extends far beyond these crude, diagnostic stipulations: its tendrils worm into every inch of the brain, body and behaviour. But when I talk about anorexia, bulimia or binge eating, these are the conditions I am describing.

While interviewing, I spoke to women suffering from a range of eating disorders, but in Beth I chose to embody BED alone. Why? Put simply, it is the story we never hear. More than any other condition I have written about, BED is trivialised – but I defy anyone to read Beth's story and maintain that her disorder is trivial. The silence surrounding BED is all the more alarming given its comparative prevalence: the most recent large-scale review of eating disorder incidence estimated that 0.9 per cent, 1.5 per cent and 3.5 per cent of women experience anorexia nervosa, bulimia nervosa and binge eating disorder (respectively) at some point during their lifetime.[19]

It is not uncommon for discussions of eating disorders to merge the different conditions into a single, homogenous group. This is, on one level, right: across the board, sufferers share core feelings of insecurity, helplessness and self-blame. Anorexia and binge eating are less opposing ends of a spectrum (as one might automatically imagine) than two neighbouring points: both involve the use of food to dull or alleviate painful emotions, with determined disregard for the body's wants and needs. However, from interviews and from personal experience, I know that there is a uniquely intense agony to binge eating, and that intense agony is shame. The condition oozes a viscous shame that clogs the throat and cakes the skin. Over the course of this project, I spoke to women about the most hidden and private of experiences, but no stories were as steeped in shame as stories of binge eating. Women *shrivelled* in shame when describing the elaborate ritual of food buying, the body bulging against the seams of clothes, and the inability to claw back 'control'. Binge eating induces self-hatred, and self-hatred brings misery, and misery begets binge eating.

There is a level of shame in anorexia – the lies and deception, the physical incapacitation, the unsavoury habits. There is also pride. On my adolescent eating disorders ward, patients had to be discouraged from 'dressing inappropriately': parading in barely-there shorts and crop tops, arms and legs like sticks of uncooked spaghetti. *Cover up? But my body is my trophy. I have worked for this.* Anorexia is obsession, isolation and tedium, yes, but it is also power, accomplishment and awe. Our culture's attribution of disproportionate 'value' to anorexia is not so mysterious: anorexic bodies are visually horrifying; extreme food denial is something few of us can manage; it is, perhaps, more strikingly 'abnormal' to eat next to nothing than to overeat. However, in emotional terms, it is absolutely false to assume anorexia to be more painful than binge eating. Both disorders demand a stunning level of time and energy to maintain – but the anorexic is rewarded with care and concern, the binge eater with dismissal. When anorexic, I felt acknowledged and noticed; my binge eating only ever engendered a sense of fraudulence and humiliation. It ripped me apart, because so little had changed: anorexia led me to isolate myself out of coldness and weakness; when binge eating, I isolated myself out of revulsion and self-loathing. The compulsive consumption of food is just as debilitating as its renouncement – but nobody sees. Nobody cares. It feels like garden-variety greed.

On the subject of shame, one might expect bulimia to hold the trump card: surely the indignity – the aberrance – of purging food can only add to the humiliation of over-consuming it? Certainly, many bulimia sufferers long for anorexia, idolising its 'simplicity' and 'cleanness'. However, among my interviewees, the lexicon of bulimia was *not* as loaded with mortification as that of 'pure' binge eating – and, of the two aspects of the disorder (overeating and compensation), it was the taking in of food that was experienced as degrading. When probed, women generally concluded that they felt their compensatory behaviours – vomiting, fasting or exercising – lent them some degree of legitimacy. *At least I am trying. At least I am real.* Shame is not proportional to aberrance: it is proportional to invalidation. BED receives so little societal acknowledgement that sufferers are left to explain their behaviour through punitive labels and harsh self-talk. *It's not that I'm unwell, it's that I'm undisciplined. It's not that I'm debilitated, it's that I'm disgusting.*

The assimilation of eating disorders into a single diagnosis not only neglects the particular embarrassment of binge eating: it suggests that any media treatment of the subject is positive, with a heightened understanding of one form of eating disorder equating to a heightened understanding of eating disorders *en masse*. Overwhelmingly, the media focuses on anorexia. Ill-conceived films and well-intentioned documentaries succumb to gratuitous shots of xylophone bones and hollow faces. Radio broadcasts are presented from the eating disorder units to which one only gains access if one's weight is sufficiently low. Magazine and newspaper articles boast pictures of bodies that could be cadavers. Over and over we are presented with *one* subsection of *one* type of eating disorder, and told: 'This is what it is to struggle with food. This is what it is to be seriously unwell.' Sometimes, these presentations are perceptive and illuminating, but they are not presentations of *eating disorders*. They are presentations of *anorexia*.

With every new film, programme or article telling the story of frail people and the flesh they starved away, another door is shut against the myriad sufferers whose weight does not reflect their inner turmoil. In their minds, sneering thoughts set up a tattoo: *See? You're not really sick. See? You're not really worthy. See? You're not really real.* This is not to say that anorexia is not worthy of attention: of all people, I am in no place to make such a statement, my first book having explored my anorexia in depth. It is to say that other eating disorders – those that do not manifest visibly on the body, those that do not result in extreme thinness – are *equally* worthy of attention. And yet they receive, at best, a cursory nod of begrudging recognition.

If there is one thing I learned from my interviews – allied with my own experiences – it is this: the way we view restrictive vs. non-restrictive eating disorders is broken. Imagine these two scenarios:

### One

You meet a friend for coffee. She doesn't look well. She is drawn; her face is sunken. Her clothes wrinkle and sag. Her collar bones protrude. She looks empty – hollow and grey and pointy at the edges. She tells you she hasn't been feeling good. She has felt very low. She says she hasn't been eating – she has barely been eating at all. Sometimes, she hasn't eaten anything for days on end. She has been starving herself, waking up weak, fainting before bed. She can't eat. She has lost a lot of weight – she knows this. She wants to lose more. She thinks she has more weight to lose. Food has taken over her life.

What do you say? What do you think?

### Two

You meet a friend for coffee. She doesn't look well. She is drawn; her face is puffy. She tugs at her clothes. She crosses her arms over her stomach. She looks fuller than usual – as if her outline has been stretched. She tells you she hasn't been feeling good. She has felt very low. She says she has been eating too much – far too much. Yesterday, she ate a full bag of pasta, a block of cheese, a pint of ice cream, two packets of biscuits, three bags of crisps and enough chocolate to make her sick. All in the space of a few hours. The gorging is a crazed, desperate blur. She has been bingeing, waking up feeling bloated, going to sleep feeling sick. She can't stop eating. She has gained a lot of weight – she knows this. She is humiliated by it. Food has taken over her life.

What do you say? What do you think?

For most, the first scenario is a straightforward presentation of anorexia nervosa: severe, debilitating and worthy of medical treatment. What about the second? Are you looking at illness, or poor self-control? Do you advise a visit to the doctor, or a summoning of willpower? Anorexia and binge eating disorder should be seen as two sides of the same coin – equally agonising, equally serious – but, at a societal and medical level, they are not. At best, they are interpreted as 'degrees' of eating disorder: binge eating the least serious; anorexia the most; bulimia kicking its heels somewhere in the middle. At worst, they are pushed into separate 'categories': anorexia an illness;

binge eating a bad habit; bulimia a hybrid, swinging between 'get yourself to hospital' and 'get a grip on yourself'.

Anorexia bias extends beyond the perceptions of laypeople: the section of the NICE guidelines (the UK's National Institute for Health and Care Excellence) devoted to anorexia treatment is over 1,600 words long; bulimia and BED *combined* receive little over 1,000.[20] A recent statement from Andrew Radford, Chief Executive of the eating disorders charity Beat, addressed the issue of assigning treatment on the basis of low body weight and little else:

> 'Not only does assessment by BMI [body mass index] result in a barrier to early intervention, it effectively shuts out people with bulimia and other eating disorders from accessing specialist treatment – these diagnoses make up approximately 80 per cent of people diagnosed with an eating disorder. The physical and mental risk of these other eating disorders are often as severe as anorexia. BMI 'barriers' must be urgently removed from all inpatient and outpatient services and replaced with access to treatment based on a comprehensive assessment of a person's physical and mental health.'[21]

The BED diagnosis may be dismissed because it 'pathologises a normal behaviour'. Yes – occasional overeating *is* a normal behaviour. Food is as pleasurable as it is practical, and there are times when it is all but compulsory to eat past comfortable fullness. But BED is so much more than ten too many chocolates on Christmas Day. BED is isolated, clandestine and quiet. BED is eating until sick. BED is flushing food down the toilet in an attempt to guarantee it won't be retrieved from the dustbin and finished off. BED is cancelling event after event because of seams that strain and belts that bite. BED is a sordid, sweaty self-destruction: having eaten too much, one lives too little, in response to which one is compelled to eat more and live less.

Binge eating exists in the murky hinterland between self-comfort and self-harm, problem and solution. It is an act borne of deep emptiness, and – on a superficial level – it is an effective 'filler'. The reasons for the emptiness, and the reasons why certain individuals turn to food (restriction or overconsumption) in times of emptiness, are difficult to decipher. On a logical – *bio*logical – level, bingeing is an organic sedative, granting the comfort and satiation some struggle to obtain through other means. Emotional emptiness is excruciating, and food fills us up. The pattern of overeating in response to stress, fear or unhappiness is often established early in life – many of my interviewees recounted vivid memories of childhood binges. Once one has become accustomed to burying feelings under layers of sugar and starch, failure to do so leaves one raw, frightened and itchy.

Not all eating disorders entail a physical, bodily emptiness, but all eating disorders thrive in empty spaces. An empty space may be a life devoid of activity, or a life full to the brim with joyless drudgery. An empty space may be fewer friends than can be clutched in the palm of a hand, or scores of unhappy relationships. An empty space is one without emotional nourishment; an eating disorder is not the *state* of malnutrition, but a *response* to malnutrition.

Perhaps, then, recovery lies in fullness – physical, emotional and psychological. Anorexia, bulimia and binge eating disorder are master space-occupiers, oozing and expanding to fill every inch of any plot they are given – but they cope poorly with competition. Filling one's life from the corners inwards forces the eating disorder to contract – to rise grumpily from where it was sprawled and repack itself into another space. A smaller space. One doesn't become 'too busy' to have an eating disorder: one becomes full enough to no longer need an eating disorder. The binge-friendly pockets of lonely time close up, their seams stitched together by exciting ideas and engaging conversations and kind people. The elusive power of a flat stomach is crushed by the realisation that nobody cares about the flatness or unflatness of one's stomach. The nagging, gnawing feeling of being empty inside grows smaller, and smaller still, and then smaller after that, until it is hard to believe one ever thought one could eat the world and still feel naggingly, gnawingly empty.

I have spoken to more eating disorder sufferers than I can count, and my own eating disorder has crouched on my shoulder for more than half my life. With the imperfect expertise this grants me, I can say that there is no hierarchy of 'badness', 'worthiness' or 'validity'. Just as there are torments unique to anorexia, bulimia and binge eating entail their own tortures – tortures of which we know far too little. But, at their core, eating disorders are similar. They are draining. They are difficult to maintain. They are distressing. They are loyal. They are vicious. They are soothing. They are contradictory. An eating disorder is never a testament to willpower, nor a mark of greed – it is a hunger, a fear, a confusion. It is an empty space that can be filled.

# What I wish I could tell you about my binge eating disorder

It is not about greed. It is not about willpower.

There is nothing 'fun' about binge eating. It is not something 'we all wish we could do It is a private, shameful, degrading experience.

You may not be able to see my binge eating disorder. I may eat normally in public; my weight may be average. This does not mean the disorder does not exist.

Food and weight might seem shallow, trivial things to obsess about. The eating disorder is about so much more than food and weight, but these have become my focus. That's why I can't recover just by regulating my eating or by losing/gaining weight.

My eating patterns may seem illogical, even perverse. I may resist eating in public, but eat huge amounts alone. I may avoid social occasions because of anxiety about the food involved, then stay at home and eat for hours. I may binge immediately before going out for a meal, then feel too ill to eat at the restaurant or host's house. It is all related to the intensity of my feelings: I am not being greedy, thoughtless or difficult.

It is frightening and humiliating to be controlled by food. I often feel I have no agency at all: the food insanity drives everything I think, feel and do. It makes me feel like an animal.

My eating pattern may be made up of periods of restriction, periods of 'normality', periods of bingeing, etc. I sometimes feel I am different people during these different states. I don't know which 'me' is real.

Binge eating can make me feel worthless. When I am in a bingeing cycle, my self-hatred is overpowering. I may not allow myself to wash, clean my teeth, or even sleep in a bed.

My eating disorder is cunning and insidious. I can feel determined to escape its torment one moment, but the next moment it digs in its claws and forces me to continue punishing myself with food.

Please do not tell me I 'don't look like I have an eating disorder'. There is no 'looking like' one has an eating disorder: I am likely in as much mental distress as someone whose eating disorder results in emaciation. Weight is an irrelevance.

It can be reassuring for me to hear that you don't value me for my weight or appearance. My thoughts are so all-consuming that I sometimes believe everyone will hate me if I gain weight. It is helpful to be reminded that my value is unrelated to my size.

Please acknowledge the struggle I am facing. I spend most of my life feeling my eating disorder is insignificant and invalid: that I am 'making a fuss'. It is such a relief when people accept that my illness *is* an illness: a powerful and all-consuming mental health condition.

# *Holly*

What I say now will be the truth, the whole truth and nothing but the truth. I declare it solemnly and sincerely. When I have said the truth, the whole truth and nothing but the truth, you might ask why I am not saying it in court. You might ask why I am not speaking up or speaking out or doing whatever other kind of speaking I am supposed to be doing.

I go to court every day. You do not see me take the witness stand. Nobody asks me 'oath or affirming?' There are no wigs or gowns. But I am there, in my own court, where the judge is me and the jury is me. Every day I pick and peck at myself.

***Holly, the interrogator: Right, Holly. Are you ready to tell us all why we're here today?***

**Holly, the interrogated: I want to say what happened. I want to say everything that happened. But you have to let me tell it my way. It might be mixed up. It feels fragmented in my head. I won't be able to go from start to finish. I have to tell it my way.**

This is what the world was like when I was small and whole. This is what I remember.

The sun tingles hot cheeks; knobbled limbs sprout from the PE kit shorts and T-shirt that go home on Friday and come back on Monday, clean and pressed and faded. My skin is tight with sweat and sticky with golden syrup from the golden syrup sandwiches I ate at lunchtime from the square, pink lunchbox.

After school we go out to play on the grass in the middle of the estate, Dad sitting on the doorstep, smoke billowing around him like a shroud. When I climb up on his knee and brush my cheek against his it prickles. He smells stale and I breathe in deeply. The smoke encases us in a sweet fug, burrowing into the fibres of my clothes.

Where the grass meets the pavement the ground is thick with fine, white dandelion seed, and we pretend it is snow and attack one another with compacted handfuls that disperse when they hit the air. Upstairs at number 64, Rohan's beautiful, mysterious sister Aisha flits back and forth past the window, taut midriff appearing and disappearing between outfits. Her beautiful, mysterious pop music floats down, and Sadie and I take turns at being the dance teacher, and then we fight, and she isn't coming to my party (except it is a joint party, so unfortunately she has to come). Or we hang like bats, suspended by bent knees from the bicycle rack bars, Sadie's T-shirt falling over her head, giggling deliciously as the world inverts. Or we lie, side by side, grass tickling exposed skin, bloated baby bellies swelling towards the sky. We lie so close together that the hairs on our arms brush and itch.

By 5.30 the mums are inside, kitchen windows open, pots and pans sputtering. Zack's and my dad is inside too, shaking fish fingers onto a tray. Sadie and I run from house to house, pausing, inhaling deeply and shouting, 'Ricky and Stewart – sausages! Taylor – pizza! Lola and Carys – shepherd's pie!' By 6.00 Sadie is sitting at the table in her house and Zack and I are sitting at the table in ours, *The Simpsons* illuminating our faces as we mop up ketchup with pale potato waffles. Ribena dribbles down my T-shirt and Dad pulls it over my head, and then he pulls Zack's over his head too, because he says, 'no point doing two washes.' Naked from the waist up, we take our rocket-shaped ice lollies back outside, back onto the grass, my ribs poking from the skin above my full stomach. Sadie is back as well, Baby Annabelle tucked into the crook of her arm, and Zack and Nate kick their football into us *on purpose*, even though it is Baby Annabelle's bedtime. I run up the path to tell Dad, and Ricky jumps out from the open doorway, roaring a horrible roar. My arms and legs go as stiff and plasticky as Baby Annabelle's, and the bangs in my chest are so big they hurt, and the air can't get into or out of my mouth. Ricky laughs and goes to play football with Zack and Nate, but Sadie trips him up and lets me hold Baby Annabelle, and the banging in my chest goes away. It doesn't matter. Ricky wasn't coming to our party in the first place.

Aisha's beautiful, mysterious music is a low pulse in the air. And Baby Annabelle's bulbous head is smooth against the crease of my elbow. And it is so warm and so safe and so good.

---

*Do you have a lot of sex, Holly?*

**I don't know. What's a lot?**

*Do you have sex with a lot of different men?*

**I don't think so.**

*Your friends think so. Your friend Amy said you're 'not one to hang around'. Do you remember her saying that? It was after you slept with the boyfriend before last … or was it the one before that? You didn't 'hang around' with him, did you?*

**She was drunk when she said that. I was drunk when I slept with him. It doesn't count.**

*How long had you known the defendant before you slept with him? A few months? A few weeks? A few days?*

203

**We slept together the night of the day we met.**

*Yes. And who initiated sex that night? The defendant?*

**No. It was me.**

*Yes. It was you.*

That's why all this happened. It happened because I wasn't the person I was supposed to be.

──────────

Summer. We lie side by side in the indigo night, windows flung wide to the airless outdoors. My skin is tight with the ghost of the sun, but I roll towards him all the same, wanting to be held. He has been away all weekend, at his sister's wedding. I offered to go too, but he said not to bother. We'd have to find someone to feed the cat, he said. It wasn't worth it. I thought it would have been easy to find someone to feed the cat, but I didn't say so. He texted me a picture of his sister in her wedding dress. I said she looked beautiful. He said he missed me. I glowed for hours.

He rolls towards me, the warm breeze of his breath blowing stray strands of hair from my forehead. We are so close I can taste him in my mouth: toothpaste and mouthwash and, underneath, the thick, fibrous taste of meat. He rolls towards me, wanting to roam his big hands across my chest and my stomach and lower. I don't want that tonight. I feel dirty where he touches. My skin prickles and I thrum between my legs. I want to curl away, tight in a ball, and be small and private, but he is close and his are needs palpable. They press down on me, urgent and unshakeable. I make my body loose. *He deserves this*, I think. I turn my head to the side and force my thoughts away from the heavy, suffocating closeness. *This is the least I can do.*

I don't want the low, animal-sounding noises and the hot breath in my ear. I don't want the jerky rhythm and the faint, tugging pain inside. I don't want the feeling of every inch of my space being filled with him. As he moves and tenses I feel the muscles of his stomach clench above me, and for a moment I am safe, locked in a strong, protective cage of him. He stiffens and makes a tiny, strangled sound, then falls, sweaty and slack. I don't want it. Not really. But he deserves this, so I don't say no, and not saying no is the same as saying yes. Isn't it?

———

Autumn. When he comes in from the bathroom I pretend to be asleep. Curled like a seahorse, each hand clutching an elbow, I screw my eyes tight shut. I am a child playing hide-and-seek. *I can't see you! That means you can't see me!* Sweat moistens the crevices of my body, the weight of the duvet unwelcome in the dense heat of an Indian summer. I pull the feather casing tighter around me. *I can't see you.* I force my lungs to swell and deflate in a steady rhythm. *You can't see me.*

When his fingers trail up my back, the cotton of my T-shirt is lifted, and goosebumps erupt where air hits damp skin. My in—out breathing is a caricature of sleep. My lungs are stuffed so full of air they feel tight, pressing against my ribs like balloons. His mouth is soft against my neck, and, with a jolt, I remember that I love him. We are bound together, he and I, because I love him and because he needs me.

Because I love him, and because he needs me, I stay ensconced in pretend-sleep when he tugs my shoulder, pawing insistently until I fall onto my back. I feel bare on my back, as if the layers of feather and fabric have been eaten away by his hunger. I keep my eyes shut, and he must know I am not asleep, but he does not speak. He only does.

I am not in my body. It is as if I have been siphoned out and up to the ceiling. I am hovering above the tangle of limbs on the bed, watching myself be moulded around his need. When he moves in a certain way, it looks like he is alone, writhing and grunting in a solitary bubble of sensation. The headboard of the bed makes a dull thwacking sound as it hits the wall behind. The mattress squeaks. I am glad we live alone. I worry that the cat will come in. I wish I could pause time, just for long enough to push the door shut. I don't want the cat to come in. His pyjamas are wrinkled around his knees, still covering his lower legs, and his T-shirt is rucked around his midriff. Only the sweat-sheened skin between thigh and lower back is exposed, but from my ceiling vantage point he looks terribly naked. I want to look away. He wouldn't want me seeing him like this. He isn't really like this. He can't help that he needs this.

I don't look away. I am fixated on my asleep-but-awake body and the clumsy choreography of his stops and starts. I feel strangely peaceful: the closed eyes and crushed limbs of the woman on the bed below are a long way away. It is like I am watching a disturbing film, and I know I should be upset, but I feel nothing at all. The sounds of raspy breath and skin moving across skin are muted. Occasionally, I catch a glimpse of a fraction of his face – when he twists his neck, or flicks hair from his eyes. He looks desperate. When he finishes, he presses his mouth roughly to my cheek. He needs me.

Sprawled like a starfish, one of his hands rests on my arm. His fingers are too hot. As I come back into my body, skin prickling with pins and needles, I feel very strongly that I want his fingers off my arm. I am itchy. I want to submerge myself in cool water. When I shift my hips, there is a dull pain inside. I try to peel his burning digits from my skin, but his hand clutches reflexively. I let him keep hold of me. I close my eyes.

*I can't see you! That means you can't see me!*
*I didn't say no! That means I said yes!*

---

Winter. Christmas party. When I fall onto the bed, I feel ethanol seep from my pores. We have drunk so much that our cells are rebelling, spitting the excess poison to skin level. It makes us shine. My lipstick has peeled off in ruby flecks, clinging to my tongue and chin, collecting in the chapped grooves of my mouth. My cheeks are ruby too – 'drunkface', we called it as teenagers, as we dumped empty cider bottles in overflowing dustbins and held cold cans of Coke against hot skin. We couldn't sneak home from the park until drunkface had subsided. If you split an egg onto my cheek it would frazzle.

He moves like a heavy, half-drugged bear, clanking open the buckle on his jeans, and I twist an arm to pull down the zip of my dress. It is size 'optimistic/delusional': my breasts spill from the top, bulging and puckered with goosebumps. When I stand up, I feel every pint and glass and shot swilling around inside me, sloshing from one side of my stomach to the other, and I stumble. Always alert, he clamps an arm to my waist, and the muscles are full and hard against my back, and I am so touched he has stopped me from falling that I take his face in my hands and kiss him. I kiss him hard, mashing together our dozy lips, and he tastes of cider and mulled wine spice. His face prickles. When I pull away I am dizzy and slightly sick. I sit on the bed, kick off my shoes and breathe heavily, the liquid inside swishing like a spirit level. And then he pushes me back, one big hand on my chest, and my head meets the pillow with a soft thud.

I do not pretend to be asleep. My eyes are misty but wide as he mounts the bed, the elastic of his pants snapping as he wrestles them down. When he climbs on top of me, fluid and acid rise in my throat, and I wonder how angry he would be if

I threw up in his face. I focus on forming my stomach muscles into an iron cage, locking in the liquid that wants to escape. When he claws at my barely-there underwear, I move to pull it back into place. I move to curl onto my side. I move to press my legs together. His hand takes my wrist, clasping so tightly I can feel the tissue tenderise. In that moment, I am made of memory foam: the vice of his fingers will leave me patterned with grooves. When I look at his face it is contorted with urgency, like the face of a hungry baby. *Can you just stop moving,* he wants to say. *I am busy. I am otherwise engaged.* And I know that his hand, too tight around my wrist, and his plans, too sharp inside my body, are not meant to cause me pain. My wriggly, inelegant aliveness is an irritant, in the way of what he needs me to be. He wants me to be silent and pliable. My underwear is around my thighs and my back is flush with the mattress and his knee has forced my legs apart. I am silent and pliable.

I could go back up to the ceiling: remove myself from the brutal, messy inelegance of the bed and become an observer. But I worry that if I leave my body now I might never return. I feel strongly that, if I am to stay alive, I must stay here. And so I stay, teeth clenched so tight my head pounds with pain, drunkface burning against the cool pillow, and with every sigh of the mattress and thump of the headboard I think this will be the moment, this will be the one, this will be the time I am ripped in half. The movement feels like the slam of a car door, or the impact of a body flung against a wall. His face is twisted and puce, his hair slicked back with sweat, his breath coming with grunts and spit.

Afterwards, I sit on the toilet, naked. I feel fat. The skin on my wrists and neck and the insides of my thighs is tender, ready to bloom into purple-blue bruises come morning. Veins sprawl like ugly webbing underneath my surface, and I am raw and meaty and horribly ugly. My insides have been sanded away. When I stand under the shower, the water rushing down the drain is pink. I put on clean underwear and long-sleeved pyjamas while my body is still wet. The material sticks to me, adhering to every bump and curve. I sit back on the toilet seat and tug the top over my knees, stretching the fabric until it hangs like a sheet.

When I climb back into bed, his arm finds me and brings me to him, and I make the decision to let him comfort me. I am sore and scared, and I need comfort, and there is no one else but him. In the past I would always have let him comfort me, and I do not want to believe that what happened tonight has cleft my life into 'before' and 'after' with such finality. I let him comfort me because I didn't say no. If I had said no, it would have changed everything and nothing. The scene unfolding on the bed – my body, unfolded on the bed – would have been identical, except that it would have been loaded with layer upon layer of dark, scary meaning. And I am scared of that dark.

We lie, entangled, my chin tucked underneath his head, his full, hard arm muscles tight against my back. The fug of sex and alcohol hangs in the air and between the fibres of my clothes, and the great, greedy evil crouched in the corner casts its shadow over us like a shroud.

I didn't say no. But I didn't say yes.

---

*So, the defendant subjected you to non-consensual sex on multiple occasions. Indeed, he believed sex to be his right, regardless of your willingness.*

**Yes. That's exactly how he thought of it.**

*If someone doesn't consent to sex, does that make it rape?*

**I'm not sure.**

*Rape is rape, Holly. If someone doesn't consent to sex, then it's rape, isn't it?*

Yes. Rape is rape.

*And rape is a crime, isn't it?*

Yes.

*And, if you are the victim of a crime, what should you do?*

It's not always that simple.

*Non-consensual sex is rape, isn't it? Rape is a crime, isn't it? Crimes should be reported.*

But you know I didn't—

*You didn't report multiple crimes to the police, did you, Holly? You didn't report any crimes, did you?*

No.

*Why not?*

I don't know.

*Perhaps there <u>were</u> no crimes. Did you and the defendant have sexual relations on a number of occasions? Yes. Did you explicitly withhold your consent on any of those occasions? No.*

I didn't want to do it. He must have known I didn't want to do it.

*Is the defendant a mind reader, Holly?*

No, but—

*Your friend Danielle Woods …*

What? Why are you talking about her?

*How would you describe your relationship with Danielle Woods, Holly?*

She's a friend.

*How would you describe the defendant's relationship with Danielle Woods, Holly?*

They're friends too.

*That's not what you said to your friend Amber, is it, Holly? On the night of the 15th of December, at the party you attended with the defendant?*

I was really drunk.

*'He's been flirting with Danielle Woods all fucking evening.' You said that, didn't you?*

I might have. I was drunk.

*You felt threatened by Danielle Woods, didn't you?*

It wasn't like that.

*You felt threatened by Danielle Woods, and angry with the defendant for 'flirting with her'. You decided to get your own back, didn't you Holly? You decided to cry rape.*

I didn't. I know that's how it might look, but I didn't.

*But an isolated incident wasn't enough, was it Holly? No, that would seem too random – too hard to fathom. Who's honestly going to believe that a devoted, loving boyfriend can turn into a repugnant sexual predator in the space of a single evening? You needed to flesh out your story, didn't you, Holly? Provide some background, invent some previous …*

Is that how it looks? Is that really how it looks?

*Yes, Holly. That's exactly how it looks. And yet, despite all your careful planning, your story still doesn't add up. Because, if this man were really so monstrous, why did it take so long for you to become upset by the monstrosity? Why did this alleged rape 'destroy your life beyond repair' when the other alleged rapes had had no apparent effect?*

They did have an effect. It all had an effect.

*Your story doesn't fit, Holly. You're lying.*

It was insidious. It would have been easier if it had been cut and dried, but it wasn't. When it started, I could convince myself it was normal for him to do stuff I didn't want to do. He made me think that was just how sex worked when you were at that point in a relationship. I thought it was normal for me to have to do it even when I didn't want to. He's a man, I'm a woman. I thought that was how it worked. But then, this time, the time after the party … It was different. Everything about it was different. I felt like my body got torn up. It was nothing like the other times.

*So the previous incidents were just 'sort-of' rape, were they? 'Grey area' rape? 'Not-really-rape' but also 'not-really-not-rape'?*

Perhaps in a way—

*Rape is rape, Holly. You said so yourself.*

That's why all this happened. It happened because I didn't do the things I was supposed to do.

---

*Can you remind us of the date of the alleged assault, Holly?*

It was the 15th of December 2017.

*Thank you. And would it be fair to say that, after the assault, you were … upset? Distraught? Terrified? Traumatised?*

Yes. All those things.

*And your feelings towards the defendant? You must have been frightened of him?*

Yes. I felt frightened.

*You must have wanted to get as far away as possible, as quickly as possible. Is that right, Holly?*

Yes. I did.

*Thank you. What's this, Holly?*

It's something I've signed. I signed for a parcel.

*That is definitely your signature, is it, Holly?*

Yes.

*And whose address is that, Holly?*

My old address. The flat. Where I used to live.

*It's the flat where you used to live with the defendant, isn't it, Holly?*

Yes.

*The same flat where the alleged assault took place?*

Yes.

*What's the date on the card?*

The 21st of December.

*And the year?*

**2017.**

*So you were at the flat that day – almost a full week after the assault took place?*

**Yes.**

*So you were … what – collecting some clothes? Dropping off your key?*

**No.**

*What were you doing there, Holly?*

**I was still living there.**

*You were still living there? Still living in the flat from which you say you wanted to get as far away as possible, as soon as possible?*

**I was … I was very confused …**

*Could you tell me what this is, Holly?*

**It's like … property details.**

*Details for which property, Holly?*

**The flat. The same flat.**

*Could you read the highlighted line, Holly?*

**'Charming, characterful one-bedroom flat located—'**

*Sorry, did you say 'one bedroom'?*

**Yes.**

*And is that true? The flat has just the one bedroom?*

Yes.

*And that would be – what – a twin room? Two single beds? A single bed and a sofa bed?*

It's a double room.

*Oh. But we've already established that you stayed in the flat for a full week following the alleged assault, haven't we?*

Yes.

*So where did you sleep during that time?*

In the bed.

*Oh. I see. So the defendant slept … On the sofa? In the lounge? In the bathroom?*

He slept in the bed too. We slept together.

*You slept together? You continued to share your bed with a 'rapist'?*

Yes.

*Why on earth would you have done that?*

Because there was only one bed. And I had nowhere else to go.

That's why all this happened. It happened because I didn't think the way I should have thought.

---

In the flat there is only one bed, and I have nowhere else to go, and my brain is so liquid that I cannot see past these two absolutes. I can't leave or start sleeping on the sofa. I can't ask him to leave. He is so much bigger than me. He could kill me.

If I leave, he will find me. I cannot leave for the same reason I couldn't say no. I am too frightened.

For a week I am hot and dizzy with fever. My face is clammy. My head pounds. I feel as if nothing in the world is real. Outside, in the street, Christmas lights illuminate shop fronts and their winking seems snide. I want to rip them down. *It shouldn't be Christmas. Who is letting Christmas happen?*

When he is at work, I sleep in fitful bursts of minutes, crying when I feel his weight crush me flat. I open my eyes and he is not there: I am covered with a blanket, not a body, and the breath rasping in my ears is my own. At night, I stay awake, alert as a prey animal. If his fingers brush against me in even the smallest, sleeping touch, bile rises and white noise roars. I sit in the bathroom, resting my face against the cool, tiled wall. I want to run away or sleep forever. *But it has only been a week. It will get better.*

I need to go to the doctor. I need to go to a refuge. I need to go to a different country. I have nowhere to go. The fever has abated, but I do not return to work. I rake my hands through my hair and it comes away in thick, dry clumps. I cannot eat; I can barely swallow. I sit in the same position for hours, bug-eyed, staring without seeing as the horror film plays on a loop in my head. I want to pour bleach on myself; scrub my skin from head to toe; take huge, quenching swigs of disinfectant. *I feel dirty, I feel dirty, I am dirty.*

They must know I am dirty when I go to the clinic, because they cover the bed in fresh white paper before I sit down. *They don't do that for anyone else. Only for me. I am a contaminant.* The nurse in the pale blue tunic tells me her name is Sandra. I tell her my name is Sadie. I choke out words that prickle my tongue and hang in the air like fumes. I tell her I am scared I could be pregnant. I feel like a robot. Sandra asks many questions and I give few answers. She is polite but bored. Sweat pools at the creases of my knees, sticking me to the bed-paper. Suddenly, I am lying down, legs splayed inelegantly, but I don't remember moving. Sandra approaches me with a fistful of lethal-looking swabs, and tells me to relax. *That's what he used to say. That's what he used to say. That's what he used to say.* I find a scrap of voice, lodged behind a wisdom tooth, and make a strangled sound. Sandra puts her hand on my shoulder. I twist my head and vomit onto the lino flooring. *But it has only been a month. It will get better.*

Instagram tells me he is on holiday in Mauritius. He looks smooth and strong and unworried. I feel screwed up and chewed up and spat out like gristle. There is not a waking moment when I am not thinking about it – but 'thinking' is the wrong word. You *think* about what to cook for dinner, or how to travel to work, or what to buy your friend for their birthday. I am not *thinking* it. I am *living* it. In the outside world there could be rainbows or thunderstorms or weddings or funerals or national disasters or an apocalypse, but inside there is only rape.

I see it. There is a blank, white projector screen filling my field of vision, and on the screen I am brutalised again and again in high definition, high resolution, colours and noises saturated and amplified and exaggerated until they feel too big for my irises to contain and I am sure my eyes will explode. I see odd things: the books on the bookcase, whose spines I teased from the darkness and whose titles I repeated like defunct talismans while it happened. I see the overflowing washing basket crouched in the corner, and remember that I thought about the washing, that I must do the washing, that it was good that I'd not yet done the washing because that meant the next day I could put these clothes in the washing and get them clean. I see the small patch of damp I noticed, crouched in the corner of the ceiling, and I feel damp inside.

When the images rise to a crescendo, I taste them. Food turns mealy: instead, I taste his breathy gasps; the salt of his moon-illuminated skin; the blood that filled my mouth when I clamped teeth to tongue to keep me in my body. I can taste the salty sweat that prickled when I licked my lip. I can taste the sour bile that rose in my throat. At the back of my throat, where the pipes join up, I can smell it. Fear and greed and alcohol. Sex smells biological, but rape smells chemical.

I can hear it, no matter how much noise there is around me. The inside-sounds are not loud, but they are insidious. It's like how, even if you can barely hear someone speaking, you can still hear the sibilance. Outside-sounds are soft and gentle and watery; inside-sounds cut through them like a razor. There is a rhythm to the sounds: creak-slap-grunt-pant. Squeak-rustle-growl-groan. Ugly, messy body-sounds. Air hooked in and puffed out in snorts and sighs.

Perhaps I could manage the seeing and tasting and smelling and hearing, but I feel it, too. The pain is paralyzing, as if a lit cigarette were being held to my skin, scorching new holes in me. I can feel his hands on my wrists and his breath on my face and I feel horribly, terribly full as my body relives the horrible, terrible night. *But it has only been a few months. It will get better.*

LinkedIn tells me he has a new job. His employment profile is solid and impressive. I am paper-thin, and my employment profile has a hole that gapes wider by the day. I can't go to work. I can't even get to the bus stop. Every man whose eye I catch is an attacker, a rapist, a predator. The imagined assaults feel viscerally real. *Did I walk down the street unharmed? Or was I grabbed from behind, forced up against a brick wall and violated? Which is real?* Entering a lift with a man is a nonstarter – who would hear my screams? Sleep is impossible: when I close my eyes I am back there, silent and pliable, the desecration playing out garishly behind my lids. I wake from nightmares soaked in a grisly mixture of sweat, tears and urine, my body shaking like a forest of leaves. Sometimes, I cannot close my eyes at all, unable to tolerate the images projected onto the backs of my lids. Even the split-second of blindness before I sneeze sends me into dizzy panic. I shower ten times a day, scrubbing myself red-raw and still feeling so dirty I expect the towel to be streaked with grime when I scrape it across my skin. For long periods I float up and look down on myself from the ceiling. I am not her any more. I am not in that body.

Sometimes when I open my eyes, offcuts of nightmare still bouncing around my skull, I cannot move. I cannot make my frightened soul re-enter the body that is home to so much hurt. I coach myself through tiny, fractional movements – flexes of fingers, wriggles of toes. It can last for hours: the juddering, halting coming-to, dipping one toe into the water of embodiment then scurrying away, scared of falling in. I can usually get to the bathroom by late morning, the kitchen by early afternoon. By evening, I might have drunk a hot drink, and been thawed around the edges. And then it will be time for sleep again, and time for another nightmare. If I manage to speak, I cannot be sure how it will sound. It is like there is a time delay between the making of words in my mouth and the hearing of them in my ears. I am off-kilter, uncalibrated. I sound drunk or deaf. *But it has only been a year. It will get better.*

Twitter tells me he has lots of opinions about Brexit. His jokes are relaxed and confident. I am tense and timorous. Do you remember how it felt when you were little, and you went downstairs in the middle of the night, and you finished your cup of cold water and the darkness made familiar shapes evil? And you knew the looming shadows were cast by the table and the ironing board and the branches outside the window, but the darkness latched onto your fear, making it bigger and bigger until the stretched membrane burst and the fear was everywhere, clutching at your lungs, pummelling your stomach, and you ran up to bed certain that, at any moment, claws would clasp your ankles and drag you down to somewhere deep and black? That blood-bashing, heart pounding terror is my steady state. Like a faulty car alarm, I descend into panic with each tap from a falling leaf and brush from a gust of wind. My arms and legs go plastic. The bangs in my chest are so big they hurt me, and the air can't get into or out of my mouth. There is never enough oxygen. The banging never goes away. I am *always frightened*.

When life looked like this just one or two months after it happened, I thought it would get better. I thought it was impossible to exist in this state for longer than a few weeks. But I was wrong.

I was raped two years ago, and yesterday, when I was choosing pasta in the supermarket, I felt him inside me. It was the second time that day, and the seventh time that week. On Monday, I was in the pub with a friend, and we were sitting opposite a blank, white wall, and I watched my brutalisation unfold like a film on the empty plaster. Last week, I was ordering coffee in a café, and I heard a voice that sounded like his, and it was happening again, and I ran.

Facebook tells me he has a new girlfriend. In the picture, she presses her lips to his cheek, and I feel the stubble against my own mouth. He has a new girlfriend. He has a new victim. I look at the numbers on the screen of my phone, and imagine dialling emergency services. *I should want to Speak Up. I should want to Speak Out. I should want to make sure this never happens to anyone else.*

I press the button on the top of my phone and the screen goes black. I don't want this to happen to anyone else. But more than that, I want it not to have happened to me.

---

*But you loved him, didn't you? The defendant. Did you love him?*

**Maybe. Probably. In a sort of way.**

*Can you tell me what this is, Holly?*

**It's a print-out. Of text messages.**

*Do you recognise those text messages?*

**Yes.**

*Who are they from?*

**Me.**

*And who are they to?*

**Him.**

*Could you read the first message out loud?*

**'I am so lucky to have met you. I love you so much it makes me crazy.'**

*Could you read the second message?*

**'Last night was amazing. Thank you for being wonderful. I love you so much.'**

*'Last night was amazing.' That's what you wrote in the message sent on the 8th of June 2016 at 10.24am. What were you referring to? What had happened on the night of the 7th of June 2016? What had been 'amazing'?*

**I don't want to say.**

*Had you watched an amazing film? Been to an amazing restaurant? Had an amazing night's sleep?*

**We had sex.**

*I see. You had sex. Sex that was 'amazing'. Is that right, Holly?*

**Yes.**

*Did you say 'no' to that 'amazing' sex?*

**No.**

*Had you said no to sex before that?*

**No.**

*Had you initiated sex before that?*

**Probably.**

*Who initiated sex that night, Holly? The night of the 'amazing sex'? Who initiated sex that night?*

**I can't remember.**

*Well, it was a long time ago. Let's try a more recent date ... Say, the night of the 15th of December 2017. Who initiated sex that night? The night the alleged assault took place?*

**I don't think ...**

*Who initiated sex that night, Holly?*

**I kissed him. I only kissed him.**

*So you initiated sex that night? The night you claim you were raped?*

**I just kissed him. I'd had a lot to drink.**

*You certainly had. A huge amount to drink.*

**We'd been to a party. We'd both been drinking.**

*I imagine with that much alcohol on board it must have been quite difficult to stay 'with it'?*

I was drunk. I wasn't unconscious.

*What did you wear to the party, Holly?*

Sorry?

*What were you wearing? The night of the party and the alleged assault?*

Erm ... A dress. A blue dress. It was ... It was kind of silky ... It had—

*What dress size are you, Holly?*

About a size twelve. Sometimes a fourteen. Usually a twelve.

*What size was the dress you wore to the party, Holly?*

Ten.

*Did you make a mistake when purchasing the dress? Pick up the wrong size by accident? Did you try to return it?*

No.

*No. You intentionally bought a dress at least one – if not two – sizes too small. Why did you do that, Holly?*

I just ... I think I ...

*The dress was very tight, wasn't it? Left nothing to the imagination. And that was your aim, wasn't it? You deliberately dressed provocatively, in too-tight clothing, in order to be sexually appealing to the defendant on the night of the party.*

It wasn't like that.

*Where did the dress come down to, Holly?*

What do you mean?

*Was it knee-length? Ankle-length?*

It was shorter than that.

*Oh. So, just above the knee, was it?*

It was quite short.

*Did you feel self-conscious in your short dress, Holly?*

A bit. Like you said, it was quite short and tight.

*So I imagine you behaved with a certain modesty at the party, didn't you? Made sure there was no reason for you to unnecessarily expose yourself?*

I didn't really think about that.

*No. You didn't. In fact, you behaved provocatively, repeatedly moving in such a way that your body was exposed to male guests, and, in particular, the defendant?*

I didn't mean to do that.

*Some might say you were as good as inviting the defendant into bed with you then and there. Do you think that's fair, Holly?*

I never wanted this to happen.

*Holly, you've said that when the defendant began to remove your underwear, you felt 'so frightened of what he would do you were nearly sick'. Is that right?*

Yes. Yes, that's right.

*You feared for your wellbeing – perhaps even for your life. Is that right?*

Yes. Yes, I did.

*You would have done anything to stop the defendant from doing, in your words, 'what I knew he wanted to do'. Isn't that right?*

**Yes.**

*Did you say no?*

**What?**

*When it became clear that the defendant wanted to have sex, did you say no?*

**I ...**

*You wore an intentionally provocative outfit. You behaved in an intentionally provocative manner. You drank so much you could barely function. You deliberately aroused the partner with whom you had repeatedly initiated sex in the past. The partner you loved 'so much it made you crazy'. And then – according to your story – you suddenly decided that you were not, in fact, a willing party, but a potential victim of assault. You feared for your safety. You would have done anything to prevent the attack from happening.*

**I ...**

*Did you say no, Holly?*

**I didn't say yes.**

That's why all this happened. It happened because I didn't say no.

———

The grass in the middle of the estate hasn't been cut or watered all summer. Perhaps it has never been cut or watered. It is turning to scrub: brown and sparse. In between the stretches of brittle blades, there are patches of dry earth, caramel-coloured and laced with cracks. Outside number fourteen, toddler toys are strewn underneath the tree – blocks and bricks and a pram with three wheels and a grubby pink trike. Sadie never moved out. We kept in touch, on and off, talking without hearing each other's voices. She was about to move into the city centre to do a fashion course, but plans change. It turned out I wasn't pregnant, when I went to the clinic pretending to be Sadie, but the real Sadie was. While I was cowering from Sandra's swabs, the real Sadie was holding her real baby in the crook of her arm, like she used to hold Baby Annabelle on lazy summer evenings. Sadie's Mum says she wishes Sadie had had a chance to see the world. I wish I hadn't.

Dad comes out to the step, a bottle of beer in each hand. He gives one to me, and I put it down on the concrete paving. Dad doesn't know I don't drink any more. Dad doesn't know I am not me any more. He swigs deeply, and I wonder whether he always drank so much, and smoked so much, and, if so, why I never noticed before. I wonder why I never noticed how small the estate was, or how dirty our toys were, or how Dad was a broken man, trying to patch up a motherless girl and boy with all the sweets we could eat and all the television we could watch. It's so quiet here without the beautiful, mysterious pulse of Aisha's music, and I wonder what happened to Aisha. Aisha went out into the world, like me. I hope she didn't get hurt.

Dad tells me that the fish and chip shop down the road has been replaced with a Thai takeaway. He tells me that our old dustbins have been replaced with wheelie bins. He doesn't ask why his daughter has been replaced with a grey shadow. I want to curl up in his words. They are so warm and so safe and so good.

Dad should have been the most influential figure in my life. He was the one who packed my lunches and cooked my dinners and took me swimming on Saturdays and washed the Ribena out of my T-shirts. But the most influential figure in my life was the man who raped me. The person he was and the things he did have altered me more profoundly than anything that went before and anything that has come since. I am a different person now. And I search and I search for a silver lining, but I can't find one. I look for what he has given me, and I find only what he took.

When I came home, a week ago now, it was the first time I had been back to the estate in years. Dad looked at the grey of my face and asked, 'What happened, Hol?'

'I grew up,' I said. I didn't grow up. I hunched down. I shrank in. I twisted on myself, turning from the world like a photophobic plant turns from light. I will leave the estate in a few days. I can't be here. I can't be in a place where things were once so warm and safe and good.

Dad lights a cigarette, and smoke bloats around us like a shroud.

'Do you need any money?'

'Yeah.'

'OK. I can do that.'

'Thanks.'

'Can I do anything else?'

'No. I don't think so.'

'OK. Have you got a plan?'

'I think I'm going to move to the seaside.'

I like the idea of living where the air is fresh and cold. I think that is where I will knit myself back together.

'OK. By yourself?'

'Yeah. By myself.'

It is always 'by myself' now, Dad. I am always by myself. There was someone, a few months ago – a soft, harmless boy with soft, red-brown hair – but I had to stay awake all night to watch him. Once, deep in sleep, his hand brushed across me and I started so violently I fell out of bed. I ended it the next day. The truth is, there is no one who can heal the wounds my rapist inflicted – and no one who can fill the gap he left. When I was raped, I gained swathes of fear and paranoia, but I lost, too. I lost someone I had loved with a deep, breathless love. Please don't ask me how or why. It didn't make sense. I just loved him, Dad.

We met up, you know. I'm mad, aren't I? But I missed him. He took everything from me, and I missed me, too. Perhaps I thought if I saw him he might give me some of myself back. He was smaller than I remembered, sitting on the sofa in the corner of the dingy coffee shop. There were people all around. He was gangly. I always thought he was strong. He *was* strong. I remember the muscles, swelling against my back. He wasn't a monster, Dad – was he? In my head he had been a monster, but then suddenly he was just a person. He was small.

I wish I had only known him as a rapist, but I knew him as a person, too. He took me to Brighton for my birthday. He bought me a St Christopher charm, suspended from a silver chain. He said it would protect me, and he never told me that I would need protection from the hands that fastened it – snap – at the back of my neck. He made me love him so much that I lost track of where reluctance became resistance, where yes became no. He eroded me in small, simple ways.

We didn't say much when we met, though I had planned so many words. I wanted to tell him that I had started a master's course and had to drop out because exams make me anxious and, since he did what he did, when I get anxious I dissociate. I walked into the first exam, uncapped my pen and watched it, suspended from limp, unmoving fingers. It took half an hour to will enough strength into my body to walk out. I didn't want to be raped again, sitting there, frenetic scribbling all around me, but the anxiety would have sent me straight back to that place. It always does. Before we met up, it had felt so important for me to tell him that it was the perfect course – the perfect degree, the perfect university – and that I couldn't do it because of him, and that that made me angrier than anything. But when I looked at him, coiled and defensive, the anger leeched out through the soles of my feet. I felt tired. I felt sad. We drank our coffees and spoke in short, tight words. Outside the café, he patted me on the back and I flinched, and he rolled his eyes.

I wish I was angry. I wish I hadn't wanted to meet him. I don't still love him, Dad – how could I? But I don't hate him. Somehow I can't. I'm sorry, Dad. At every point, at every turn, I have not been who I should have been.

A car drives past, spilling low, foreign music, and Dad rubs a hand across the prickles of his beard.

'You know I love you, don't you, Hol?'

I know it.

'Yes.'

When I live by the seaside, I will live alone. I will find a job that is the same every day – as a waitress or receptionist or cashier – and I will make enough money to keep a small room warm and a small appetite sated. I will walk a lot, every day, on the beach, and I will breathe cold, clean salt into my lungs until they press against my ribs like balloons. Life will be duller than it has ever been before, and more solitary than it has ever been before, and purer than it has ever been before, and when I open my curtains in the morning I will see the sea. Perhaps that will be my silver lining. Perhaps it will get better.

'But it's basically just a nasty memory, isn't it? We all have nasty memories. It shouldn't take that long to forget it.'

## Post-Traumatic WHAT Disorder?! Your Guide to Kicking This Pesky Problem to the Kerb Double Quick!

### *Stage One: Immediately Following The Trauma*

OK, OK, so something bad has happened. If you're reading this guide, it was probably something Really Bad – something that made you feel you were at risk of death or serious injury, an experience that was prolonged and inescapable, etc. We're gonna call it The Trauma, and yep, we get it. It was Really Bad. Cry me a river. Dry those tears and pull yourself together. We're *recovering* here!

Straight after it happens, you're probably going to be pretty down. You'd better get used to the feeling of sand coating the insides of your eyelids, because you're not going to be sleeping much. You should probably cancel any upcoming engagements, because people are not going to want to spend time with you for a while. You are going to be a *zombie*. You might become unwashed, unfed, unkempt – but it hardly matters, as you'll be spending very little time in your body for the moment. Most days, you'll float above yourself, wondering how the rest of the world is so busy and buzzy and blooming when you have shrivelled and shrunk. Most days, you will be a ghost. It's all good! We're *recovering!*

Nightmares? You'll have nightmares so vivid you'll wake yourself with screams and sweat. Flashbacks? You'll relive The Trauma multiple times a day, multiple times a night. Sometimes there will be triggers – sounds or smells or sights that send you hurtling back in time – but sometimes the flashbacks will come from nowhere. And when they come, you'll need to escape whatever situation you're in pronto, because you will be *back there*.

You will be right back in The Trauma, and there will be nothing you can do to escape. Don't sweat it! Others have it much worse, right?

Have you ever boarded a theme park ride, and ascended to its peak in your rickety cart, and then realised on the whooshing descent that you didn't want to be on the ride after all? There's nothing you can do, is there? You're in it, and it's whirling and clanking, and the bile is rising in your throat and you cannot get off. That's Stage One. Get used to it. Stop *fussing*.

### Stage Two: 1–2 Months Post-Trauma

Congratulations! You've survived Stage One. Good news: from here on in, things are going to get a whole lot easier!

Remember that Really Bad thing that happened the other month? The Trauma? Doesn't seem so bad any more, does it? Too *right* it doesn't! We're *recovering* here! Sure, it has occupied your every waking, sleeping and in-between moment for the past 4–8 weeks, but any day now you're going to find it receding into the background. Sure, sure, it was a Really Big, Bad Thing and you probably feel that life can never be the same after such a Really Big, Bad Thing. Well, you're wrong. Get with the programme.

You know those self-indulgent symptoms you were experiencing? The nightmares, the flashbacks, the memories that gripped your body as well as your mind? They were permissible in Stage One, but now's the time to shake them off. Remember, The Trauma happened a while ago, and you've got to get back on your feet. Feeling sorry for yourself just ain't gonna cut it any more!

OK, yes, you're probably going to have some residual 'experiences' at this stage. There might be days when you feel you cannot push The Trauma from your mind. You might be finding it hard to leave the house, convinced that everyone and everything is out to get you. You might be scared in a way you weren't scared before: patently aware of your own fragility. But let's get one thing straight:

The Trauma was *a long time ago* now. It's time to pull up your socks, tie back your hair and *move on*.

### Stage Three: 3–6 Months Post-Trauma

At this stage, The Trauma should really be little more than a memory. It happened *months ago!* It's in *the past!* If you find yourself experiencing symptoms from Stages One or Two, it's time to implement some tough love. Why *the hell* are you still letting this affect you? Why are you still allowing yourself to be controlled by this?

You're probably coming up with all sorts of reasons as to why your continued struggles are *perfectly acceptable*.

'It was the worst thing that has ever happened to me – it was the single most significant experience of my life.'

'It changed my entire view of the world. I have had to recalibrate every belief I held about people's motives, intentions and powers.'

'I'm not the person I was before it happened. It changed me. How can I go back to being who I was before when I *am no longer who I was before?*'

*Wake up.* That's not how it works. Experiences don't hold that kind of power – *you* are the one in the driver's seat! It doesn't matter how scared or shocked or appalled you were. It doesn't matter that you're surrounded by reminders of The Trauma that make it impossible to forget. It doesn't matter that your world was tipped sideways the day you opened that door or walked into that room or started up that car. It's been *ages*. You should be *over it*.

### Stage Four: 6–12 Months Post-Trauma

Hoorah! Excellent news! Your programme is complete, and you are fully recovered! *Great work!*

232

At this stage, there should be no noticeable difference between your current and pre-Trauma lives (though feel free to consider yourself older and wiser – that one's on us!). Your memory of The Trauma can now sit comfortably alongside its fellows in the memory bank – perhaps next to a recollection of your graduation, or a childhood trip to the circus? Put it somewhere nice and cosy, make it feel at home – that memory holds no power over you any more!

Remember how you once thought you had been changed irreversibly by The Trauma?! Isn't that *funny*?! Don't blame yourself – after something Really Bad happens you're all at sixes and sevens, and you find yourself thinking some crazy things! You might have thought that The Trauma would affect you for *years*, assaulting you with thoughts, feelings and sensations as vicious as the assaults of the original event! You might have thought The Trauma would alter your course in life, preventing you from making trips, or taking exams, or getting a job! You might *even* have thought that The Trauma would have a lasting effect on your ability to form relationships! Weren't you *silly?* Weren't you *quaint?* All you needed was to pull yourself together and let time work its magic, eh? Sure, it affected you pretty badly in the immediate aftermath, but just look at you now, less than a year later! You're *right as rain!* You're *over* it!

'That's the thing. It's not just a nasty memory
I can forget. It's not like that at all.'

Most mental illnesses develop incrementally, squeezing tighter over months or years; post-traumatic stress disorder (PTSD) can enter a life in a moment, and cleave it irreversibly into 'before' and 'after'. In some cases the trauma is prolonged and repeated – years of childhood abuse, recurrent exposure to horrifying situations as a member of the emergency or armed forces. In others, a single incident beds in and breeds destruction on an epic scale. 'Trauma' can last for less than an hour; the defining, most intense traumatic 'moment' can last for less than a minute. PTSD can last a lifetime.

My conversations with PTSD sufferers felt subtly different to other interviews. I could not ask: 'Can you tell me about the development of your PTSD?' in the same way I could explore the spiralling of depression or anxiety. That is not to say that PTSD does not 'develop': like all mental illnesses, it takes its course, and that course is characterised by periodic deteriorations and improvements, but, in most cases, at the heart of the disorder is a single incident of horrific assault, attack or accident. This is one of the particular cruelties of PTSD: its development is swift and brutal.

The other cruelty of PTSD lies in its dependence upon other people. PTSD is unique in the level of agency held by those outside the sufferer. Not every case is clear cut: the PTSD that develops following, say, national disaster is not precipitated by any one individual, but in Holly's case and many others there is an attacker. The difference between naturally contracting seasonal flu and being intentionally injected with the virus is the malicious intent of the latter scenario: Holly was *given* PTSD. There is a unique depravity in an incident from which the powerless emerge debilitated, while the powerful walk unscathed.

Of course, Holly's story captures just one of the incidents that can give rise to PTSD. The disorder can stem from any experience perceived by the victim as serious or life-threatening:

military service is renowned, but many develop the condition in response to experiencing – or witnessing – road accidents or physical assaults. In choosing which 'trigger' to depict through Holly, I was entirely guided by the experiences of my interviewees: although not all PTSD sufferers I spoke to had experienced sexual violence, the majority had.

The prevalence of sexual assault among my interviewees was surprising and saddening. It is an evil that ties together women of all ages, all colours, all backgrounds – and it is one that is growing. In 2016–17, Rape Crisis centres in England and Wales responded to their highest ever number of helpline calls in a single year: nearly 4,000 a week.[22] Ninety-three per cent of service users were female, and 36 per cent were aged 25 or younger. Although this may partially reflect an increasing awareness of what constitutes appropriate vs. inappropriate sexual behaviour, the extent of the increase in those accessing specialist Rape Crisis services (29 per cent above the same period in 2015–16) suggests a serious and growing problem.

Interestingly, discussions of sexual abuse arose throughout my conversations with interviewees, not just in those conversations with PTSD sufferers: the experience was tucked into the pasts of a huge number of women. There was no perfect correlation between the severity of their experiences and developing PTSD, nor did developing PTSD signal a 'weakness' of character. Different people were affected by similar experiences in different ways. Before this project, I naively envisaged the relationship between trauma and PTSD as a push-button – 'If you experience trauma *this* severe, you will *always* develop PTSD.' It is not so. In Holly's case, the water is further muddied by the repetitive, cumulative nature of 'attacks', as is so common in domestic violence. Why should one incident trigger a post-traumatic stress response when previous, similar incidents did not? Do experiences accumulate, eroding the ability to cope, or is each incident tackled afresh? If one experience does not result in full-blown disorder, is a 'traumatised' response to an equivalent experience invalidated? These were among the questions my interviewees asked themselves.

In Holly's story, I wanted to capture the conflicting feelings many of my interviewees reported about the abuse they had experienced. The 'courtroom' scenes take place in Holly's mind, between the parts of her that are 'victim' and 'abuser', but they can also be taken as a nightmarish imagining of the persecution she fears she would face if she pursued legal action against her attacker. Among many of my interviewees, there was a feeling that, unless they had been the 'perfect victim', they had no right to seek justice. What would the 'perfect victim' look like? When discussing sexual assault *in general*, women knew all the right answers: that it doesn't matter what she was wearing, or how much she'd had to drink, or whether she knew her attacker, or whether she 'led him on'. It doesn't matter where the attack happened, or what she did afterwards, or how loudly, insistently or decidedly she resisted sex. Lack of consent is lack of consent; assault is assault; rape is rape. But, when probed as to their feelings about their *own* attacks, women turned on themselves, hurling judgements they would not dream of making about others. Again and again, I heard:

'I kissed him first. I wanted him to like me. I shouldn't have done that.'

'He was my boyfriend. It would have been different if he had been a stranger. But we had slept together lots of times before. We were together.'

'I was dressed really provocatively. I was behaving really provocatively.'

'I didn't report it straight away. I should have reported it straight away. If it was really that bad I would have reported it straight away.'

'I didn't say "no" properly. He might have thought I wanted it. It was my fault.'

*It was my fault.* As we see in Holly's internal courtroom, sexual violence victims are often their own judge, jury and executioner, punishing themselves for being scared, for being vulnerable, for being female. When women do bring rape and sexual assault claims to court, there are certain safeguards in the legal system; for example Section 41 of the 1999 Youth Justice and Criminal Evidence Act restricts the circumstances in which evidence relating to a complainant's sexual history can be revealed. But, for the majority of my interviewees, the costs of officially reporting their assaults were deemed greater than the benefits. They were afraid of attackers, who, in many cases, knew their whereabouts and were unlikely to be held in police custody following allegations. Their abusers were part of their social circle, and they feared the havoc that might be wrought if they spoke up. They knew that police questioning could be a traumatic experience in and of itself, and that the chances of the case being taken to court were minimal; the chances of conviction even smaller. They did not have enough angry energy to see the process through. They feared a 'he said/she said' stalemate.

Holly's PTSD stems from a collection of discrete moments, likely summing to less than an hour in total; the resulting disorder encroaches on every inch of her life for weeks and months and years. Fundamentally an anxiety disorder, Holly's PTSD shares many symptoms with Freya's generalised anxiety: the perception of a suffocating lack of safety; the exhausting excess of adrenaline; the dense, close fear. I was also struck by the vividness of the world PTSD sufferers occupy – flashbacks, bodily memories and nightmares mean that trauma is not locked into the past, but mingles with the present, constantly making itself known. It is for this reason that the concept of being able to 'get over' PTSD within a matter of months is so ludicrous: how can one recover from something that, according to the mind, is still being lived?

Many of my interviewees reported dissociation – both during the original trauma and as a post-traumatic reaction. They described floating above their bodies, feeling a haunting absence of pain or distress. Some subjects credited this dissociation with their very survival, feeling that, had they 'truly experienced' the trauma, they might not have lived through it. Others felt that, had they been more fully dissociated during trauma, they might not have developed PTSD (there was a powerful sense that, when dissociated, one does not 'really feel' or does not feel 'as strongly'). However, *post*-traumatic dissociation was rarely experienced as protective: sufferers felt wrenched from their bodies, despite wanting to remain connected. As Holly describes, dissociation is an overly sensitive alarm: during trauma, it removes the victim's mind from danger; afterwards, it is triggered by innocuous events, barricading the sufferer in a box of silence. It is a crazed, overly assiduous effort to keep the psyche safe, but it leaves chaos in its wake. I spoke to women whose lives had been jolted off course by dissociation: how can one hold conversations, or attend job interviews, or take exams when one is 'not there'?

The derailment that results from severe PTSD is profound, and came across strongly in my interviews. Although they were, almost unanimously, devoid of resentment or self-pity, many sufferers found themselves deposited into an existence they had neither planned nor expected, having to accept that their lives had been drastically re-routed. When Holly was 'small and whole', she did not imagine a future in which she would be anything other than 'bigger and whole': she did not imagine a future in which she would be hurt and lost. This is PTSD: it picks you up, turns you inside-out and drops you back down, tender as a peeled grape. The world chugs on, bombarding you with the same hits and knocks and challenges as ever, with little understanding that every bump bites into your newly fragile flesh. It is a cruel disorder.

It is hard to inject the kind of levity necessary to balance such dark subject matter. Holly's story was painful to write; I imagine it is uncomfortable to read. In cases like this, as readers, we can feel we deserve some pay-off for the horror we have taken in. We want a small light to illuminate the darkness. I cannot provide this light, given my interviewees felt PTSD to be a disorder that 'has no silver lining': it is not my place, and not their truth. Holly's story does not end with 'full recovery' or 'resolution' because these were not states described by my interviewees. It ends with hope, because my interviewees were bravely, admirably hopeful. Many had achieved a level of recovery that, while imperfect, allowed them to function more normally than they had thought possible in the depths of the disorder. It would be audacious to suggest that anyone should be 'grateful' for this half-normality, but these women were overwhelmingly level-headed about their situation, appreciating progress without dwelling on the ground left to cover. It was humbling to witness the quiet courage with which they accepted new paths, and set to work on the task of knitting themselves back together.

# What I wish I could tell you about my PTSD

My PTSD triggers are many and varied: some might be obvious; some might seem obscure. If I become triggered by something, please don't ask me to explain why. Just accept that, for whatever reason, that sight/sound/smell/taste has become associated with trauma for me.

Please don't ask me to talk about what happened. If I need or want to share any details, I will, but I have to be the one to decide. The traumatic event is probably the most private, painful thing in my life: being asked 'So what is it?' makes me feel invaded.

My PTSD sometimes makes me feel like a house that was set on fire. It can be repaired, but the damage is enormous. Reconstruction takes time, and the house won't be exactly the same as it was before it was burnt.

I can feel exhausted all the time. Even if the trauma was months or years ago, some days it will take all my energy just to process the feelings it has left me with. I am not being lazy: I am trying to field the impulses to fight, fly or freeze.

No matter how long it has been since the trauma occurred, when I am in the grip of a flashback it feels as if it is occurring now.

You probably don't have PTSD from seeing a spider or going to a boring lecture. It's best not to say that you do.

Please don't require me to behave in a particular way surrounding my trauma. If I was the victim of an attack or assault, I might want to pursue legal action, but I might not.

I will have thought long and hard about this. Please never suggest that, because I don't want to report it, it must not have happened.

I may find it hard not to blame myself for what happened, even if – on a logical level – I realise it was not my fault. I find it helpful to be gently, repeatedly reminded that I am not to blame. Please try not to be frustrated with me if you feel that the message is not going in: my self-blame runs deep, and it is hard to let it go.

PTSD can affect me in ways you might not have predicted. I may seem chaotic, self-destructive or introverted. I may have strings of hospitalisations. I may go silent for months. Some of my behaviour is unrelated to PTSD, but a lot of it does stem from trauma. I need you to understand that I am not trying to be deceptive, evasive or manipulative. I am trying to deal with the fact that I still feel torn in two.

# *Maya*

When was it?

I know when it was.

It was at a friend's house, after school. We were deep in a sickly teenage infatuation with baking. When my fingers plunged into the sticky mulch of oats and syrup in the mixing bowl a gluey mess crept onto my sleeve, and friend laughed and squealed and yanked the material up to my elbow to avoid it meeting a sugary end. She looked down at my arm and stopped laughing. It was the loudest silence I'd ever heard. We looked down together at the skin, decorated with streaks and slices of red and pink, criss-crossing angrily over one another, puckering like fish-skeletons where stitches once held me together. Hot, hot blood was beating in my ears. She looked like she was going to vomit into my flapjack mixture and so I yanked away the bowl because there was no way in hell she was ruining my flapjacks. I yanked down my sleeve and didn't care that it got crusted with oats and syrup. I wanted to say something, and I think she wanted to say something, and because we both wanted to say something we said nothing. Nothing at all. We carried on as if everything was fine and normal, and I burnt the flapjacks, and we ate them and pretended they didn't taste of soot.

No. It was after. I know when it was.

It was at university. Another home-but-not-my-home. Another friend sat across the table, nursing a mug of bitter tea. I twittered about how I was *just so stupid* and how it was *hilarious really* because I ought to be, like, *expelled* or something because I couldn't manage *any* of my work, and it was all just *so funny* because *everyone else* was managing *just fine* but I was *really not managing at all* because I was just *too stupid*. I talked too fast and giggled too much and grinned too widely when my insides weren't gabbling or giggling or grinning at all. I saw the worry in her kind brown eyes, and I burrowed back under the cover of silence. She watched me scratch-scratch-scratch at the skin on my wrists, flaking off old scabs and laying the foundations for new ones. And, just as I was leaving, she said, 'Your wrists look really sore.' And I spoke without speaking, saying, 'it's nothing' when we both knew it was something. And she told me to go to the chemist. To get some antiseptic cream. To make sure they didn't get infected. And I smiled and said I would, and we both knew I wouldn't, and I don't know whether the charade made us feel better or worse.

No. It was after. I know when it was.

It was at my first grown-up flat. A grown-up home full of hard, wooden floors and harsh, hidden thoughts. A friend had said she would drop round one evening, and I had said, 'Yes, lovely, you must, please do drop round one evening,' and then she had only gone and *actually dropped round one evening*, like a *nut job*. When I opened the door I was wired and jittery. I couldn't speak. I danced on the balls of my feet like a spooked sparrow. I hugged her, and my body was tight and tense, and I left trails of blood down the back of her coat. Because I had been by myself, you see. And 'by myself time' had come to mean 'locking myself in the bathroom and dissecting myself' time. You see? The poor friend had had to snap into action, poking my neck for a pulse, emergency services on loudspeaker between us. The next thing I knew she was squeezing my shoulder as doctors examined exposed tendons and I leaked dark pools of liquid life onto the floor of a hospital cubicle. They knew me.

It was Attempt Number Three. She rattled off my name, address and date of birth as I gulped down oxygen from a plastic mask and visited me the next day, when I was clean and scrubbed and installed in a bed on a ward, bandaged from elbows to fingertips like a budget-gloved boxer.

Yes. I think that was when it was. That was when people started to worry.

———

After Attempt Number Five, they do not let me go home. They send me to a psychiatric ward. I arrive late at night, but people are awake and working as if it is day. Strip-lights illuminate the corridors, and the glass-walled cube of the nurses' station is bright and busy. The space around the station is shadowy: three mud-coloured sofas bordering a low table. They are made of the sort of material you could wipe clean with a cloth if you spilled a drink on it. A blanket-swaddled figure lies on one of the sofas, eyes wide and staring. At the border of the room, a tiny person hunches on a beanbag, glaring and wary as a cat. She reminds me of my friend's dog, who is so scrappy he doesn't look like a dog at all, but like a wild, overgrown squirrel. The image swims up to the front of my mind as the bulbous eyes of the beanbag girl meet mine. She is a shrunken straggle of limbs, her hair a mass of rat tails. Her skin is the colour of strong tea and her features are delicate, like they have been carved with the point of a pin, but her eyes are bold, their sockets gouged deep into her face. It is as if handfuls of clay have been removed from the round of her head, the holes filled with liquorice. In the gloom, there is no white to those eyes: no iris; no pupil. Only black. She doesn't really look like a person at all.

The burly paramedics who drove me here in the rattling, cattle-van ambulance stand awkwardly under the glare of the strip-lights. I think it unnerves them, this sick mind sanctuary.

They run their eyes over the walls of the day room, which are plastered with peeling foil transfers – butterflies, inspirational sayings, Marilyn Monroe quotes. They clear their throats and shift their feet, visibly anxious to return to the broken bones and haemorrhaging peptic ulcers of the patients in the main hospital. The nurse who rode with me in the van, presumably brought along in case I tried to top myself in transit, is assiduously working her way through a packet of gluten-free biscuits. She waves through the glass to the ward nurses, who are tapping their keyboards and pretending not to see us.

At last, the door to the station swings open and a pale, kind-faced ward nurse introduces herself in an Irish burr. The paramedics scrabble for the right way to say goodbye to a lunatic. Ambulance Nurse's well wishes are warm with care and thick with biscuit crumbs, and I watch three backs retreat down the corridor towards the air-locked exit. The kind nurse picks up the rucksack my sister brought when she visited me in the main hospital. She empties the contents onto a table, chattering as if it is not the middle of the night and this is not a secure unit and she is not combing my belongings for anything I could use as a weapon or suicide bid. She confiscates my phone charger, sewing kit, scissors, painkillers, can of coke, chewing gum and hair ties. She lets me keep the underwear my sister brought to the hospital in a plastic bag, but takes the plastic bag itself. With a business-like lack of embarrassment, she moves towards me and goes to slip her hands into my pockets, her body close and comforting. My brain snaps awake and I jerk away, plunging my own hand into my pocket and bringing out my razor blade, cupped in my palm like a baby mouse. I hold it tenderly, snatching a glance at her confused face. 'Careful. Don't cut your fingers,' I whisper. My voice is gruff and small.

When I have packed all the non-contraband back into my rucksack, the kind nurse leads me away, past the beanbag girl, whose gaze hasn't wavered since I arrived. As we walk by her I do a tiny wave. It dies in the space between us. Like the nurses in the station, she doesn't wave. The kind nurse takes me down a long corridor with rooms leading off either side. We reach the door at the end of the corridor. Another home-but-not-my-home.

There is a bed and a shelf and nothing else. The room is as empty as a shell with no snail inside. High up in the far wall there is a window of glass that looks three inches thick, and outside the night is black. Light comes from a single, flat circle of bulb set deep in the ceiling. The sheets on the bed are made of the sort of shiny, slippery material you can't tie in knots. The floor is linoleum: pale blue and slightly soft. I cast my mind back, riffling through the blur of the past few days. *Did I commit a crime?* I don't remember committing a crime. *Why am I in a cell?* I don't know why I am in a cell.

'Will I get you anything, Maya?' the kind nurse asks, a hand resting lightly on my shoulder. *I don't know. Will you?* I shake my head, and hear the swing of the door as she leaves, and when she returns she is holding a white tablet that I put inside me without asking questions. We are sitting on the edge of the bed, and I don't know how we got there. The kind nurse touches her hand to my back in one last ration of warmth, and I am so close to flinging my arms around her neck and curling myself into her chest like a child. I don't. I stay still as a statue as she rises and tells me to sleep well, and I don't tell her how highly unlikely it seems that I will sleep at all, let alone well, and I don't ask her why no one has read me my rights, and I don't dive to the floor and attach myself to her leg as she moves to leave the room, whimpering and begging her to stay, though all these things parade across my mind as possible courses of action. I just lift my hand in a tiny, pointless wave when her back is turned, and watch as it too succumbs to the great, wave-devouring vacuum in the air between us.

I don't have any pyjamas. I am wearing blue jeans and a yellow T-shirt and a grey hoodie and white trainers. I take off my trainers and coil the laces inside. I unpick the plaits holding my hair from my face. Then I pull back the slippery sheets and climb into bed, drawing my knees as close to my chin as my jeans will allow. It feels foreign to sleep encased in denim. I put up my hood and tug the body of the jumper out and over my legs until it encloses the whole of me, like a soft, grey contraband carrier bag. My eyes are heavy, as if the lids are being dragged down towards my toes, and my head is thick and foggy. I am glad I put the white tablet inside me without asking questions. It feels so wonderful to be falling sleep.

---

### Production: On the Border
### Scene One: Absence Is Different to Inaccuracy

[*Wide shot. The medical room of a psychiatric ward. MAYA is sitting on a high bed swinging her legs. The JUNIOR DOCTOR sits at a desk opposite her, examining a coloured chart. She is young, with bandy, adolescent legs and raffish hair.*]

[*We hear MAYA's 'inner voice' as voiceover.*]

**Junior Doctor**
What's your appetite like?

[*MAYA shrugs evasively.*]

**Junior Doctor**
You're quite underweight. Do you get your period?

**Maya [*inner voice*]**
Bloody body. Bloody body and its bloody blood. As it happens, no, I don't get my period much. At least, I don't think I do. I lose track. I barely notice the bleeding when it does happen, much

less when it doesn't. But, I suppose, if I really think about it, it seems like a while since I last had that feeling of tiny, dripping loss. I couldn't say how long. Two months? Four months? Six?

[*MAYA nods.*]

**Maya** [*outside voice*]
Yes, I get my period.

**Junior Doctor**
Oh. Right. OK then. Good.

[*The silence stretches. MAYA continues to swing her legs. The paper on the couch underneath her rustles.*]

**Junior Doctor**
Are you feeling OK?

[*MAYA nods.*]

**Maya** [*inner voice*]
I'm fine. I want you to leave me alone. But when I say 'leave me alone', don't you dare even *think* about *actually* leaving me alone, OK?

[*JUNIOR DOCTOR brings one knee up to her chest, wrapping slender arms around it. She scrolls through the notes on the computer screen, making a soft snicking sound with her tongue against her teeth.*]

**Junior Doctor**
OK. So. According to our notes, you were admitted to the general hospital on the 21st of March following a paracetamol overdose. You admitted yourself at around 11.30pm, having walked to the hospital from your home. You had also cut your left arm, and this was sutured in A&E. While in hospital, you were treated with the paracetamol antidote, and were medically stabilised, but didn't feel able to return home safely. This was your twelfth admission to the general hospital over the past eighteen months – four of your previous admissions were for intentional overdoses, and the remaining seven were for self-harm. Your only psychiatric diagnosis is …

[*She loses her place on the page for a moment,
then finds it again.*]

#### Junior Doctor
Borderline personality disorder.

[*MAYA is looking at her fingers, writhing in her lap.
Her body is tense. She is like a coiled spring.*]

#### Maya [*inner voice*]
Can't you see them? Can't you hear them? The words
– every last measured, sterile one of them – are jangling
around the room. 'Sutured' is weaselling its way into the
first-aid box, fashioning itself a bed out of gauze bandage.
'Antidote' is rattling the door of the medicine cabinet,
incensed to find it locked. 'Intervention' is mincing up and
down the far wall, pretending to examine the colour-
coded charts on the Mental Health Act, as if their contents
aren't already committed to memory. And bang in the
middle of the room, tall and sneering and bad, 'borderline'
is crossing its arms and pinning me under a hard stare.

#### Junior Doctor
Are there any … inaccuracies? In what I've just told you?

[*MAYA shakes her head.*]

#### Maya [*inner voice*]
No. Absence is different to inaccuracy.

[*The JUNIOR DOCTOR rises.
She speaks to MAYA, but we cannot hear her.*]

[*MAYA lies back on the couch, and the doctor examines
her, pressing a palm to her stomach. MAYA turns her
head to face the wall. She blinks slowly, heavily. The
sounds of the real-life scene are muted – only MAYA's
inner voice is audible. It is clear and calm.*]

### Maya [*inner voice*]

There weren't any doctors there on the morning of Attempt Number Five, when I left my flat and walked to the supermarket to buy one box of paracetamol, then walked to another supermarket to buy the next box of paracetamol, then walked to the pharmacy to buy the final box of paracetamol. There weren't any psychiatrists there to take notes when I popped the pills out of the blister packs one by one, until the pile on the bathroom floor was definitely large enough to kill me twice over. There weren't any nurses there to offer me water from plastic cups as I necked the pills three at a time. There weren't any surgeons there to admire my handiwork as I expertly sliced through skin and fat and redness in my arm until a bright white tendon was exposed for three clean inches. There weren't any paramedics there to look shifty as I bound the wound in a grubby handkerchief, packed an overnight bag and walked to the hospital. None of this is in my notes.

[*JUNIOR DOCTOR motions for MAYA to sit up. She sits back down at her desk. MAYA slips off the couch, slips from the medical room, and slips through the ward, fingers trailing along the walls. Her inner voice monologue continues as we follow her through the day room, down a long corridor.*]

### Maya [*inner voice*]

There was a receptionist I vaguely recognised, and who vaguely recognised me, yawning at her terminal when I glided up to the front desk at A&E. There was a receptionist who grew impatient with my tears and silence, and whose eyes rounded when I shrugged off my jacket and crimson cascaded to the floor. There was a doctor or a nurse or a porter who folded me into a wheelchair and whisked me through to triage. It felt like home. They wound bandages so tightly around the seeping wound I thought I might never feel my fingers again. There was another doctor or nurse or porter who asked whether I'd taken tablets, and when I nodded yes asked how many, and when I didn't answer asked whether it was more than twenty, and when I nodded yes jabbed a needle into my non-bandaged arm and sent icy fluid dripping through me. And, when the anaesthetic had been injected and I'd been sewn back together and the icy fluid had been dripping through me for long enough to neutralise the poison swilling around inside, there was a solemn psychiatrist who asked me whether I wanted to die.

I nodded. Lying in bed on the acute medical ward, arm chilly with antidote, skin puckered by 22 stitches, I nodded. Yes, I nodded. Of course. Of course I wanted to die. Because – let's face it – you'd have to be pretty screwed up to pull this kind of stunt if you didn't want to die, wouldn't you? To pull this kind of stunt at least once every few weeks, just because sometimes you need to put your body in the same agony as your head? Just because sometimes you need to lie in a hospital bed and have people lavish you with the sympathy that seems to fill a wicked, needy little hole inside you? Just because sometimes you worry that people are forgetting you, forgetting how much you need, and you feel like the only way to remind them is to shut yourself back in the 'invalid' box? Just because sometimes you crave the sterile safety of a medical ward? Just because sometimes you need people to know you are not OK? Just because?·

[*MAYA reaches her bedroom. In the room, she pulls back the bedsheets, climbs into bed. She hugs her knees to her chest, making herself small. Her eyes are dull and staring. Camera comes in close on her face.*]

#### Maya [*inner voice*]
When he asked me whether I wanted to die, I nodded. Because you'd have to be pretty screwed up to pull this kind of stunt if you didn't want to die. Wouldn't you?

## CUT

On the ward, time lasts for twice as long as it should. Breakfast television blares across the main room – the 'day room' – for at least twelve hours each morning. In front of the chirpy presenters and moving diagrams of easterly winds, beanbag girl crouches in her beanbag, eyes flicking from side to side. Other women drift in and out of the room through doors that punctuate the walls. One wears a head-to-toe sheep costume under a biblical-looking hessian tunic. She scribbles manically in a notebook, and when I peep over her shoulder I see pages blackened by angry nonsense scrawls. Another performs an elaborate yoga routine on the floor next to the sofa, cackling and muttering. It all unfurls to the backdrop of the nurses, sitting in the nurses' station, studiously pretending not to be there.

For the first week or two on the ward, I don't speak. I shuffle backwards into a cocoon of silence. Silence is safe. Silence is calm. Silence is soft, and makes people treat you softly. In my silence, I feel protected by an impenetrable barrier between me and the rest of the rough, noisy world. It ends unremarkably. By the end of a week or two, I have been satisfactorily restored to factory settings – my emotional timbre brought down from a dizzying high to a numb low. Happily, my remastering of verbal communication allows me to take full advantage of the packed activity schedule the ward has to offer. The packed activity schedule is run by an occupational therapist who looks like a Geography teacher.

## Bored? Check out our super-fun schedule of super-awesome activities!

### *Mondays: Music Therapy!*
Drop in and enjoy a room full of instruments and unstable people who can't play instruments!

A man from the men's psychiatric ward is very participative in music therapy. One Monday, he launches into a heartfelt solo vocalisation – with guitar accompaniment – which starts as a song about religion and ends as a song about brushing his teeth, and it isn't really singing and isn't really guitar playing and isn't really a song at all but laughing isn't really allowed. I could never be a music therapist – something inside me would rupture from all the not-laughing.

### Tuesdays: Art Therapy!
Pursue your creative endeavours with the earnest, bespectacled occupational therapist who looks like a Geography teacher!

In art therapy, Geographer-therapist puts little pots of foam stickers on the table and tells me, in great detail, about how I can make a birthday card from foam stickers and coloured card. While I make a birthday card from foam stickers and coloured card, he gives me a quiz from a pub quiz book. I think the quizzes were designed to be group activities, but I am the only patient who ever attends art therapy. I never know the answers to the questions. I never tell him that it isn't anyone's birthday.

### Wednesdays: Yoga!
Limber up and stretch it out!

Nope.

### Thursdays: Gardening!
This week, we're growing tomato plants!

I grow some excellent tomato plants.

### Fridays: Choir!
Featuring hits from One Direction, Jessie J and Katy Perry!

Choir could be renamed 'duet practice for Maya and Geographer-therapist'. Other women sit on the sofas holding lyric sheets, but they rarely sing. If Geographer-therapist and I entered

*Britain's Got Talent*, we would inevitably win. The sob story would be second to none.

Sometimes, when I'm singing 'Last Friday Night', or visiting my tomato plants, or making my umpteenth birthday card for no one's birthday, the whole thing feels hilarious. *I don't belong here!* I must be part of a candid camera show or social experiment. The mirth rises up inside me like a bubble, and I feel light and bright and effervescent. *I don't fit in here.* I cannot imagine ever feeling bleak again. But then, when the bleakness comes, it comes like a piece of heavy cloth thrown over me. My sister calls on her lunch break, her voice strained with exhaustion and despair. 'You've got to stop this, Maya,' she says. 'You're ruining all our lives,' she says. 'It's selfish,' she says. 'Selfish and attention-seeking and manipulative,' she says. I *hate* her. I disconnect the call and dissolve into a mulch of misery. I keen in my slippery bedsheet cocoon. At least it's safe in here. *I don't fit in out there.*

The friend whose coat I stained with my sliced wrists during Attempt Number Three comes to visit. She was on holiday when I made Attempt Number Five. When she left I was in my flat, and when she came back I was here, in prison. I don't know who informed her of my change of address. Her face is tender with tears and, for a moment, everything is right. She has come to visit me. She is worried about me. She is crying about me, so she *must* care about me. I want all her care, all the time, all for myself, and now I am glad about the pill-swallowing and the arm-slicing and the cell of a bedroom and the preposterous parade of therapies because I feel special. I take her into the canteen (where we are allowed to sit at weekends because that's where they set up the table football, and weekend table football is a basic human right). We watch sheep-tunic woman beckon over one of the men from the men's psychiatric ward and show him the bottle of brandy she has somehow slipped between her tunic and her onesie. My friend asks why Attempt Number Five happened. I can't say 'because I couldn't go to work'. I can't say 'because I was worried people were forgetting about me'. I can't say 'because unless I'm tortured and wounded I don't know who I am'. I can't say 'because I don't fit in anywhere'. All I can say are frothy phrases about 'everything being too much', when what I really mean is that nothing was too much. That's what was wrong – *nothing*. I feel *nothing*. Other people live in 3D, but my world is flat, and over time the absence of distress has become distressing. *Nothing*. That's exactly what is wrong. I am awash with nothing.

She looks tired and faraway. She looks down at her lap. She says she wishes I could see what a good person I am. Her voice sounds limp and close to disintegration, like a wet piece of paper. I wish she wouldn't say kind things; they make the guilt peck, gannet-like, at my gut. I am *not* a good person. If I were a good person I wouldn't look at her worried eyes and feel a jolt of joy inside, but I do. Because she is worried about *me*. She cares about *me*. That's how I know I am a very bad person. I know she has her own knot of guilt, pecking at her insides, because she is thinking that perhaps if she had done more to support me Attempt Number Five might not have happened. Perhaps she thinks Attempt Number Five was my huge, overblown way of punishing her for not seeing or doing or being enough. Perhaps she is right.

Before she leaves she hugs me tight as a vice. I love being held. It is not because I crave the attention, or even because of the comfort of warm envelopment. It is because I feel broken, and I need someone else – someone strong and solid – to hold the shattered pieces together. I whisper, 'I'm sorry,' and she murmurs, 'What are you sorry for?', and I don't answer because I don't know. I watch as she leaves, through the door cleaving the unit from the rest of the world, and I snuffle down a sob. My broken pieces clatter to the floor too fast for me to gather them up and stick myself back together. No matter how much I suffer and how much she cares, she can still leave the suffering behind when visiting hours are over. I can't.

I pad back into the day room and sink into the corner of a mud-coloured sofa. It is evening. Outside, thick clouds are soaking up daytime and spitting out night. Earlier, yoga girl leapt up from her floor-based calisthenics and grabbed the television remote, flicking until the screen illuminated with the fluorescent faces of characters on the toddlers' channel. It must have been six, seven hours ago – maybe more. No one has thought to change it back. We sit, tired and old, in front of *Peppa Pig* (plus entourage). It is rather an exciting episode. Peppa has been invited to Suzy Sheep's birthday party. The graphics are bright, and the day room is dim, and the irony of the cast of cartoon animals, their voices slicing through the purgatory of the unit, is dark. Laughing is not allowed. I go to the nurses' station, and wait for fifteen minutes before one of them cracks and stops pretending not to be there. I ask for a sleeping pill, and I go to bed.

---

### Production: On the Border
### Scene Two: Bad Person

[*Wide shot – medical room. MAYA is standing, back to camera, socked feet flat on the platform of a set of scales. The IN-CHARGE DOCTOR stands beside her, noting her weight. IN-CHARGE DOCTOR is middle-aged. She oozes a quiet authority.*]

[*MAYA steps off scales, hoists herself onto examination couch. Camera tracks down her body. She is scrawny: depleted-looking. She leans back, palms braced on the couch behind her, and her ribs protrude from her T-shirt. Her skin is slightly grey.*]

*Her hip bones are like hatches, jutting into the space between
her body and the waistband of her jeans. Her skin is stretched
tight over her skull. Her face looks sharp and equine.*]

[*IN-CHARGE DOCTOR sits at desk, adding to MAYA's computerised
notes. She does not look at MAYA when she speaks to her.*]

### In-Charge Doctor
We're still quite concerned about your weight. It says here that
you don't always make it into the canteen for meals. Why is that?

[*MAYA shrugs.*]

### Maya [*inner voice*]
When I'm empty, my thoughts are clearer. When I'm empty,
my feelings are quieter. *I'm just hungry*, I can tell myself. *If
I wasn't hungry, I wouldn't feel empty. And I'm choosing to be
hungry, so I'm choosing to be empty. It's as simple as that.*
Being tummy-empty stops me being *empty*-empty.

[*IN-CHARGE DOCTOR taps at keyboard some more. She rests her chin
on her fist and stares at computer screen. She does not look at MAYA.*]

### In-Charge Doctor [*neutrally*]
The fact is, Maya, you're not really trying. Are you?

[*IN-CHARGE DOCTOR looks at MAYA. MAYA holds her gaze.*]

### Maya [*inner voice*]
Why are your words angry when your voice
is not angry? Am I bad or not?

### In-Charge Doctor
What have people told you about borderline personality
disorder, Maya? Do you know what it is?

[*MAYA's eyes drop to the floor. She folds her arms across
her chest. She shrugs almost imperceptibly.*]

### Maya [*inner voice*]

I remember the other doctor, at the other hospital. I remember
how the label came out of his mouth and went into my body
and how it felt like he said, 'Do you know what, Maya? We've
finally got to the bottom of all this – all this "self-harm" and
"suicide" and "misery" business. We've finally dug our way
down to the root of your problem and – do you know what
we've found? *Nothing*. That's what we've found. *Nothing at all.*'
I remember how I felt like saying, 'Yes! That's just it! *Nothing!*
That *is* the problem – the *nothing*!', but I knew from the way
his lips were curling and his words were snarling that he wasn't
meaning what I was meaning – that he was talking about
*nothing* in the sense of *not a thing*, while I was talking about
*Nothing* in the sense of *absence* and *empty* and *hollow*. 'And do
you know what that means, Maya?' I felt like he'd said: 'That
means we have our answer. And that answer is that you're *just
not a very nice person.*' Because – 'personality disorder'? What
else could anyone mean by 'personality disorder' except …

### Maya [*outside voice – whispering*]
Not a very nice person.

### In-Charge Doctor
Ah. I see.

[*MAYA buries her chin in her chest. IN-CHARGE DOCTOR swivels her
chair to face MAYA. When she speaks, her voice is soft and steady.*]

### In-Charge Doctor
You know, Maya, a famous American therapist once said that
people with borderline personality disorder are like people with
third-degree burns over 90 per cent of their bodies. It's become
a bit of a cliché now, but it's still valuable, I think. She said that
their emotional 'skin' is gone. They feel every tiny touch like an
acute agony. It makes them very, very sensitive to things the rest
of us might think of as very, very small. Feeling overwhelmed by
an ordinary situation can trigger a quite extraordinary reaction.

### Maya [*inner voice*]

Three weeks ago I was sitting on my bed, dressed in my pyjamas, pouring pills into myself like pebbles into a jar because I couldn't go to work, and I didn't know why I couldn't go to work but I knew that I couldn't go, and I didn't know how to explain that I couldn't go to work but I knew that I couldn't go, and at that moment nothing in the world mattered except creating a watertight excuse for not going to work.

### In-Charge Doctor

This vulnerability makes the world a very scary place, and different people develop different means of easing the fear. Some find they are quick to seek care and attention, particularly from those of higher status than themselves.

### Maya [*inner voice*]

This morning I was scratching a layer of skin off the underside of my wrist, and presenting the pink, weeping square of exposed tissue to the kind nurse, and breathing in her powdery smell as she bandaged me up, and wanting nothing more than to tuck my head under her chin and curl into her chest. This is what I do. I suck up every scrap of warmth she shows me and desperately try to invite more, greedily mining her for affection. The hunger for her attention is raw and shameful. It is push, pull, push, pull – I want her and need her and want not to need her and need not to want her ...

### In-Charge Doctor

Some find they grow angry easily: they become too busy hating the world to fear it any more. Others form intense, dependent attachments to friends or partners, and feel desolate if these relationships experience even slight turbulence. Sometimes, the strength of the emotions you feel can send you into a state of what we call 'dissociation', where you are not consciously present in the world.

### Maya [*inner voice*]

A week ago, I was standing in the canteen, waiting in line for my splat of food from the dinner lady, and someone jostled behind me, the edge of their tray nudging my back. I wheeled around and flung my tray, and the plastic plate skidded across the floor. I roared as if my body had been forced into an electric socket, then melted onto the floor like cold custard. A burly nurse scooped me into a small, solitary room on the ward and brought me lukewarm cottage pie. I spat out the mush of mince and mashed potato because I didn't have the energy to swallow. Fat tears came in wracking sobs. I leant over my plate and watched clear fluid spill from my face into my lunch. *Why am I here? What did I do?*

### In-Charge Doctor

We also know you can feel very frightened that you are going to be left all on your own.

### Maya [*inner voice*]

'You'? Why are you saying 'you'? Is this what I am? Is this me?

### In-Charge Doctor

Sometimes this is because you really *have* been left alone, as a child or an adult, but usually it is just a feeling, without obvious cause. We don't know where it comes from, but the fear is completely real, and the need to pull people closer – sometimes by doing desperate, destructive things – is overwhelming. Sometimes you hurt yourself – even attempt suicide – in order to show people how much you are hurting, and how much support you need.

### Maya [*inner voice*]

Last week I was sitting in the rice pudding-smelling canteen with my friend and feeling the cavernous distance between us and wondering what else I could do – how else I could harm myself – to close that gap to the hair's breadth I needed it to be …

**In-Charge Doctor**
We know you go in and out of hospital, because
you hurt yourself frequently. This might be because
you feel safe and secure in hospital—

**Maya** [*inner voice*]
Blue NHS signs at the roadside, flooding me
with calm and longing ...

**In-Charge Doctor**
—or it might be because you feel ambivalent about whether you
want to live or die. You have very set ideas about the sort of
person you *should* be, and when it proves impossible to live up
to your ideals there may even be a sense of *deserving* to die.

**Maya** [*inner voice*]
Fantasies so intricate the wrench of reality gives me
whiplash: a moment of intense, irascible anger. If I
can't be perfect what's the point in being at all?

**In-Charge Doctor**
You struggle with impulsivity – doing things without thinking them
through beforehand – and this can lead you to be reckless with
the risks you take, especially when it comes to your self-injury.

**Maya** [*inner voice*]
Cool fingers running over the map of veins in my
wrist. And a voice telling me: *Go on – just slice through
it. Do it. What's the worst that can happen?*

**In-Charge Doctor:**
You view the world in absolutes. Things are wonderful
or terrible; people are saints or devils ...

**Maya** [*inner voice*]
Six years old, Mothers' Day, ugly sugar-paper cards saturated
with PVA: 'Dear Mummy I love you always except for when
you shout at me because then I hate you, from Maya'

[*IN-CHARGE DOCTOR pauses for a moment.*
*She uncrosses her legs.*]


**In-Charge Doctor**
The last thing we know about borderline personality disorder
is that, while it is by no means true to say that all sufferers
will experience all symptoms, it is true to say that *most*
sufferers will feel a deep, fundamental emptiness inside,
which can make you feel totally alone and isolated.

**Maya [*inner voice*]**
If you opened up my chest, you would find an empty cavity.
Did you know that? Most people have a heart and lungs and
a soul in their chests. But if you cracked my ribcage down the
middle and opened it like a set of double doors, you would
find a hole in my chest big enough to hold the world.

**In-Charge Doctor**
You find it difficult to 'fit in' with the rest of the world,
because, no matter how able and together you seem
on the outside – and many sufferers are *exceptionally*
talented, successful people – you cannot escape
the feeling of there being *nothing on the inside.*

[*Throughout IN-CHARGE DOCTOR's speech, MAYA has been
tipping further and further forward. Now, her head rests low on
her chest. Her tears are coming thick and fast and silently. IN-
CHARGE DOCTOR takes a tissue from the box on her desk and
tucks it gently into MAYA's hand. With her head still down, MAYA
blots at her face. Her words break through unexpectedly.*]


**Maya [*outside voice*]**
Selfish. And attention-seeking. And manipulative.
That's what it is. That's what I am.

[*MAYA begins to sob, noisily and messily. Her body convulses.
IN-CHARGE DOCTOR rests a hand gently on her knee.*]

### In-Charge Doctor [*softly*]

Sometimes your behaviour can *look* attention-seeking and manipulative. It can look as if you want endless cossetting and cuddling and special treatment from those around you, and as if you are using calculated methods of obtaining those things.

But it isn't a want, is it, Maya? It's a need. It is a *need* to be noticed, cared for and reassured, not just a *desire* for special privileges. That need can feel desperate and all-consuming, like a baby's need to be held and protected. Manipulation is about coldly, deliberately extracting things from other people; that's not what you do. You act on impulses to do things you think might grant you some modicum of comfort and reassurance.

And, while those impulses may be ill-thought-out, and may end up affecting others, the deliberate controlling of others' behaviour for personal gain simply *does not come into it*.

### May [*outside voice*]

But it still makes me a bad person.

### In-Charge Doctor [*emphatic*]

It makes you *feel* like a bad person, Maya. It makes you *feel* guilty, and cast out, and lonely. You feel like the world is a frightening, perplexing place, and everything you do – every person you cling to and every habit you form – is your way of trying to sail your ship through the storm inside. You're trying to do what all of us are trying to do – it's just that your concourse is choppier, and your ship is easier to destabilise.

### Maya [*inner voice*]

I am five, being sent to the naughty step for some minor transgression, sitting down and slamming my head against the wall with such force the world turns black. I am seven, joined at the hip with the first best friend, refusing to sit next to her at lunchtime after she goes to someone else's house for tea. Twelve, waking up and immediately screaming with distress, bawling over and over again to my helpless mother, 'I can't, I can't, I can't pretend for another day, I can't pretend to be normal, I can't I can't I can't ...' Twenty, daring myself to stand closer and closer to the edge of the deserted late-night platform as the trains zip past, dangling a foot into the abyss. Twenty-three, poisoned and bleeding, relief seeping into my bones as I am folded into a wheelchair and whisked away from the burden of having to cope. Just for a moment. Because no – it wasn't always like this. There was a time before the slashed wrists and pickled liver and hospital wristbands – but that time wasn't *better*. That time was *only lonelier*. Because maybe it isn't fair to drag people into my despair by strings of concern, but what else can I do? No one can bear to be lonely forever …

[*IN-CHARGE DOCTOR breaks the silence.*]

**In-Charge Doctor**
In my experience, people with borderline personality disorder are exceptionally perceptive, sensitive, empathetic and thoughtful individuals. You care deeply about others, and your capacity to love and be loved is unusually expansive. But you need help to feel safer inside. The things you're doing to achieve some inner stillness – things like hurting yourself, or not talking, or not eating – work very well for a very short time. And, for me, that isn't good enough. It's less than you deserve.

**Maya** [*inner voice*]
I need to lift my head. There are so many tears. I'm all blocked up. I can't breathe properly …

[*MAYA cautiously lifts her head. She winces. IN-CHARGE DOCTOR passes her a tissue.*]

**Maya** [*inner voice*]
The pain is blooming in my spine. The light is so bright in here. I need to blow my nose. I need to get rid of the gunk clogging me up …

[*MAYA blows her nose. The sound is loud and wet. She gingerly touches her eyelids and cheeks.*]

**Maya** [*inner voice*]
My face is so swollen. It hurts to touch it …

[*MAYA raises her head a little higher. She is bedraggled and blotchy. Her eyes are glazed.*]

**In-Charge Doctor**
Maya?

**Maya** [*outside voice*]
I don't try to be a bad person. It just happens.

**In-Charge Doctor**
I don't think you're a bad person, Maya. I think you're a sad person.

**Maya** [*outside voice*]
I don't feel sad. I don't feel anything.

**In-Charge Doctor**
Do you want to feel anything?

**Maya** [*outside voice*]
No.

**In-Charge Doctor**
We could do some work on helping you feel things.

**Maya** [*outside voice*]
Yes please.

**In-Charge Doctor**
You look tired. Shall we leave it there for today?

**Maya** [*outside voice*]
Do I get to see you again?

**In-Charge Doctor**
Do you want to see me again?

**Maya** [*outside voice*]
No.

266

**In-Charge Doctor**
I could see you again tomorrow.

**Maya** [*outside voice*]
Yes please.

**In-Charge Doctor**
OK, Maya. Thank you for talking to me.

**Maya** [*outside voice*]
Thank you for listening.

**Maya** [*inner voice*]
Thank you for hearing.

[*Close-up on MAYA's face.*]

**Maya** [*inner voice*]
Outside the medical room, on the ward, I can hear the faraway sound
of someone banging on the door to the nurses' station, and I can
picture the faraway sight of the nurses pretending not to be there.
The television buzzes its low, constant tune. Outside the ward, in the
canteen, there is a clank and clatter of plates and pots. It must be
close to dinnertime. Soon, the cutlery will be jangling from the locked
kitchen to the serving hatch. Outside the unit, in the real world, it is
raining. Heavy drops thrum down, hard and insistent against windows.

[*MAYA blinks heavily. Her exhaustion is palpable.
She looks directly into the camera.*]

**Maya** [*inner voice*]
The sound is dull and mellow and soothing,
on the border of my mind.

**CUT**

———

'But it's mainly manipulation, isn't it? It feels
like an excuse to call it an illness.'

## The Borderline Myth! Everything You Need to Know Before Embarking on Life as a Master Manipulator!

1. Are you ready to struggle with relationships? You are going to struggle with relationships *big time*. Friendships, partnerships, any-kind-of-ships! They don't feel like celebrations of human contact: they feel like a ghastly parade of opportunities for *rejection, humiliation* and *abuse!* You are going to perceive yourself as *chronically unlovable* and *unattractive*. The way you think about people will be up-and-down, love-or-loathe, as if your vision only allows you to see them in black and white. If someone shows you a tiny snippet of kindness, you will cling to them like a limpet. If someone does something you don't like, you will never want to speak to them again. You can't see people as variable entities: you see only goodies and baddies. It's no big deal. It's just a giddying, sickening merry-go-round.

2. Ever worry about abandonment? Buckle up. You're about to start seeing abandonment lurking round *each and every corner,* and abandonment is the most *excruciatingly terrifying* thing you can imagine! Even *thinking* about abandonment will contort your mind in paroxysms of *pure, unadulterated agony!* Your existence will become shaped by the fear that, at any moment, you could be left entirely alone. It's no big deal. It's just a relentless, haunting terror.

3. Thought you could guarantee the unconditional love and care of those closest to you? Think again. You need to get your head around the fact that, unless you work to keep them close,

everyone will drift away. How to keep them close? *Show them that you need them!* Tell lies to make people *envy* you. Tell lies to make people *pity* you. Hurt yourself or threaten to. If people seem disinterested in you, or more interested in someone else, you will feel like your heart is being wrenched from your chest. You will feel you are being plunged into a *nightmare world* where your *darkest terrors* are made real! An explosion will erupt inside. There will be anger and tears. It's no big deal. It's just a desperate, helpless bind.

4.  Emotion regulation? You can wave goodbye to that old friend! Now, a minor disappointment is a life-altering catastrophe; a small misfortune is an unbearable disaster; an insignificant mistake is proof of your worthlessness. Emotions are experienced with maximum intensity, for minimal reason: you will cycle from *jubilant* to *despairing*, *hopeful* to *hopeless*, *high* to *low* multiple times per day. It will be *gruelling!* It's no big deal. It's just an exhausting, bewildering rollercoaster.

5.  You're in luck! You've got a new calling card! Impulsive behaviours. Where to begin? Binge eating, drinking, drug-taking, money-spending ... They are itches you need to scratch. They will add to the instability that hallmarks your new existence. But remember, any relief gained from this self-medication will be temporary: recklessness may grant you brief periods of elevated mood, but overall you will be left feeling low, tortured and ashamed. All the more reason to do it again! It's no big deal. It's just a pointless, circular compulsion.

6.  You've heard of self-harm, right? Attempted suicide? Meet your new bedfellows. You'll be using these neat little tools for all manner of purposes. The traditional 'cry for help' is always a winner – nothing like a spell on a hospital ward for

communicating your despair! White dressings, white gloves – you feel like a black hole. You gulp down the small ration of care and you hunger for more. But the drive to self-destruct runs deeper: it is more than a need for gentle hands, wrapping you in bandages. Your life has become draining, bruising, bewildering. You feel worthless, flawed and disgusting. Self-harm is self-hatred, suicide is escape. It's no big deal. It's just a forlorn destruction.

7. Reality? It's all relative. When your emotions get too big and strong to handle, you're going to need to check out of the world. Time will slow down or speed up. The room will contract or expand. Your vision will be sharpened or blurred. Nothing will feel real. You can call it dissociation. It's no big deal. It's just a sort of madness.

8. You will feel empty inside. You will be unable to articulate the emptiness you feel inside. You will feel as if your organs have been scooped out with a shovel. You will feel you lack a soul. You will change who you are depending on who you are with, because you have no stable self to inhabit. That's why your emotions will be close to the surface: there is nothing to push them down. There is no reassuring ballast of selfhood. You will long to feel full and warm, but no matter how much love and care you receive you can never fill the emptiness. You will feel subhuman. It's no big deal. It's just torture.

> 'That's the thing. It's not just being
> manipulative. It's not like that at all.'

I'm sorry Maya's departure was abrupt. We could have stayed with her longer – followed as she was released from the unit and tasked with mending a life wrought apart at the seams. We could have crouched at the air-locked entrance to the ward, waiting to see whether she would return in a week, or a month, or a year. But somehow it felt right to leave in the middle of the story. In many ways, a personality disorder is just that: an elongated middle-of-story, without a clear-cut beginning or end.

Most psychiatrists use a system of diagnosis that identifies ten separate personality disorders, but borderline personality disorder (BPD) was the only (diagnosed) subtype experienced by my interviewees, which is why I have focused on it here. The abstractness of the term 'borderline' has led to the rebranding of the disorder with the more descriptive 'emotionally unstable personality disorder' (EUPD). This term gives a more immediate impression of the core struggle: sufferers often feel they are in a constant state of high emotion, which can change with little warning or provocation. I have chosen to use the term BPD, rather than EUPD, as the people I spoke to always identified themselves using the former label.

BPD is enrobed in misconception. A good chunk of the time, it is confused with bipolar disorder (they share the same first letter, but little else). Sometimes, the misgiving is more alarming, equating BPD with psychopathy. Mention of the illness can be a catalyst for an extended and impassioned diatribe on the 'ridiculous' proliferation of spurious psychiatric diagnoses currently recognised by medical professionals. If one mined the depths of the diagnostic and statistical manual or international classification of diseases, one might indeed find details of disorders that seem questionably specific or obscure, but the BPD diagnosis is neither questionable nor spurious: it describes a real, complex set of symptoms experienced by a real, complex set of people.

A personality disorder affects an individual's patterns of thinking, feeling and behaving – in other words, how they exist and function in the world. The term 'personality' encompasses one's beliefs and values, one's way of relating to others, one's self-image, and the way one deals with situations. If we acknowledge that a personality disorder disturbs these fundamental, day-to-day processes, it is easy to see how profoundly debilitating it can be. In other chapters, we have seen conditions that derailed sufferers by dysregulating mood (Abby), establishing dangerous behaviours (Georgia), and compromising the grasp on reality (Yasmine). Maya is derailed on all fronts: BPD makes mood labile, prompts unstable behaviour, and destabilises one's presence in the 'real world'.

Although, like any psychiatric disorder, BPD can only be officially and accurately diagnosed after medical consultation, the internet yields a plethora of self-diagnosis questionnaires, posing questions such as: 'Do you have long-term feelings of emptiness and loneliness?' and 'Do you have sudden and intense feelings of aggression, and find it difficult to control your anger?' A string of yeses does not constitute a BPD diagnosis, but these are the same broad criteria psychiatrists hold in mind when assessing patients for the disorder. However, these symptoms plainly overlap with those indicative of other conditions. When is binge eating an 'impulsive behaviour', as in BPD, and when is it part of BED or bulimia pathology? Feelings of chronic emptiness are described by sufferers of both BPD *and* depression, while alternate periods of intense joy and intense misery could contribute to the building of a bipolar-type picture. On paper, aspects of Maya's presentation could easily be mistaken for Abby's, Beth's or Yasmine's. This is one reason why a diagnosis of BPD must be assigned with caution and rigorous assessment.

Perhaps more than any other category of mental health condition, personality disorders stoop under the weight of societal prejudice. A BPD diagnosis can feel like a declaration that there is something wrong with who you are – because what is 'personality' if not 'who you are'? And what is 'disorder', if not 'something wrong'? In the eyes of the unsympathetic, BPD is read as shorthand for 'manipulative': just as we saw Harry berate Abby for her 'selfishness', BPD sufferers are frequently criticised for attempting to wrap the world around their little fingers. For therapists, BPD patients can represent a challenge. Patients at the mercy of extremes of mood often present the therapist with extremes of behaviour, alternating between charming and charmless with alarming fluidity. Their black-and-white view of the world can also lead to black-and-white treatment of the therapist – one week they are adoring and effusively grateful, the next they are chilly and resentful. Although trained in professional detachment, therapists are human, and are sometimes affected by this intensity. Certain private clinicians refuse to treat the condition at all, and most impose a limit on the number of BPD patients they see at any one time. Life as a psychiatrist, psychologist or psychotherapist is, without doubt, challenging, and perhaps the enforcing of such boundaries is a wise act of self-care.

However, the apparent proliferation of negative BPD-related attitudes in the purely medical community is disturbing, as the self-destruction that is part and parcel of BPD leads sufferers into frequent contact with emergency/primary care services. In a study of the attitudes of registered psychiatric nurses, 89 per cent perceived people with BPD as manipulative, with 32 per cent reporting that sufferers 'made them angry'.[23] Perhaps most concerningly, only 44 per cent of nurses asserted that they knew how to care for people with BPD. This prejudice spans the disciplines. Patty Fleener, a US social worker, gives a chilling description of the anti-BPD stigma she encountered on adult mental health wards:

'When I was a social worker I would roll my eyes when someone mentioned BPD. Why? Because that is what all of my co-workers did. I was educated by my co-workers of how horrible borderlines were. Did I have my own experience with them? Nope. Did they? Nope. But if you rolled your eyes you were showing others that you were well educated about this population. You knew enough about this disorder to know that the borderlines were horrible people and hard to manage. When in real life, I knew nothing of this disorder.'[24]

Krawitz and Watson, of the New Zealand mental health commission, echoed this sentiment:

'[BPD patients] may already be disliked before they have even been seen. Clients in treatment are often embroiled in clinician attitudes which are derogatory or deny the legitimacy of their right to access resources. Studies have demonstrated that clinicians have less empathy for people meeting diagnostic criteria for borderline personality disorder than other diagnostic groups, and make more belittling comments [about these people].'[25]

A broad social discussion of BPD is necessary because of what the disorder represents: the maligned face of mental illness. It is one thing to express wholehearted support for your depressed sister as she sits unobtrusively beside you, suffused with sadness, too numb to talk over the television. It is one thing to hold your girlfriend's trembling hand as her mind and body are mauled by panic, feeling her vulnerability coursing through your entangled fingers. It is something else to continue to love and care for someone whose disorder makes them behave in ways most would find unpleasant and disturbing; to maintain sympathy and understanding in the face of lies and crises. People with BPD often find themselves supported when their symptoms are socially acceptable, but admonished when their disorder becomes difficult or distasteful. This is why it is important to show the challenging behaviour mental illness can entail: if the 'unpresentable' face of conditions such as BPD goes unpresented, we hold sufferers to unrealistic standards: 'You are allowed to be affected by your illness but only in an inoffensive/endearing/interesting/adorable way, and never in a way that inflicts confusion/discomfort/embarrassment/inconvenience on others.' BPD is a prime example of a disorder that causes sufferers to behave 'difficultly' – but this does not make them any less worthy of care or concern than those whose problems manifest 'acceptably'.

When professionals and non-professionals reduce BPD sufferers to their most challenging symptoms, they misrepresent a group of people who are vividly, vibrantly alive. They are fiercely bright and often self-reflective. A mental illness is never an asset, far less an accessory: the trope of the beautiful, broken woman, made alluring by her kooky instability, is never helpful. But there is so little favourable representation of BPD sufferers, it is difficult to worry about painting an overly positive image. Their lives are difficult, because they *do* teeter on a fine line, and on one side of that line *does* lie a well of torrid, painful emotion, inciting desperate, extreme behaviour. But on the other side of the line – on the other side of the border – is a life characterised by empathy, enthusiasm and warmth.

## What I wish I could tell you about my BPD

I am not a bad person. I am a person struggling with disordered patterns of thinking, doing and being.

You don't have to understand how it feels to be me. Most of the time, I'm not sure I understand myself. You just have to accept that being me is bewildering, frightening and intense.

Acting on impulses grants me temporary relief from negative emotions. This is why I find it so hard to resist doing impulsive things, even when I know they are not helpful long-term. In the moment, all I can think about is escaping the horrible feelings.

When I feel a connection to someone, they are elevated above everyone else. It can be an excessive, obsessive fixation. I want to do everything I can to gain the affection and esteem of that person. I don't mean to play people off against one another, but sometimes I feel I have eyes for only my current 'favourite person'.

I am constantly afraid that people will abandon me. Over the course of my life, lots of people have cut ties with me, because they have found my behaviour strange, unstable and difficult to manage. This has only increased the paranoia. That is why, when I love someone, I cling to them, wanting every inch of their time, care and affection.

Sometimes I have fits of enormous anger, but I am not an angry person. When the anger takes over, it feels foreign, as if the rageful person is not really me.

I am not doing things 'for attention', but I do crave care and concern. Sometimes, I go to great lengths to obtain that care and concern – for example, by lying or making threats. My need feels so desperate it is hard to stop myself doing these things.

I need a lot of reassurance. I need to be told that you don't hate me, and that you are not going to leave me. I know it can be exhausting and probably frustrating, but I am like a leaky bucket: I find it difficult to hold on to calmness for any period of time, so I need a lot of topping up.

It helps when you give me validation by acknowledging that my struggles stem from a real, serious illness.

I know I sometimes do and say things I shouldn't. This is usually because I am panicking, or my emotions are controlling me, and I don't think before acting or speaking. The most valuable people in my life are those who understand that I don't do these things to be nasty or cruel, and who are able to forgive me.

Sometimes I feel all alone in the world. I have often been treated with suspicion and contempt as a result of my illness, and this has made it hard for me to trust people.

Please don't call me toxic. I'm a person, not a chemical.

# Presences and Absences

I have only told seven stories from the 70 I heard, and I have only heard 70 of the several million similar stories that exist worldwide. Even with this sample, there were experiences I could not assimilate directly into the narratives of my characters – and I was loath to insert experiences where they did not fit.

Who else, then, did I meet?

I met women who curled their spidery, late-twenties limbs into knots on their beds as we spoke, compelled to make themselves small. They shrouded themselves in flower-patterned duvets and flicked on string after string of fairy lights when the sun streaming through the window began to die, illuminating photo collages of grinning girls. They talked about the degrees they had accumulated and the jobs they were doing and the adult lives they were leading, and they fiddled with the plaits in their hair.

> 'I was only twelve when it started. I was only twelve when I was stunted. How could I have moved on? It was like falling into a vortex. I didn't grow – I shrank. One of my friends just had a baby. We're the same age, but I'm not old enough to have a baby. How could I have got to that age by now? It's been ten years. I haven't been doing life. I've been doing anorexia.'

I met women afraid to describe the auditory and visual hallucinations that plagued them, because 'that's not something we talk about'. Women who stepped aside in the street to allow non-existent passers-by right of way; women who sensed taunting, giggling voices rising from the shadows cast on the pavement. Women who heard their names on the tannoy at work, dutifully reported to Aisle Nine, and were met with raised eyebrows and muttered comments: 'You do know that didn't really happen, don't you?' Women who walked beside main roads and were suddenly surrounded by horns and expletives.

'I was only doing what it told me to do. I was only doing as I was told in my head. One minute I was walking along, the next: *Cross. Don't look. Just cross.*'

I met women whose throats closed and hearts pounded in the middle of classes, in the middle of the office, in the middle of a conversation. Women who would gasp for more oxygen, more oxygen, more oxygen, until their blood became so saturated with oxygen they felt dizzy and sick. The threat of panic hung over them, brooding and black.

I met women who hurt themselves to soothe themselves. Who sanded away their skin with nail files as children, curled up in bed around their habit while other children curled around soft toys.

'It calmed me down. It was a way for me to muffle all the overwhelming feelings I was having. It made things seem manageable again.'

I met women who burned their wrists on radiators, giddy with the rush of pushing themselves past the pain.

'I'm always so conscious of my wrists, nowadays. They're always there – of course they are – and I can always feel them there. It feels so unnatural not to be hurting them; not to be hiding them … It's such thin skin …'

I met women whose heads bore the angry, scarred-over scabs of head-banging so violent it broke the fragile skin on their scalps.

'It felt like the only way to silence the thoughts. My head was so noisy – so noisy all the time. When I smashed it against the wall, there was a second – just a second – when everything was too busy jangling about to make any sound. And when that second ended, I would smash it again. I wanted to bang my head until I passed out, because that seemed like the only way to get rid of the thoughts for any longer than a second.'

I met women whose lives had been blighted by chronic and debilitating physical illness that had spooled into mental distress, such as migraines so painful they left the sufferer incapacitated.

'When I was little, I never missed school. If I was ever ill, I made my Mum take me to school anyway, so I could explain to my teacher that I wasn't going to be in because I was ill, not because I just didn't want to be there. But, with headaches, I didn't care any more. I couldn't care. It hurt too badly. I would be in bed all day, every day, and mostly I couldn't tell how much of it was headaches and how much of it was depression. They felt sort of similar.'

'My parents were very worried. I wasn't that worried. I remember thinking: *If they tell me I've only got – say – ten or fifteen years to live, I won't be sad. Seems like quite a lot to me. Definitely long enough …*'

I met women who cast back to past behaviour and winced. Women whose internal anguish had pushed them into thinking and saying and doing things they readily identified as irrational.

Although these women never renounced responsibility for their actions, in some cases they marvelled at the extent to which the things they had done had felt like they occurred outside of their own control, with some even referring to an 'alter ego':

> 'I recognise her now – BPD me. She's so different to the normal me. I think she was around a lot with my ex-boyfriend. I made things very difficult for him for a while – I could send him up to 100 texts a day. I don't really know what I was looking for. Reassurance, I suppose. I was so scared he was going to leave me.'

For those who had engaged in subversive, 'inappropriate' behaviour while unwell, there was a self-perpetuating element to their shame and confusion.

> 'It's not like I didn't know it was wrong to steal – of course I knew that, everyone knows that. But I went into a place of desperation, I suppose. I was so desperate that I didn't feel like the wrongness of it mattered any more. And then, in times when I felt better, I'd get hit with how bad it was – what I had done – and feel even worse about myself, and that would make me even more desperate.'

> 'I lie all the time. I lie like I breathe. I lie so much I can't remember what's real and what's not. It's a horrible thing to admit, because no one wants to think of themself as a liar. It's such a terrible thing to be, and yet – logically – I know that's what I am. For me, I think the lying happens because I feel so, so unhappy with who I am. I hate everything about myself. So I lie in order to be someone different – someone who has had different experiences, achieved different things … just someone better, really.

Sometimes I suppose I lie to get attention. Having people's sympathy is a big thing for me. I feel like sympathy is something I really, really need, because if people don't pity me they might stop caring about me. But obviously I always know that I'm not the person in the lies – deep down I mean – and I also always know that I'm not an honest person. Which I hate. It's like, the better the person I create with the lies, the worse I know myself to be on the inside. The bigger the gap between the two people, the worse I feel. And the worse I feel, the more I lie. It isn't an excuse, but it is a reason.'

Who, then, did I not meet during the course of my interviews?

I met no one miserable. Women who had experienced – or were experiencing – deep, profound misery? Yes. *Miserable* women? No. They carried their misery on their shoulders, rarely complaining about the weight, much less expecting others to carry it for them. They sat beside it at meals, rarely objecting when it gorged and left them to starve. They tucked it into bed next to them, rarely retaliating when it pushed them to the floor in sleep. They did not fight against their misery with the force one might expect, but nor did they wallow in its company. Yes, sometimes they succumbed to the embrace of their illness – being 'too anxious', 'too depressed' or simply 'too unwell' to engage in a daunting task can be a relief as well as a restriction. But for each moment's solace they sought, there were a hundred attempts at disentanglement, a hundred quiet disappointments. The majority of women co-existed with their misery in brave resignation, without dwelling on its unjust invasion of their lives. They were living with misery; they were not miserable.

I met no one humourless. There is, I have come to realise, humour in even the darkest situations, and to acknowledge it is not to disrespect the darkness. The women I met held stories that made me shiver, and yet – when they recounted curling into the foetal position, grieving over a pan of burnt rice, or inventing bizarre tales of extreme-sports-gone-wrong to explain self-harm scars – their eyes twinkled. Some things are just funny. These women solidified my conviction that allowing oneself to laugh about one's problems isn't callous or heartless. To shroud mental illness in po-faced solemnity is wrong. We approach all other human behaviour with appropriate, affectionate humour: to suppress this humour would be to segregate the mentally ill from the human. The women I met did not have to demonstrate their suffering through purse-lipped, low-voiced 'suffering as theatre'. Mentally ill behaviour can be absurd: when something is absurd, you can laugh about it. Most of my interviewees laughed easily and often. This did not invalidate the tears shed moments before, because feeling sad does not preclude one from ever feeling joy.

I met no one weak; I met people excessively concerned about *appearing* weak. They berated themselves repeatedly for 'making a fuss', convinced that the hours they spent paralysed by their demons betrayed an 'inability to cope with life', and that this 'inability' was a personal failing. Comparisons to 'other people' were rife:

'I kept thinking: *Why am I struggling so much? Other people don't find university this stressful. What's wrong with me?*'

'I suppose I thought I must be a really, really useless person. Because why should I be so desperately sad all the time? I had nothing to be sad about. Other people had much worse to deal with, and they coped a lot better than me.'

'I thought: *Other people don't hate themselves as much as I do because other people don't make as many mistakes as I do.*

I thought: *It makes sense that I want to hurt myself like this, because I'm a terrible person – other people aren't.'*

It is a cliché to say that those who endure mental illness are strong, and more of a cliché to refer to 'strong women', as though female strength were an anomaly. The women I met were perceptive, generous, considerate and highly attuned to the subtle undercurrents – the thoughts, feelings and motives that bubble beneath every person's surface – to which many of us are blind and deaf. They were not lazy, wilting under paltry burdens: they were fighting to stay afloat despite immense downward pressure. Were they strong? They were better than strong. They were real.

I met no one useless – although, again, concerns about *appearing* useless loomed large. These women were, in most cases, highly intelligent, competent and accomplished. Although, for some, mental distress had a detrimental effect on performance at work, school or in another field, for others there was a sharp contrast between what happened 'on the outside' and what happened 'on the inside'.

'I remember feeling like before I went to work I had to put this bodysuit on – I would say a mask, but actually it felt like it extended to my whole body – because I had to be this confident, capable person for the whole day, but actually I knew that wasn't who I was inside. Sometimes it would feel like I was just pouring myself into this other persona, because I wasn't even really a proper person at all – I was just like jelly. There was nothing really there. So, when I was at work, or out at social occasions, no one would have known there was anything wrong. Even when I was spending my full hour's lunch break crying in the staff toilets and only sleeping two hours a night and writing endless new-and-improved suicide notes, no one would have known there was anything wrong. That was very important to me. Like, obviously they would have known there was something wrong if I had killed myself, but ... I don't know. I guess I wouldn't have been around to deal with the fall out if that had happened. If people found out there was something wrong while I was still alive – still working there – I would have had to see them all the time, all the time knowing that they knew ... I wouldn't have been able to bear it. I would feel so ashamed. So I kept on with the routine of fine-on-the-outside, not-fine-on-the-inside. As soon as I could take the suit off I just spilled out into a soup of despair. It carried on for a long, long time. It felt like the sensible, responsible way to be behaving.'

I met no one lazy. I met no one whose reasons for not leaving their bed/not completing academic work/not holding down a job/not doing 'what they were supposed to do' was 'I just can't be bothered'. It was only ever 'I just can't'. The *can't* we refer to when we speak of mental illness is as profound and definite as the *can't* associated with physical impairment. A person with two broken arms can't carry a suitcase; a person with anaemia can't produce red blood cells at will; a person with asthma can't breathe properly – they just *can't*. In the same way, there are times when a person with depression can't make it to work; a person with anxiety can't leave the house; a person with bipolar disorder can't suppress a surge of mania – they just *can't*. To accept the temporary limitations of those suffering from mental illness is not to solidify them as permanent impairments, just as accommodating a temporary physical illness does not invite it to become a chronic condition. We do not worry that carrying the broken-armed person's suitcase for them will mean their arms never heal, and we shouldn't worry that giving the depression sufferer a day off work will mean they never recover. Just as broken bodies can often be healed, so can broken minds. Some physical impairments are alleviated with a straightforward treatment, and some mental illness sufferers respond well to courses of medication or therapy. Other physical impairments require lifelong monitoring, and other mental illnesses warrant long-term control. Neither ailment is brought about by laziness, and neither should be attacked with authoritarian discipline for fear that anything else is 'giving in'.

I met no one selfish. This was, perhaps, the subtlest discovery. The women I met were, in many cases, introverted and introspective. Prone to a high level of self-examination from a young age, most were unusually self-aware, but even in childhood this self-awareness tended to manifest as self-blame.

> 'I thought about myself all the time when I was little, but it was always about what was wrong with me – how I could be better, what I was not doing well enough … that sort of thing. I thought every bad thing happened because of me. I was always examining myself and finding flaws. It never stopped.'

For those who had not experienced heightened introspection in childhood, mental illness had often brought self-focus. The experience of psychological distress is so engaging and all-consuming, one cannot help but become entrenched in oneself and isolated from the outside world.

> 'I felt so far away from everything and everyone else. I was always stuck inside myself. I know everyone's always stuck inside themselves in a way, but it felt … I don't know. It felt more so. I did always think about myself,

but not because I wanted to. Not in a good way – I only
ever thought about myself in a bad way.'

These women were not selfless martyrs – at times, we are all
selfish, and they were no different. However, their concern for
others' welfare was striking. Almost everyone I met had a strong
drive to protect those around them, a heightened sensitivity to
the feelings of the rest of the world.

'I didn't want to tell anyone about my problems ... What
would that have been like for them? I didn't want to make
them unhappy. I didn't want to be a burden.'

'Sometimes I did think about killing myself. Sometimes
I did – you know – want to. But then I always thought
about someone having to find me. Someone having to
deal with me. And I couldn't do that to someone else.
I didn't care about hurting myself, but I did care about
hurting other people. It wouldn't have been fair of me to
make them suffer just because I chose to suffer.'

'There were people around me going through difficulties
and I needed to support them. I needed to be the strong
one. So of course I couldn't talk about what was happening for me. It wouldn't have been fair. I didn't want to
draw focus away from them. They needed it more than
me. So I just kept quiet and tried to help everyone else
and not think about myself too much.'

People suffering from mental illness are not saints. That misconception blows dangerously close to the 'beautiful, broken girls'
trope: the portrayal of unstable young women as soft, fragile
and flawless, simply too delicate to cope with the ugly stresses
and strains of life. The women I met were the first to condemn

their own behaviour as, at times, irrational, impulsive, incomprehensible and – yes – ugly. It is my belief that those suffering from mental illness are not attention-seeking, but attention-*needing*: their behaviour comes from a place of crazed, desperate determination to communicate internal distress. People who starve or slice or scald themselves do not *want* to be 'made a fuss of': they *need* to be seen and heard. In the moment, with emotions running high, the two motives can look similar, but they are worlds apart.

It is also a mistake to assume that one story of mental illness can ever be used as a template for another. Convenient as it would be for experiences of depression, anxiety and the rest to resemble one another with mirror-accuracy, one individual's story can barely be mapped onto another's. In the above example, for every person who uses self-harm, self-starvation or other self-destruction as a plea to be noticed, there are others for whom such behaviours are secret rituals, hidden from the world by smiles and long sleeves. For every person who interprets diagnosis as an overdue validation of a sickness that cannot be seen, there are others for whom labels are shameful, tarnishing the 'perfect' façade. For every woman I met whose story felt familiar, fitting my emerging understanding of a given condition, there was another who gave me a different insight into the same issue.

Abby is not a universally applicable depiction of depression; Beth's struggle may look different to another person's experience of binge eating; Holly's PTSD is not 'all PTSD'. They are single stories, knitted together from multiple stories, couched in a sea of millions of stories. I do not pretend to have given a fully comprehensive overview of female mental illness within these pages: I spoke to scores of women, but *millions* wage psychological warfare every day. I cannot draw concrete conclusions as to why these conditions develop, nor how they should be treated – I would not want to. It is not my place, and that was not my aim. Through this book, I hoped to grant an insight into the lived experience of a handful of disorders, shining a light into the corners usually shrouded in shadow. I wanted to tell stories. I wanted to explore how it feels to be marooned, helpless, on the rocks – but also to capture the moments in which one can rise, feel the sun on one's face, taste the salt on one's lips and stand on legs that are battered but strong. All I can do – all I have done – is amplify the voices that often go unheard.

# REFERENCES

1.  Stansfeld, S., Clark, C., Bebbington, P., King, M., Jenkins, R. & Hinchliffe, S. (2016). Chapter 2: 'Common Mental Disorders'. In S. McManus, P. Bebbington, R. Jenkins & T. Brugha (Eds.), 'Mental Health and Wellbeing in England: Adult Psychiatric Morbidity Survey 2014'. Leeds: NHS Digital.

2.  The Welsh Government. (2016). 'Welsh Health Survey 2015'. Retrieved from: gov.wales/statistics-and-research/welshhealth-survey/?lang=en [Accessed 21/09/17].

3.  Bell, C. & Scarlett, M. (2015). 'Health Survey Northern Ireland: First Results 2014/15'. Retrieved from: health-ni.gov.uk/sites/default/files/publications/dhssps/hsni-firstresults-14-15.pdf [Accessed 21/09/17].

4.  Brown, L., Christie, S., Gill, V., Gray, L., Hinchliffe, S., Ilic, N. & Leyland, A.H. (2015). 'The Scottish Health Survey 2014'. Edinburgh: The Scottish Government. Retrieved from: gov.scot/Publications/2015/09/6648/0 [Accessed 21/09/17].

5.  McManus, S., Hassiotis, A., Jenkins, R., Dennis, M., Aznar, C., & Appleby, L. (2016). Chapter 12: 'Suicidal Thoughts, Suicide Attempts, and Self-Harm'. In S. McManus, P. Bebbington, R. Jenkins & T. Brugha (Eds.), 'Mental Health and Wellbeing in England: Adult Psychiatric Morbidity Survey 2014'. Leeds: NHS Digital.

6.  Office for National Statistics. (2016). 'Suicides in the United Kingdom: 2014 Registrations'. Retrieved from: ons. gov.uk/peoplepopulationand-community/ birthsdeathsandmarriages/deaths/bulletins/ suicidesinth eunitedkingdom/2014registrations [Accessed 26/01/18].

7.  Conwell, Y., Duberstein, P.R., Cox, C., Herrmann, J.H., Forbes, N.T. & Caine, E.D. (1996). 'Relationships of Age and Axis I Diagnoses in Victims of Completed Suicide: A Psychological Autopsy Study'. *The American Journal of Psychiatry*, *153*(8), 1001–8.

8.  Eisenberg, D., Downs, M.F., Golberstein, E. & Zivin, K. (2009). 'Stigma and Help Seeking for Mental Health Among College Students'. *Medical Care Research and Review*, *66*(5), 522–41.

9. Shipherd, J.C., Green, K.E. & Abramovitz, S. (2010). 'Transgender Clients: Identifying and Minimizing Barriers to Mental Health Treatment'. *Journal of Gay & Lesbian Mental Health*, *14*(2), 94–108.

10. Kessler, R.C., Berglund, P., Demler, O., Jin, R., Merikangas, K.R. & Walters, E.E. (2005). 'Lifetime Prevalence and Age-of-Onset Distributions of DSM-IV Disorders in the National Comorbidity Survey Replication'. *Archives of General Psychiatry, 62*(6), 593–602.

11. Nutt, D. J. (2008). 'Relationship of Neurotransmitters to the Symptoms of Major Depressive Disorder'. *The Journal of Clinical Psychiatry*, *69*, 4–7.

12. Sullivan, P.F., Neale, M.C. & Kendler, K.S. (2000). 'Genetic Epidemiology of Major Depression: Review and Meta-Analysis'. *American Journal of Psychiatry*, *157*(10), 1552–62.

13. Holtzman, N. S. (2017). 'A Meta-Analysis of Correlations Between Depression and First Person Singular Pronoun Use'. *Journal of Research in Personality*, *68*, 63–8.

14. Depression and Bipolar Support Alliance. 'Recovery Steps'. Retrieved from: http://www.dbsalliance.org/site/PageServer? pagename=wellness_recovery_steps. [Accessed 23/11/17].

15. Hawton, K., Rodham, K., Evans, E. & Weatherall, R. (2002). 'Deliberate Self-Harm in Adolescents: Self-Report Survey in Schools in England'. *BMJ*, *325*(7374), 1207–11.

16. Klonsky, E.D., Oltmanns, T.F. & Turkheimer, E. (2003). 'Deliberate Self-Harm in a Nonclinical Population: Prevalence and Psychological Correlates'. *American Journal of Psychiatry*, *160*(8), 1501–8.

17. Sullivan, P.J. 'Should Healthcare Professionals Sometimes Allow Harm? The Case of Self-Injury'. *Journal of Medical Ethics.* Published Online First: 9 February 2017. doi: 10.1136/medethics-2015-103146

18. Hill, A. (2009, 25 October). '"Assisted Self-Harming" Offered in UK Hospitals'. *Guardian*. Retrieved from: https://www.theguardian. com/society/2009/oct/25/self-harm-hospital-assisted [Accessed 23/08/17].

19. Hudson, J.I., Hiripi, E., Pope, H.G. & Kessler, R.C. (2007). 'The Prevalence And Correlates of Eating Disorders in the National Comorbidity Survey Replication'. *Biological psychiatry*, *61*(3), 348–58.

20. National Institute for Clinical Excellence (2017). 'Eating Disorders: Recognition and Treatment' (NG69). Retrieved from: https://www. nice.org.uk/guidance/ng69 [Accessed 12/01/18].

21. Sangster, S. (2016, 5 August). 'The Destructive Truth About Eating Disorder Services'. *The National Student*. Retrieved from: http://www.thenationalstudent.com/Opinion/2016-08-05/the_destructive_truth_about_eating_disorder_services.html [Accessed 11/01/18].

22. Rape Crisis England and Wales. 'Rape Crisis England and Wales Headline Statistics 2016-17'. Retrieved from: https://rapecrisis.org.uk/statistics.php [Accessed 14/02/18].

23. Deans, C. & Meocevic, E. (2006). 'Attitudes of Registered Psychiatric Nurses Towards Patients Diagnosed with Borderline Personality Disorder'. *Contemporary Nurse*, *21*(1), 43–9.

24. Fleener, P. (2011, 1 August). 'Stigma and Borderline Personality Disorder' [Blog post]. *My Borderline Personality Journal*. Retrieved from: https://myborderlinepersonalityjourney.wordpress.com/2011/08/01/stigma-and-borderline-personality-disorder-by-patty-fleener-m-s-w [Accessed 30/05/16].

25. Krawitz, R. & Watson, C. (1999). 'Borderline Personality Disorder: Pathways to Effective Service Delivery and Clinical Treatment Options'. Mental Health Commission.

# ACKNOWLEDGEMENTS

For a long time, I had very little faith in the manuscript that became this book. I will always be grateful for the kind advice I received from two wise writers: Leon and Frankie Arden. Your insight and encouragement were invaluable. Also, thank you to one of my oldest friends, Livvy Utley, who read an embarrassingly rough approximation of my early chapters, and was unreservedly (undeservedly) enthused.

It has been a pleasure and privilege to work alongside such excellent people on this project. Thank you to Hattie Grünewald at Blake Friedmann: your initial interest has been matched by your sensitivity, perceptiveness and enormous skill throughout the publication process. Also, thank you to the many people at Icon (and beyond), who have scaffolded this book at various points and in various ways: Michael Sells, Ruth Killick, Victoria Reed, Lydia Wilson, Lucy Cooper and Ellen Conlon. Most of all, Kiera Jamison: put simply, I could not ask for kinder, cleverer editor.

If I have communicated nothing else in the preceding pages, I hope I have shown that mental illness ebbs and flows, lurking in the shadows for longer than one might imagine. The process of researching for this book spanned some time, during which my own mental health was not always good. I was supported during a particularly low period by two people, Clare and Rose. Your help was generous, and I am sorry it was a difficult time.

Juggling a book and a degree has been a challenge I have met with tears, tantrums and very shoddy essays. Since I started studying, I have been lucky enough to be taught (and counselled) by Rebekah, Hannah and Laura, three exceptional tutors who have gone above and beyond to maintain my (fragile) equilibrium. I have also been enormously touched by the unselfish enthusiasm of some dear friends: Kate, Miranda, Tsvetana, Becci, Alice, Sophie and Rosalind. And then one person has had to put up with more fretting, moaning and anxious fixes than anyone else. Everyone needs a wingman, and I have the best in the business. Thanks, PWM. I'd be lost if truth be told.

Of course, in the case of a book like this, there is a 'thank you' that overshadows all the others. Without the women who bravely agreed to speak to me, there would be no book. So many people were involved in the construction of these stories – from those who were interviewed to those who provided feedback. The majority wish to remain anonymous, but by name I can thank Danielle Freeman-Grantham, Stephanie Mallett, Gemma Ward, H. Beverley, Zoe Longbottom, Helena Miles, Lee Shu En, Niamh Gordon, Iman Ahmedani, Katie B., Lucy, Marie, Anita, Kaya, Isabella, Mani, Rowan, Lottie, Shay, Felicity, Amira, Carolina and Lissy. Thank you for letting me speak with your voices.